Since studying journalism at RMIT in Melbourne, Kathryn Bonella has worked as a journalist in television and print. She moved to London eighteen months after graduating and spent several years freelancing for *60 Minutes* as well as numerous English and American television programmes, magazines and newspapers. She returned to Australia in 2000 to work as a full-time producer for *60 Minutes*. She moved to Bali in 2005 to research and write Schapelle Corby's autobiography, *My Story*, and *Hotel K*.

www.kathrynbonella.com

Also by Kathryn Bonella

Schapelle Corby – My Story
Hotel K

SNOWING IN
BALI

THE INCREDIBLE INSIDE ACCOUNT OF BALI'S HIDDEN DRUG WORLD

KATHRYN BONELLA

Quercus

Some of the people in this book have had their names changed to protect their identities.

First published in 2012 in Australia by Pan Macmillan Australia Pty Limited
1 Market Street, Sydney

First published in Great Britain in 2013 by
Quercus
55 Baker Street
Seventh Floor, South Block
London
W1U 8EW

A CIP catalogue record for this book is available
from the British Library

ISBN TPB 978 1 78206 265 3
ISBN EBOOK 978 1 78206 266 0

10 9 8 7 6 5 4 3 2 1

Text and plates designed and typeset by Ellipsis Digital Limited, Glasgow

Printed and bound in Great Britain by Clays Ltd. St Ives plc

To the holiday-makers who think they're going to paradise . . .
All isn't as it seems

CONTENTS

CONTENTS

AUTHOR'S NOTE

Because of the nature of the revelations contained in this book, some names have been changed in order to protect the identities of the people involved. This includes instances when they are referred to in quoted media articles.

FOREWORD

There's something about Bali . . .

. . . And drug dealers

They're a perfect fit – with Bali's myriad hotels, sun, surf, millions of tourists, an endless stream of the world's biggest drug bosses and a strong culture of corruption, the party paradise is the ideal place to play the drug game.

That is, until you go down.

You are living the dream until you bust and all the reality comes so fast and so bad . . . this game is fucking dangerous.
– International drug boss, busted in Bali in 2012
with nearly a kilo of cocaine

Snowing in Bali has evolved organically out of my other two books, *Hotel K* and Schapelle Corby's *My Story*. I think of them as my Bali trilogy, as each one was inspired by the previous and there's a crossover of characters and themes in all three.

Writing Schapelle's book opened my eyes to the bizarre, crazy world of Hotel K. Sitting in the jail every day for a couple of months interviewing Schapelle, I saw the sex and the violence first hand, and the experience of getting to know many of the prisoners inspired *Hotel K*. The subsequent researching for and writing of *Hotel K* gave me insight into island life, and the fact that outside the white walls of the jail, Bali shared many of the same issues. Despite its *Eat Pray Love*-esque image, corruption was endemic, violence rife, and the drug dealers were cleaning up, selling both on the island and sending drugs overseas, especially to Australia. Bali is located in a strategically perfect spot for international trafficking and its millions of tourists serve as a perfect camouflage.

Snowing in Bali took about 18 months to research and write. Over that period, I spent time with gangsters, drug dealers, pimps and hookers to get a feel for the dark side of the paradise, which invisibly infiltrates everywhere. But it was the access I got to the island's international drug dealers that was most riveting. There was no question their stories were the ones to tell, especially as more and more of the island's dealers agreed to talk to me; participating in one-to-one interviews, often sitting for days at a time while I recorded their stories.

My entree into this unique position was largely due to my previous book – it had introduced me to dealers in jail, who put me in touch with people outside, most of whom knew of *Hotel K*. Some had read and liked it, with one person even photocopying it to pass around. It was also proof that I wasn't an undercover cop.

Of course I don't condone what they do, but I found the drug dealers fascinating, and mostly highly intelligent, educated, multi-lingual and cultured – with a penchant for the best: top restaurants, French champagne, high-class hookers, luxury villas and hotels, first-class travel and designer clothes. Many were surfers, who had come to Bali chasing the perfect waves, and found an ostensibly easy way to fund their lifestyles in paradise.

As you'll see, the main characters tell their stories, with graphic – sometimes very sexually explicit – details of their drug fuelled party lifestyles, as well as their secret tactics to move drugs through the airports and evade police. Once the dealers started warming up and trusting me in their interviews, it was amazing – they just talked and talked and talked, often coming back the next day to talk some more. Most told me they were speaking of many things for the first time – as I'd promised not to use their names. I learned that even among their close dealer friends, these guys don't swap stories – their lives are infused with deep paranoia, especially when they're using coke. They also know that if another person in the drug game gets busted, often their only leverage is giving someone else up (or cash). So it was that some of these dealers were almost bursting to tell their stories, often with a gleam in their eyes as they recalled some moments. Rafael, in particular, seemed to want to talk as a kind of confessional and joked at one point that it felt like I was his psychiatrist. I offered a non-judgmental ear, and that was the key.

I should mention that for some of those I spoke to, I paid them a financial contribution for their time, which was undoubtedly also an incentive.

A couple of the dealers were also motivated by a heartfelt desire to show young kids who might be thinking of getting involved in the glamorous life of fast bucks, hot women and orgies, that in the end, it's not worth it. Literally, within a second, life goes from heaven to hell.

*

I first met some of the dealers during *Hotel K* research when I went to the Super Maximum Security Prison on Nusakambangan Island to interview Juri and Ruggiero whom I'd got to know in Kerobokan Prison while working with Schapelle. It was there that I met Marco, a very funny and gregarious man, who is on death row for trafficking 13.7 kilos of coke in a hangglider frame. When he was busted, he'd fled the airport and was on the run for two weeks. In jail, he cooked me lunch – pasta and steak (he'd spent time in a Swiss cooking school, and it was delicious). I also met his death-row compatriot Rodrigo, who was Marco's polar opposite – very quiet and sad, with huge black circles under his eyes. I was introduced to Rodrigo in the church, and he was very polite, but didn't say much. I was told he'd been crying all morning, and that this was typical.

I went back to Nusakambangan for *Snowing in Bali*, but was busted on day two with my digital recorder. Although the prison boss was very polite, he knew of *Hotel K* and was fearful I was writing an exposé on his jail – which would indeed make interesting reading, but I wasn't. He allowed me back inside for 20 minutes to say goodbye, but I had to conduct the rest of my interviews with Marco on the phone.

I was also introduced to fugitive dealer Andre, living on a false passport in Bali, after he'd escaped from jail in Brazil. He was dead keen to tell his story, and even some day go on *Banged Up Abroad* – a television show he regularly watched to get tips on what-not-to-do. He was an extremely intelligent and good looking guy, well educated, with three sisters in Brazil – two of them doctors. Like most of the dealers I met, Andre could have chosen any career he wanted, but he chose to traffic drugs.

It appeared to be a direct line to a glamorous life – until it flipped to a tiny prison cell. I spent many long days over several weeks interviewing Andre – including doing follow-ups over a few months – until the day he got spooked. Some Bali dealers, had heard he was talking to a journalist and, given his fugitive status, he panicked that they'd give him up.

Nyoman, the Laskar gangster and pimp I spent time with, introduced me to his fake drug dealer friend, Wayan. Both of them talked to me about how they didn't like their jobs, but had no choice. They were poor: the pimp lived in a tiny room called a *kos* – smaller than most Australian bedrooms – with his wife, toddler son and newborn baby girl. He took me to an illegal cockfight (a daily event in the back streets of Seminyak), where I saw the cops show up and leave – after they got their cut. Nyoman's wife was employed, spending up to five days sewing tiny little sequins on a dress, for which she would receive about $10. I later went to the Seminyak shop and saw the dress with a price tag of several hundred dollars.

With the average monthly Balinese salary not much over $100, even for those working in the big hotels, it's not surprising that corruption is endemic. And, for the drug dealers, this makes life easier – with their huge amounts of cash, there are few rules that can't be broken and money can be spent on land, villas or restaurants without anyone asking where the cash came from. For those hiding out in Bali – and the dealers told me there are many fugitives – living in luxury villas, spending their proceeds of crime or even running legit businesses is easy.

*

Earlier this year I was outside Kerobokan Prison on the second night of rioting by inmates – they'd taken it over, and locked out the guards after they'd fled their posts when the rioting had started. It was an 'only in Bali' experience. Across from the jail is a sales yard for huge concrete Buddhas – it was full of soldiers with submachine-guns held ready leaning against the huge Buddhas. It was a perfect visual metaphor for the contrasts that exist on the Island of the Gods.

One night I had a call from a prisoner I'd met during the writing of *Hotel K* – he was still in jail, although no longer in Kerobokan, but asked me to meet him at a popular café, the Bali Deli, for a drink. I arrived to find him, the prison boss, and four other prisoners all sitting at one of the deli's cabanas. After drinks, we got into a government car, with its official red number plates, and drove the prison boss to his favorite karaoke club in Sanur. On the way he sat in the passenger seat singing along to a Rihanna music DVD playing on the dashboard. After dropping him off, we went to the stylish Potato Head Beach Club. At about 1 a.m. the prison boss called, waking up the prisoner-driver who was asleep on a mattress near the swimming pool. The guys left, picked up the boss and went back to jail. The next week, that night's driver was busted while out of jail, selling drugs, and quickly confessed that he'd bribed the boss to get out of jail. The boss was sacked, and the inmate had further charges brought against him.

The Bangli Prison warden accused of taking bribes to allow a convicted narcotics dealer out of his cell has been captured on video at a drug party with the prisoner and a prostitute, police said on Thursday. Police made the discovery after examining closed-circuit television footage from the Boshe VVIP Bali Club Bali in Kuta.

    – *Jakarta Globe*, 13 May 2011

It is a good example of why the landscape in Bali is ideal for drug dealing. With cash, the laws are very flexible – although clearly it doesn't always work – as *Snowing in Bali* will reveal.

I hope *Snowing in Bali* is an exciting read – but more than that, I hope it shows however glamorous it may appear to be on the outside, for those involved in drug dealing there are usually no happy endings.

CHAPTER ONE

ISLAND OF THE SEX GODS

As the two Australian models sashayed into one of Bali's trendy restaurants, past a table of cut-bodied surfers, they gave flirtatious looks to one guy in particular. His six-pack abs, dazzling smile and beautiful face gave him a shiny allure. Tonight the models were out for some fun, and they'd hit the jackpot – the sexy surfer they were zeroing in on was one of Bali's biggest cocaine dealers.

All the guys at his table were international drug bosses, out for their usual night of fine dining, drugs and girl-hunting. None of them missed the obvious come-on the models gave their friend Rafael. None was surprised, either – he was always being hit on by sexy babes. Tonight they were urging him to ask the girls over to their table, but he was being coy.

The girls weren't. Now seated, they were flashing smiles at Rafael. Wasting no time, they sent a note scribbled on a napkin via the waiter: 'Come to our table?'

'Go over there, man. You're crazy if you don't,' Rafael's friends hustled.

'Okay, okay.' He pushed back his chair and walked across to the girls.

'We've seen you on the beach at Uluwatu and think you're hot,' the blonde one flirted.

Rafael was used to this shameless vamping. The Island of the Gods seemed to provide a pass on arrival to relinquish usual inhibitions – the copious drugs and alcohol imbibed also turbo-charging the hedonistic free spirit, ensuring an endless smorgasbord of willing girls.

The line was big, you know . . . sometimes I have to choose; today I'm going to take this one, tomorrow this one . . . was very easy to catch girls. First I was good looking, well dressed, you know, clean. I have a kind of shining, hunter-like . . . some kind of smell or some look that attracts the girls. And I have something to make more interest . . . I can observe . . . beautiful girls, they love drug dealers. They have this fantasy to fuck the drug dealers.
– Rafael

Rafael was a woman's fantasy – a mix of sweet and dangerous, charismatic but gentle-natured. He was a nice bad boy. Up close, it was impossible to miss the large diamond in his tooth, the €25,000 steel, black and gold Rolex wrapped around his wrist, and the tattoos across his chest and down his arms.

Tonight, as usual, he was wearing his 1-kilo gold necklace that hung below his breastbone, framed by a black Armani shirt open to the waist, flaunting his six-pack torso and large chest tattoo of a heart with wings. 'It means my heart is free to fly wherever it wants.' With a splash of Paco Rabanne XS his babe-luring outfit was complete, and when he walked into Bali's bars and restaurants, heads turned, people called, 'Rafael, Rafael', and girls flirted like crazy.

> *Rafael was the boss: really rich, big car, big gold chains, tattoo on both arms, diamonds in the teeth ... you see, he is a drug dealer, like he has a sticker 'drug dealer' across his forehead.*
> – Andre, fellow drug boss

Rafael had built a mansion on the beachfront, designed to his exact fantasy specifications, including a diving board off his upstairs bedroom balcony and an ocean vista from his bed. 'I can see the waves from my pillow.'

He was a member of the exclusive Canggu Club, Bali's nod to the Hamptons – a sports club with sprawling facilities, for rich expatriates or tourists staying in expensive villas with membership, to dine, play tennis, do yoga or just drink martinis under poolside umbrellas. Rafael used the gym and did drug deals over lunch.

He also had a fleet of motorbikes, including a Harley, and a car that started by pushing a button on his key before he got into it, 007-style, which was useful for quick escapes from police or women.

With his flashy toys and partying lifestyle, Rafael was conscious of registering on the police radar, but for now he was blasé and winning – both as one of the island's top cocaine traffickers and a babe magnet. Tonight, like most nights, he had a few parties to choose from.

The two Australian models were asking him to come to their

villa later. They'd just finished a four-day fashion shoot on Bali's beaches, and wanted to party until sunrise before flying out. 'Bring him with you, but just him,' one of the girls said, pointing to Rafael's friend Bras – a dark and handsome Brazilian who flew often to Bali with bags of quality marijuana from Amsterdam.

'It's going to be a special party, you won't want to miss it,' the other model said, giving a wink. Unclasping her handbag, she showed Rafael ecstasy pills and a plastic bag of cocaine, unaware there was a fair chance the drugs had actually come from him. Rafael instantly saw it was bad quality, cut and mixed, brownish in colour, unlike the pure shimmering white stuff he trafficked from Peru.

'That isn't too good. Hang on,' he said, dashing off to the toilets. In front of the mirror he pulled a tiny ziploc plastic bag of half a gram of coke out of his ponytail, where he usually kept several hidden.

'Here's a small present,' he said back at the table. 'I'll bring more to the villa tonight.'

About an hour later, he made excuses to his friends, who hated missing a party. He rode home on his Honda 750 Africa twin to grab 10 grams of coke, then met Bras at a spot they'd chosen when he discreetly told him about the party, and they sped off to the models' villa in up-market Seminyak.

The high concrete walls outside concealed the stark beauty inside. Stepping through the large wooden doors was like entering another world. Moonlight sparkled on the large pool, the gardens were soaked in soft ambient lights, and loud rhythmic music was pumping. This was one of Bali's rapidly spawning super-high-end luxury villas.

Rafael's eyes shot to some vigorous splashing at the end of the swimming pool, where two people were fucking. After absorbing that for a moment, he glanced up and saw a stunning array of beautiful, semi-naked girls, coming towards him, slinking in and out of the shadows. It was as if he'd walked onto a glamorous porn movie set.

The blonde from the restaurant materialised in front of him, in a string bikini. She stretched up to place a Hawaiian-style *lei* around his neck, rubbing her breasts against him and running her fingers along the *lei* to pull him close. She kissed him hard on the mouth, then whispered, 'Hello, baby.' He didn't resist. Another beautiful girl started tearing open his Armani shirt and stroking his torso, crooning, 'Sexy body. I love your tattoos.' Rafael glanced across to his friend Bras, who was getting the same pampering.

I was like, shit ... how good is this.

The two girls with Rafael were becoming more horny and aggressive, thrusting themselves against him to the beat of the music, kissing his stomach, stroking his groin and undoing his jeans. 'Come on, baby, let's take your pants off,' one breathed in his ear as the other pulled down his jeans. 'Come on.'

The Don Juan was now out of his comfort zone. 'No, please, I don't have underwear.'

I was not feeling comfortable with the situation. I was feeling, fuck ... you know, out of control. It became crazy ... I have two girls kissing me, they take off their bikinis, the music was high, they jump into the pool, pull me in and they attack me a little bit. It was a very crazy situation.

Rafael wasn't enjoying himself; rather being naked in the pool, with two sets of breasts, hands, lips and tongues rubbing against him was strangely emasculating.

Another model came to the edge of the pool and tried to push a blue ecstasy pill – popular in Bali for being super strong – into his mouth. 'No wait, wait, I can't take a full one,' he insisted.

'Come on, your friend's already taken one. Just relax, let's party.'

I took the ecstasy, bit it in half and put half in her mouth, but she was already high . . . sweating. Then I started to feel a bit dizzy in the pool. I say, 'Please wait.' The two girls were too much, they were all over me, sucking my neck, pulling my dick, hugging me, like raping me. I was a bit uncomfortable, freaked. I cannot even get hard.

So I say, 'Wait, wait, stop, stop.' I escape from the girls, jump out of the pool, and I see my friend was already lying down on the sun chair by the pool with three beautiful girls on top of him; one was kissing him on the mouth, another one was giving him a blow job . . . When I see that, I think, 'Damn, what am I doing? I'm too slow. I should relax and enjoy. I should not refuse.'

I go to the table, drink some water and take a line and then, boom, I feel the ecstasy effect. I was like, 'Whoa,' I start getting

hard, horny, excited and then I jump back in the pool and start
playing with the girls. And then we all jump out and I start to
kiss one, sucking her pussy, and then they suck me. Was good,
you know. I was with two girls, having sex, they were kissing
each other too, and then the other three girls with Bras all came
onto the deck, all changing positions like a big orgy.

In the humid Balinese night air, fuelled with coke and ecstasy, combined with sexual exertion, they were all overheating, feeling hot and clammy, prompting one of the girls to stand up and suggest moving into an air-conditioned bedroom. On their way, the girls grabbed cold drinks from the fridge.

Rafael fished the coke out of his jeans and spooned generous lines on the bedside table. He loved to share his coke with hot girls, magnanimously declaring, 'This is on me tonight.'

The models quickly enmeshed into a tangle of beautiful bodies, kissing each other, kissing Rafael, every so often breaking away to snort a line of cocaine off the bedside table, then rejoining the writhing orgy. The room was filled with moans of sexual pleasure, sporadically changing to orgasmic screams. The mix of blow and pills was the perfect prescription for hot, uninhibited sex.

* *Cocaine makes people real horny, if it's good coke. For men it's*
like an aphrodisiac; men get a hard-on and don't come, can fuck
for hours. For me, the best combination was coke and ecstasy;
you get sensitivity on the skin and horny and you can fuck for
hours; but it's very addictive.
  – Alberto, Bali drug dealer

Rafael hadn't stopped for two hours and was now with one girl against the wall, while the other two girls were entwined on the other side of the bed. Suddenly, he needed a break.

I was, 'Whooof . . . I gotta go in the pool.' I am sweating, high from the ecstasy, and haven't stopped. I jump in the pool and feel better. Bras is still outside talking to one girl. I say, 'Hey, Bras, come inside, man, let's do some lines.' He comes in, we make some more lines while the two girls are still sucking one another on the bed, ignoring us.

Two of the models were wrapped in towels, sitting on the edge of the bed taking turns to do lines. Bras politely waited for his turn, then leant over to snort a generous line – a move that would soon dramatically end the night.

I say, 'Fuck, my friend is not well, he is starting to OD.' I see his lips are the same colour as his skin. I say, 'Bras, let's drink a beer man, beer is good.' And then he says, 'Please, Rafael, let's go from here. I don't feel good. Take me to get some fresh air on the bike, man.'

I say, 'Come on, man, I don't want to go. I want to stay here, have a good time. Are you crazy? Take beer, take water, breathe. Come on, man.'

Then he starts to throw up and I say, 'Fuck, let's go to the toilet,' and the girls were afraid, I was afraid, and then I say, 'Guys, I go. I'm going to take him out to get fresh air on the back of the bike. I'm sorry. Ciao, ciao, bye-bye.' . . . Escape.

After several minutes on the bike, with the night air rushing into his face, Bras started improving, but Rafael wasn't thrilled about leaving the night unfinished.

'Fuck, you *bencong*, you pussy. Why are you like this, man? Why did you take too much?'

'Oh sorry, sorry, but please take me home.'

Rafael had no choice. As they sped along Kuta beachfront, the sun was starting to rise across the water. There was a stillness on the streets, the witching moments of shift change between the ghosts of the night – hookers and clubbers – going to sleep and others waking up. By the time Rafael reached Bras's room at Bali Village Resort, it was daybreak.

Weariness was now starting to hit Rafael too. He slumped onto Bras's lounger and fell asleep, confident there'd be plenty more orgies with random sexy girls to fuck.

When you're really fucked up on drugs, really high, you lose all inhibitions. You just feel really horny, you meet someone at a club, have chemistry, you can fuck in front of other people, you don't care. And that's what happened a lot. There were a lot of orgies in Bali.

– Alberto, Bali drug dealer

CHAPTER TWO

COMING TO PARADISE

Surfing, sex and cocaine were Rafael's passions, but the sport of Hawaiian kings had come first. As a child he had natural flair on a board, riding Rio's waves with grace and agility. The rush of hurtling down a breaking wave, and sense of freedom quickly had him hooked – the same potent emotions that drug trafficking later induced. But surfing was his first love and the young boy dreamt about one day going to a faraway tropical island called Bali.

When his chance came, typically it involved a girl. Flying home from a surf comp in South Brazil, he flirted with the flight attendant and before hitting the tarmac, he had her number. Soon they were dating and the girl put her hot new boyfriend's name down to share the airline's free flights for staff-plus-one to anywhere in the world.

Before long they hit the skies to Bali. Rafael fell in love, but more so with the island than the girl. After a month's holiday, she flew home alone. The sunshine, palm-fringed beaches and the perfect waves spoke to his heart. This was the faraway island he so often dreamt of as a boy.

I was like, 'Wow, my god, beautiful place and good waves, very good waves.' I thought, I love this place, I want to stay here.
   – Rafael

He quickly met other like-minded westerners, who offered him a golden key to stay in Bali and pay for his dream life. Being a drug runner would be far more lucrative than his first run with a bag of sarongs. He'd taken the colourful fabrics to Rio to sell and flown back to Bali with cash, but quickly ditched the rag runs for coke runs.

It started on the beach. A bunch of surfers and expats from across the globe hung out, played music, danced, and smoked marijuana at a hotel fronting Kuta beach, dubbed 'the club'. Every afternoon, music blared from speakers, while guys played frescoball on the sand and girls sunbaked topless. Marco, a dark-haired hang-gliding champion from Rio, barbecued fresh fish and sold top-quality grass he trafficked from Holland, euphemistically trademarked 'Lemon Juice'. A rich Balinese man, a member of one of Bali's royal families, gave the crew carte blanche to use his beach hotel, joining them daily for a smoke.

This guy smoked marijuana every day – the whole day. This is crazy, because drugs get the death sentence, but the Balinese guy can smoke in front of everyone. He doesn't care about tourists, doesn't care about staff, nobody can touch him.
   – Andre, drug dealer

Unless you were a hot girl, or had a connection, it took time to become a club member. Rafael spent several days coming out of the surf and walking past with his board tucked under his arm before being welcomed to join the club's cool crew. Soon afterwards, he was offered a drug run.

They were a very close gang. It's hard to go in, to even say hello, because I think they are so cool, these guys. I want to be friends, you know. They didn't open the door. They were always rude. And then I met them on the beach one time and we smoke together.
– Rafael

Marco, the charismatic wisecracking Lemon Juice dealer, sold Rafael a small bag of grass for $100, and knew he'd be a perfect mule, or horse as they started calling runners when the word 'mule' got too hot. Rafael possessed all the traits to slip invisibly through customs. He was smart, well-travelled, white, western, good looking and a surfer – meaning no cover story needed for frequent trips in and out of Bali with surfboards. Marco, always on the lookout for a new horse, made his pitch on the beach one afternoon.

'Hey man, what you doing here in Bali to make money?'

'Not much, selling sarongs,' Rafael replied.

'You want to make some real money?'

'How?'

'Easy, you fly to Amsterdam, bring marijuana back, and I'll pay you $5000.'

Growing up in the cocaine gateway of South America, where drug busts were daily news, meant Rafael knew what the job was, and felt insulted. 'Come on, man, you think I'm a mule? I just want to buy a bit, and that's it,' Rafael snapped.

Marco persisted: 'Man, you look like a movie star, the cops are never gonna stop you. It's easy; you can hide the grass inside the surfboard bag. Easy money, little risk – come on, brother.'

His slick talk didn't work. Rafael turned him down flat and walked back to his nearby bungalow angry. But it had ignited a spark and for weeks he watched Marco's horses blithely coming with kilos and leaving with cash. He started selling Lemon Juice, freelancing as one of Marco's many sales people – paying Marco $500 an ounce, and making $100. They became good friends, and Rafael saw the intricacies of the game up close. Before long, he decided to give it a shot.

'Okay, man, let's go,' he told Marco on the beach, 'but I want to invest some cash, be a partner too.' For Marco that was no problem. It was often how deals were done, with several investors in one run, and at this point it was blue-chip. So, in the sun, on the sand, they struck a deal. A few days later, Rafael flew out of Bali to the marijuana capital, Amsterdam.

I was very confident. I say I can do this, no problem, they're not going to touch me because twice I've flown into Bali and they never even looked at me.
– Rafael

This was the mid-1990s, when Bali customs was lax, and before a rash of big airport busts and draconian life and death sentences were imposed. But there was one sobering, stand-out case that most surfers across the globe knew about – the notorious case of Frank De Castro Dias. Frank was doing a coke run to Bali but foolishly slipped up. As well as 4.3 kilos of cocaine embedded in his two surfboards, he was carrying a saw to cut the boards open. It created suspicion and got him busted. After paying a bribe of $100,000, he was sentenced to nine months in Bali's Kerobokan Prison, instead of the prosecutors' requested ten years.

Indonesian customs officials on the resort island of Bali have arrested a Brazilian accused of smuggling 4.3 kilograms of cocaine hidden in his surfboard, a customs official said on Saturday.

    – Reuters, 15 January 1994

Frank's bust exposed and ruined for a while the method of using surfboards to carry drugs to Bali, as boards suddenly got more attention. But drug traffickers constantly worked creatively to stay that one critical step ahead of authorities, by devising new tricks. On this first run, Rafael was using the so far undetected method of stitching the grass into the lining of a surfboard bag. His insouciant confidence only slipped when his bag came through Bali's airport with a large cross slashed across it in chalk. It gave him a scare, but didn't stop him.

I freaked out a bit, but when they say, 'Open the bag,' I was acting very calm, smiling. They asked, 'How many boards inside?' I say, 'Three.' 'Okay, you can go.' Oh shit yes! Close. 'Ciao.'

    – Rafael

Winning his first hand of Russian roulette was always going to ensnare him in the game. In days his cash balance had rocketed from zero to $5000, giving him precious freedom to live his dream life, spending several months cruising the islands of Lombok, Sumbawa and Sumatra, surfing from dawn until dusk. At nights though, he contemplated his next move, especially as the cash started running out.

Rafael was never going to be just a horse. He was smart and savvy, with a fierce confidence and strong ego. In Amsterdam, he'd closely watched as the master drug packers stitched the dope into the lining of the surfboard cover, using exactly the same holes they'd unpicked so that the alterations would be invisible. Like many horses before and after him, Rafael was ambitious and believed he could play this game on his own. But like most complicated things that looked easy, it wasn't, and the assumption that it was easy was why many mules got busted.

> I start thinking, 'Mmm, fuck, I can do this myself. I don't want to ever carry any more. Fuck off.' Then I meet these Peruvian guys in Bali, and then they say, 'Forget ganja, man, play with coke, it's much more money.'
> – Rafael

Life was about to get beautiful.

Sitting on the tiled floor of his Bali bungalow, Rafael slashed open the lining of the Billabong surfboard bag and extracted the plastic bags of shimmering cocaine. He opened up one and put a little on his fingertips. He sniffed. His eyes shone. It was 100 per cent pure. Amazing. He'd flown to Peru to meet the supplier, buy it, pack it and then give it to a horse to carry back to Bali, where the deal was to take place. Carrying it himself was a job too risky and lowly paid for Rafael, when he could now be a boss.

Later that afternoon he was going to make his first bulk sale to an Australian surfer. The guy was buying a kilo for $48,000 – 48 times what Rafael had paid for it. He spooned the cocaine, bit by bit, onto a small digital Casio scale, then put it into a plastic Bintang supermarket bag. After measuring 1 kilo, he tightly folded the plastic bag and wound tape around it. It was crude. It was early days and he would become more sophisticated. But today he just slipped this first bag inside a second plastic bag and threw a handful of dirty clothes on top. If anyone stopped him, he'd say he was going to the laundry.

He jumped into his rented Suzuki Jimny, picked up his contact, who'd set up the deal, and sped to the five-star Inter-Continental Hotel on the beachfront. Dark thoughts started to creep across his mind. He snuck a look at the Indonesian next to him, eyeing him suspiciously. He could be working a sting with the buyer, or the buyer could be an undercover cop. He felt intensely nervous. This game was new to him, but Rafael knew he was breaking the rules – trusting an Indonesian guy he barely knew and switching drugs for cash directly with a stranger.

But he had to trust his instincts. It had felt okay when the Indonesian insisted he came to meet the Australian buyer. He was potentially a goldmine, interested in future direct deliveries to Sydney – where the price per kilo could shoot to more than $120,000. The stakes were high, but this was a risk worth taking. The winnings could be a bottomless piggy-bank.

They drove into the hotel, valet-parked the red Jimny, and then walked alongside happy, suntanned tourists into the capaciously grand lobby, carrying the flimsy plastic supermarket bag of blow.

I go with my Bintang shopping bag, in jeans, T-shirt and flip-flops, to the room and shake hands with Australian guy. He says, 'Did you bring the coke?' I say, 'Yes.' He says, 'Where?' I say, 'In the bag.' Then he laughs. 'Are you crazy, man, why don't you put in better bag, a backpack or something?' I say, 'Ah, man, this nobody is gonna check – dirty clothes.'
   – Rafael

Rafael was keen to get in and out fast. He quickly rifled in the bag, pulling out underpants, board shorts and T-shirts, dumping them all on the polished table, then took out the precious bundle, worth more than its weight in gold, and placed it on the table. Rafael's heart was thumping. He was still on red alert to detect a trap. He was edgy. He watched the Australian, in one slick move, unscramble the combination locks on the front of his briefcase, loudly snap them open and flip up the lid. Rafael was ready to run.

I think, 'Shit, he's gonna take out a gun.'

Really, you thought that?
Yeah, because it was my first time. In those first moments I was also thinking maybe there is someone else hiding in the toilet.

*

Rafael was watching, wary, scrutinising the buyer, who was about 40 years old, clean-cut and handsome. He looked like a boss – no tattoos, stylishly dressed in jeans, Polo shirt and leather shoes, with a Rolex on his wrist. Out of his briefcase he took not a gun, but a sharp knife, using it to slice open the plastic bag, then sniff a bit of coke off its shiny blade. His mouth twitched and his eyes glistened. Rafael tried to read him, still feeling anxious.

My thoughts were going crazy, because I was really looking at the guy, really suspicious. I could see he works out at the gym, a very strong guy, and I was thinking it would be hard to fight with him, because he's bigger than me, stronger.

Rafael picked up a tiny rock, gesturing he wanted to use some. 'You mind?' he asked. It would help to settle his nerves. 'No problem,' the buyer replied. Rafael sniffed a little off his fingertips, instantly feeling better.

The buyer was now focused on testing the quality of the cocaine.

He was organised. He had all the equipment in his briefcase, like the lighter and spoon. He put some bicarbonate soda and coke on the spoon, flicked the lighter, fried the shit, and then he agrees: 'Okay, it's good. I want to take it all. How much you have?' I say, 'I have three more.' 'Okay, give me two days to get the money.'

After spooning the coke onto a digital scale to check it for correct weight, the buyer tipped the powder into three plastic ziploc bags, slid his fingers along the top of each, and placed them one by one in his briefcase. Then he snapped shut the lid and locks, and re-scrambled the combinations. 'Okay, let's go to the bedroom,' he said, breaking the silence.

Rafael trailed him out of the living room and into the bedroom. The Australian had clearly splashed out on one of the InterContinental's plush suites, which Rafael would soon discover was often the genteel way of big cocaine transactions. It had stunning ocean views, but Rafael didn't notice. His eyes flew to the four big piles of crisp $100 notes sitting on the bed – each $10,000. The buyer apologised that the last $8000 would be paid in Indonesian rupiah.

It was the first time I see bunches, like nice bunches, four together. I was like, 'Wow!'

Rafael picked up a bunch and flicked through it, checking for counterfeits or blanks. The Australian buyer sat down in an armchair, crossing his legs, telling him to take his time. But Rafael now felt he was legit and wanted to do more business, and so wouldn't be ripping him off. 'Thanks, but I'll count it at home,' he said, putting the cash into his plastic bag. They agreed to meet again in a couple of days, and Rafael left.

Two days later, it was like déjà vu. Rafael watched the Australian do precisely the same adept moves, down to snapping shut the briefcase and scrambling the locks. The one significant difference was that this time the bed was dressed with 14 bunches of cash.

*

Two months after the first rendezvous, the Australian surfer phoned saying he was again ready to deal. Rafael was keen to deliver all the way to Sydney's northern beaches this time, so he'd make more than $120,000 a kilo, the highest price anywhere on the planet. This was the reward for penetrating Australia's rigorous borders – and made it the number one global target for all drug traffickers.

A gram of cocaine in Australia costs between $200 to $500. In the United States, a gram sells for as little as $100.
  – Sydney Morning Herald, 15 September 2010

A 'generational shift' has pushed demand for cocaine to unprecedented levels, giving Australia the dubious honour of being the world's most lucrative market for the illicit drug.
  – Daily Telegraph, 2009

The day of the Sydney run started early. By 7 a.m. Rafael and his Peruvian partner, Jerome, were sitting on the floor of his bungalow packing 5 kilos of cocaine, first into plastic bags, then stitching it into the lining of the surfboard bag. It was exacting work. The faintest trace of blow on the bag could excite sniffer dogs; a mere sprinkling of dust brushing from their fingertips to the bag could spell disaster. Rafael had also heard that the potent ether smell could leach through plastic after 24 hours, so it was a race to pack and fly the same day. Tonight the flight was at 11 p.m. Only after the bag was tightly sealed was the horse allowed anywhere near it.

He was a 23-year-old Hawaiian guy, ostensibly the perfect horse – well travelled with an American passport and a strong physique that gave him a surfer look, ensuring carrying surfboards wouldn't look incongruous and create suspicion. A day earlier, Jerome had taken him shopping in Kuta to buy his clothes: Quiksilver T-shirt, jeans and skate shoes. Outfitting a horse was usual practice. They needed to look the part and it also ensured there was no trace of drugs on their clothes, given most horses were also users. When the packing was done, Rafael drove to the guy's hotel, picked him up and took him to Bali's Ngurah Rai International Airport to ensure his precious cargo safely hit the skies.

This was the Hawaiian's first big run. As he and Rafael walked from the car park he started feeling spooked. 'I don't think I can do it,' he said, looking at the doors ahead. 'There's an X-ray machine.' Rafael tried to placate him, 'No problem, my friend, this bag is X-ray-proof. It's easy.' But he was now walking very slowly. Suddenly, he dropped the bag. 'I can't do it, I'm sorry, I can't go.' They were 5 metres from the doors. Rafael took a deep breath. His mind was racing. He was confident the bag would sail through customs, but the Hawaiian's blatant fear was a classic red flag; he was sweating, almost crying, with fear in his eyes. Rafael stayed calm. He was on the brink of having hundreds of thousands of dollars within his grasp – it was just a six-hour flight away. He'd already invested $50,000. He was exhausted, but the adrenalin was surging. He had a bright idea: 'No problem, I'll bring the bag for you.' Snatching it off the ground, he walked briskly towards the doors, relieved to glimpse the horse trailing him.

I put the bag on the X-ray, I even went to look at the screen. I say, 'Come, my friend, look, no problem,' – and he came, looking at the screen and says, 'Wow, man.' . . . 'I told you, man, this is X-ray-proof. They are not going to catch you. Fuck, just go for it. Just go out of the airport and call me, but don't be like this again when you arrive in Sydney.'

As a parting gesture, Rafael ruffled the horse's excessively gelled hair, trying to make him look more waxhead and less off the set of *Grease*.

'Man, why did you do that with your hair?' Rafael gently mocked.

'I wanted to look good,' the horse said sheepishly.

'Come on, man, you look like John Travolta with this hair. You've got to look like a surfer.'

He went very happy, very easy. I say, 'See you in Sydney, my friend.'

Driving home, Rafael's heart was pumping. He felt happy, excited, sure he was about to win big. He'd fluked a crazy-low price for the coke when two naïve Peruvians flew into Bali with 5 kilos stashed in their bags, aware Bali had a strong market but with no local contacts or any idea of local prices. Someone had put them in touch with Rafael and he'd snapped up the lot for a bargain $50,000. Now he was about to say abracadabra and magically turn it into more than half a million bucks. Not bad for a fledgling career.

These guys have the best shit I've seen in my life. Even my friend from Peru says, 'Fuck, this is the best in the world. Nobody – Bolivia, Colombia – they don't have this kind of shiny shit.' It's from North Peru, not easy to find, very shiny. The best. Pure, pure. We call it 'asa de mosca' or wing of the fly. We have 5 kilos of this shit. And then we make the goal.

'Woo hoo, I made it, so easy man, no sniffer dogs, nothing,' the Hawaiian sang out as Rafael walked into his room at the Novotel Hotel in Sydney's Darling Harbour. The horse was buzzing from relief as much as cabin fever. He hadn't dared to leave the hotel room or the bag since arriving the day before.

As planned, he'd phoned Rafael in Bali as soon as he got through customs, and Rafael had taken the first available seat to Sydney to meet him. 'I want to do it again, man, I want to do it again,' he kept repeating. The fear in his eyes had turned to exultant glee. Safely through, it now seemed to him that trafficking drugs was the easiest way in the world to earn $10,000.

But for Rafael, it wasn't yet time to celebrate. He'd been given explicit, secret-agent-style delivery instructions; take a taxi from Darling Harbour to Palm Beach – about a 55-minute drive; come alone; stop at the phone booth at the front of a café on the corner; lose the taxi; call from the booth. Arrive at sunset – the surfer will be waiting. Rafael played it to the letter with only a few minor hiccups, like a protracted argument with the taxi driver against strapping the half-million-dollar surfboard bag onto the car roof, the Spanish inquisition for the entire trip, and at the end a battle to get rid of the driver, who was hanging around for a return fare. Finally, Rafael stepped into the phone box and dialled.

On the first ring, the buyer answered, wasting no time with pleasantries. 'I'm here already,' were his first words.

Rafael looked out into the darkening night. 'Where?' Car headlights blinked twice across the street. 'Fuck,' Rafael muttered, hanging up. This guy was good.

They drove to a nearby house, where the deal was quickly done. The guy tested the coke, then took Rafael to a bedroom for the cash. His heart skipped a beat when he saw the money. It was a beautiful payday. A white sheet spread on top of the bed was covered in bunches of $10,000, the brand spanking new Australian notes giving the room an acrid smell. There were more than 60 bunches, a lot more than if it had been in the agreed US currency. Rafael didn't argue, although he had specifically asked for US dollars because the Aussie dollar was low and there'd be too much cash to carry.

'You want to count it?' the surfer asked.

'Later, thanks.' Rafael didn't even look; he knew where the guy's house was now if he'd cheated him. He just wanted to leave. So he casually stretched across the bed and grabbed a corner of the sheet, then one by one took the other corners, tying them up together in a parachute-style bag. The buyer stood uneasily watching. It was a hell of a lot of cash and seeing this young guy blithely wrapping it up in a sheet rattled him. If Rafael got into trouble in Sydney and someone discovered his sheet-load of cash, it could expose the surfer too. He advised Rafael to take half tonight, and half tomorrow.

I say, 'No no, I can bring it all tonight, no worries.' 'But you can't go like this!' he says to me. 'No worries, just call me a cab. I wanna go now, the horse is waiting for me. I have to go. Ciao.'

As soon as he got back to the Novotel, Rafael raced straight up to see the horse, who was wide awake and waiting for him. Rafael handed him a Big Mac he'd bought en route, and together they sat counting the crisp notes until sunrise. The Peruvian, Jerome, arrived the next day, counted his share and flew home with the happy horse.

With a huge bundle of cash, the new playboy boss was primed to blow a few bunches in Sydney. He met up with a friend from Rio, who was living at Bondi Beach, and together they spent the next few weeks like rock stars, partying in five-star hotel rooms at night and surfing, sailing and hang-gliding by day. They took a car trip up the coast to Surfers Paradise, leaving in their wake happy hotel staff, thanks to Rafael's new habit of slinging $100 tips.

It wasn't all play, though; Rafael spent days, with the help of his friend from Rio and a new random girlfriend, changing the cash to US dollars and using their bank accounts to transfer chunks of it to Bali. It was time-consuming. Some days, Rafael went into three or four banks, with $30,000 each time, to change it into US notes.

Standing in the bank queue one afternoon, an icy shiver ran down his spine. He sensed being watched. He discreetly looked around. For the first time, he noticed all the tiny CCTV cameras. Eyes were on him everywhere. But he quickly shook off the feeling; Lady Luck was on his side, for now.

When I come back to Bali, I become a monster, because I get really rich. Fuck, everyone who comes with coke to Bali, they come to me. There were fucking so many people, man, sometimes I have to make a line. Wait, you know next week, I will sell yours, now I'm busy. Was crazy time, so much coke everywhere ... everywhere I go, 'Help me, Rafael, help me, I have 2 kilos.' I become the man who can fix, sell, you know.

– Rafael

CHAPTER THREE

SNIFF, DRINK, LIVE

You sniff, you drink, you live.
— Andre, drug dealer

The drug business in Bali was frenetic. Alberto, a friend of Rafael's, was acting as an agent, selling kilos of the cocaine and pills that were swamping the island. He wore disguises – wigs, hats, sunglasses – imagining himself as 007 as he sped along Bali's potholed roads in his rented Daihatsu Feroza. He'd drive into underground car parks, and leap from one car to another to confuse possible police tails. On a job, he'd work with the world's biggest traffickers in Bali's top hotels. Camouflaged among tourists, he would book two or three rooms simultaneously, one to hide the drugs in, another to switch the drugs for cash.

There was a time I could say, if you snorted coke here in Bali, there was a 50 per cent chance it would have come through my hands.

Really?

Yeah, we had that much here, and we had the best quality. A lot of people made millions through my hands.

   – Alberto

Another dealer, Andre, flew into Bali on false passports, sometimes gluing back his ears to look more like a photo that didn't much resemble him anyway. He darted around Bali on his motorbike wearing disguises – a Muslim hat or an Indian turban – checking into hotels to collect FedExed drug packages. He was one of South America's most wanted drug bosses.

A friend of theirs, Fabio, was fabulously rich, with a beautiful villa close to the beach. His wealth came from trafficking cocaine to Bali and then selling it in bulk to an Australian buyer or to one of the several multi-millionaire Indonesian drug bosses who worked largely with immunity in Bali, with police on their payrolls. He'd been doing it for a while; in fact, the stuff Frank De Castro Dias had been busted with embedded in his surfboards was meant for him. Fabio also ran a hip beach-front bar and restaurant, a couple of doors down from another bar owned by an Indonesian drug boss.

You would be surprised how many businesses in Bali are built on drug money.

   – Chino, Indonesian drug boss

Each afternoon Fabio bopped around his trendy restaurant, chatting up babes or selling tiny plastic bags of blow that he kept under the sarong he wore around his waist. It was the only thing he wore, as he flaunted a bare chest and muscled torso. He was notorious for his filthy bare feet, but it didn't seem to diminish his pick-up prowess. Fluent in several languages, he was rarely behind the bar, usually mingling with sexy foreign girls around the tables instead. He was highly energised, fuelled by the copious quantity of cocaine he sniffed. He kept staff on their toes, often turning around during a tableside chat to shout, 'Hey you, quick quick,' showing off that he was the boss.

Sweeping in with a surge of charisma and a bunch of friends at what he dubbed devil's hour, 5 pm, was his good friend Rafael, usually wearing board shorts, no shoes and no shirt, nicely exhibiting his six-pack torso too. Together they'd sniff a few lines, and then Rafael would help him sell a bit of coke in Fabio's pre-packed plastic baggies. He'd walk around with them in his pockets or hidden in his thick curly ponytail – for which Marco had nicknamed him 'Hair'. Rafael would ask Fabio, 'Can you see it?' and Fabio would fix Rafael's hair to better hide the bags.

That time it was a fucking game, we were not afraid, we didn't care.

Because no one had gone down yet?
Exactly. But we didn't sell to anybody we didn't know. If somebody just comes and says, 'Oh, I want some coke.' I say, 'Fuck you, man! What are you talking about? Get away or you're gonna get punched.' We just sell one by one to friends; we say,

'If you want to buy, you have to come there at sunset time; don't try to call us at 10 pm, the pharmacy is closed.'

    – Rafael

Further down the beach was their club.

The hotel was our drug club. We sell everything there, we take over the place. Sometimes I organised to meet people there ... 'I want to have 100 grams', 'Okay, meet me in the club, pm.' And then I meet there, give the coke, take the money, bye-bye. Not big deals, just small deals. Marco was dealing Lemon Juice like candy. No fear.

    – Rafael

Sprawled on the sand in front of the club were rows of Balinese *jakung* fishing boats, as well as Lemon Juice boss Marco's inflatable rubber Zodiac. He zoomed around Bali in it to avoid the choked and potholed roads. Most days he took the guys out to the best surf spots, with their five or six surfboards stacked and tied on the front. Marco, a hang-gliding professional but not a great surfer, often stayed in the boat snapping photos of the guys riding barrels. After a couple of hours, they'd pull up anchor and tear back to the club. There, Marco loved playing host, selling his Lemon Juice, standing at the barbecue with a beer in one hand, tongs in the other, cooking fish and lobsters caught that morning, while puffing on a Lemon Juice joint. All around, Balinese and westerners were smoking Lemon Juice, but it didn't stop Marco singing out, 'Come, come to eat,' to random girls walking past on the beach.

It was full of beautiful people at the club. Beautiful girls – Russians, Australians, Swedish, always some Brazilian girls – come with small bikinis, lay down, their big ass up. Everyone topless, beautiful.

– Rafael

Marco's phone rang incessantly, with surfers, expats, or tourists with connections, wanting to buy Lemon Juice. Often he'd brusquely answer, 'I'm fucking busy today, I'm in a business meeting, call tomorrow', snapping shut the phone to a round of laughs as he sat back down, smoking dope and drinking his beer.

He loved the attention and the power kick of being the island's number-one dope boss. If anyone wanted a quality smoke, he was the man, even trademarking the name Lemon Juice, and printing hundreds of T-shirts with 'Lemon Juice 100% bagus' (good) written on them in bold fluorescent lettering. Everyone from surfers and expats to rich and poor locals wore them.

I work Lemon Juice for more than 12 years. Nobody knows because the people are so stupid. I just call my friend and say, 'Let's have a drink of Lemon Juice,' but really, 'Let's smoke some pot, ganja.' That's the way, nobody knows. And then it gets famous the name Lemon Juice, everybody talks about Lemon Juice, and then I open one small Lemon Juice company.

– Marco

He organised people to sell for him, as Rafael had originally done, as well as selling it himself to friends.

With Lemon Juice he was very famous.
  – Rafael

Although most bosses kept a bit of distance from their horses, Marco liked keeping them around, reminding everyone he was the boss. It had been Marco who'd started the trend of using the word 'horses' instead of mules, initially as a typical Marco joke, using it solely for his best runners – his 'pure bloods'. But it had soon become generic for all runners and widely used by the Bali drug crews, because it was more cryptic, therefore safer.

Marco lived at the small rustic resort, Bali Village, in Legian, in fairly basic rooms nestled in overgrown gardens near the beach. The place was always bristling with his horses, and the resort was dubbed Marco's stable.

He also invited horses to the club, repeatedly using them for a gag, telling the horse to 'talk'. Obligingly, they would neigh on cue for their boss. Marco found it more hilarious every single time.

He was so crazy. Sometimes at the club I say, 'Who is this?' and he says, 'This is my new horse. Look how good he is, Cavalo relincha – like, "Talk horse, make some song"' – and the guy does: 'Neigh neigh neigh'. Marco says, 'See, my horse is very good.' I was thinking, 'Fuck, what are you doing, man? Why do you do this to yourselves?' Marco loved to fuck with the horse, put them in position; he says horse, they are shit. But he was so crazy, so funny. He made a joke with everything. Whenever I came to Bali Village, I see so

*many people around. It was his stable, full of horses, some-
times he sent two guys together the same flight with Lemon
Juice.*

  – Rafael

At this time, in the late 1990s, the island was the perfect place
to start being a drug dealer, or work in other criminal lines
that cashed in on cashed-up Bali. Tourism was booming and
the underworld was growing as fast as the number of infinity
pools. Bali was far from its sanguine, peaceful postcard image.
It had turned into a hedonistic haven for drugs and debauchery,
becoming a lucrative business island for pimps, hookers, drug
dealers, gangs and corrupt cops, police, prosecutors and judges
– who were all running rampant.

*There are a lot of fucking bad people, otherwise their jail
wouldn't be full of Balinese. If they are all so good, there wouldn't
be one Balinese in jail and there are plenty. They even have a
little Hindu temple in Kerobokan.*

  – Alberto

Most tourists flying in for a week of sun-drenched poolside
drinking, cheap massages and shopping were oblivious to the
subculture of crime. But it existed all around them. The men
in black standing at the front doors of exclusive restaurants,
clubs and bars were mostly gangsters from the island's most
violent gang, Laskar Bali – its members usually identifiable by
a distinctive three-ringed symbol tattooed between their thumb
and first finger. There were at least five big gangs, but Laskar

had most of the security contracts in Kuta, Legian and Seminyak, the prime tourist areas.

These security deals were worth big bucks, as they gave the gangs control of the drug trade. The contracts were the cause of the violent turf war that was fought constantly right across the tourist mecca, almost in a parallel universe, usually not apparent to tourists unless they got caught in the crossfire. When fights broke out in popular clubs like Bounty or Sky Garden, information was kept sketchy, with local journalists under dire threats of harm if they dared to name Laskar – all to keep the false *Eat Pray Love*-esque image intact.

Why don't you put Laskar's name in the paper?

Mostly our journalists are scared to write that group's name. That group don't like it if we write their name in our paper.

Journalists are scared?

Yeah. Scared.

Can't the police protect you?

How long can police secure you ... have you any guarantee that police can secure us for ever ... no. We say mobs or community organisation, but we don't say Laskar Bali.

But in Bali, everybody knows, right?

Everybody knows. But the big problem will come to you when you mention Laskar Bali.

What is likely to happen?

I'm not sure they won't kill me.

You think it's possible?

Possible. They can beat you on the street, run up to you, intim-idate you. So, one of our ways to protect ourselves is not to write that group's name.

– Editor, one of Bali's major newspapers

One night just after midnight, a group of Laskars turned up at a popular bar, the Red Room, in Legian, carrying Samurai swords, and stabbed a chef to death. It was a revenge hit. Laskar wanted to avenge one of its own, after a member was badly hurt a week earlier by security guards at Sky Garden Club in Legian – where Laskar had lost the security contract to a rival gang, Hercules.

The Red Room attack was strategically organised, with about ten of Laskar's Seminyak members called to a secret meeting, and told to bring their Samurai swords. These men were all physically strong, a prerequisite to being accepted into the gang, and given ID. If anyone got a call for a job, unless they had a good excuse they had better turn up. The gangsters convened in Seminyak, close to the Red Room, charging them-selves with Arak, while two went ahead to recce the bar. As soon as they gave the word that the coast was clear – no police – the men roared down Legian street on motorbikes, their faces covered by black bandanas, and their swords tucked into their black leather jackets, ready to attack. Unfortunately, this night they got the wrong man, stabbing to death the chef, whom they mistakenly took for a Hercules gangster in the dim light.

What was the problem in the Red Room?

Hercules hit my friend, in Sky Garden – not kill, but broke his head. We meet in Seminyak first, and go, fast, very fast, must be five minutes, no more; after that we run.

But Laskar killed the chef?

Yeah, wrong guy.

– Laskar gangster, Made

Tens of thugs carrying swords attacked the bar early in the morning last Wednesday. These thugs came on motorbikes and by car and went amok, attacking everything with their swords and killed Bagus Alit Edy Sastrawan (28) from Penarungan, Mengwi area. He died instantly due to a severe sickle cut. The cut stretched from his upper left lip to the inner part of his neck, and it was found that this also cut the blood vein on his neck.

'It all happened at around 00.30. The bar was about to close. Suddenly, a group of thugs came up and attacked everything around them,' an officer from Denpasar Metropolitan Police explained.

– *Denpost*, 15 July 2010

It was only when a high-profile person was involved that the frequent club violence got wide exposure, like former AFL North Melbourne coach Dean Laidley. His holiday hit head-lines when security guards at Kuta's Bounty Discotheque, where Laskar held the contract, attacked him and his family. It was vicious – the former coach was glassed in the head with a beer bottle and his son suffered a broken jaw. Three security guards were arrested.

'What the police are telling us so far is that things like this happen all the time,' Laidley told SEN [sports entertainment network] radio.

– The Age, 11 October 2011

It happens a lot over here that tourists get beaten up by security, and other tourists as well.

– Bali International Medical Centre spokeswoman
Tasya Aulia, *Herald Sun,* 10 October 2011

Crime also pervaded the hotels, with hookers allowed to work in most of them – including five-star resorts – by slinging the security guards 50,000 rupiah (about $5).

Nyoman, a Laskar gangster, was one of the tourist precinct's seven official pimps. He regularly parked his battered blue Toyota four-wheel-drive in a beach car park directly in front of the popular $300–$1600 a night Padma Hotel. Most nights the rented Toyota was full of girls in skimpy outfits, touching up their lipstick and mascara, dabbing perfume between their legs, as they took turns taking jobs.

The seven pimps cruised the streets with girls piled into their cars, on the lookout for customers to walk by or come out of clubs. They also relied on phone calls from taxi drivers, hotel concierges, bike transport guys, fake drug dealers or anyone who could snare tourists wanting sex. Whoever did got a share of the take.

Nyoman and the six other pimps had a monopoly, protected by the police, who also took their cut. The pimps owned the streets in the busiest tourist areas – Kuta, Legian and Seminyak – each paying a monthly sling of at least $400 to the chiefs at the three big police stations. The deal ensured they could work with impunity and that no other pimps could encroach on their turf without risking arrest.

But they had brisk competition from hundreds of brothels, some unsubtly disguised as massage parlours or karaoke bars, and some blatant in-your-face sex shops – dubbed aquariums – which were glass-fronted rooms crammed with girls sitting on tiered seats. These were in back lanes or nestled in the main streets of Kuta, Legian and Sanur, often alongside luxury hotels, but unless you knew they were there, you wouldn't have a clue. Taxi drivers often took tourists to the aquariums, escorting them down a laneway and taking them inside to ensure they got their cut. Dozens of girls, usually young and sometimes attractive, sat with numbers pinned onto their chests. This was fuck by number.

Aquariums, you know, they're like fish aquariums, but lady in the glass.
     – Ricky, taxi driver

Like most taxi drivers, Ricky was constantly asking his male passengers, 'You like a lady?', especially if he picked up a drunk tourist on the street or leaving a club. If Ricky got a nod, it was a great night, possibly tripling his usual daily take, depending on how well or badly the tourist negotiated. Some customers would go with Ricky to pick their own number; others would ask him to go to the aquarium alone and deliver the girl to their hotel.

Ricky happily obliged, but never wanting to get it wrong and miss out on his fee, he always asked for specifics on 'style of body' preferences. 'Fat body or sexy Coca-Cola body?' he'd ask, drawing the shape of a Coke bottle with his hands and whistling for impact. He never bothered asking about breasts, because in his experience, 'All tourists like big boobs.'

It wasn't only at night that Ricky found sex tourists, it was any time. This was business and westerners were rich, often stupid, prey. With his chirpy sense of humour belying his cunning, he worked to win tourists over. If you wanted to go fast, he'd floor it, zigzagging in and out of traffic, or go as slowly as you liked. He was super-charming, always asking, 'Tomorrow you need taxi?' Whenever he got the chance, he'd tell a guy, slyly if they were with their wife or girlfriend, that he could organise a lady. Often he'd conspire to drop a wife or girlfriend off to shop in the up-market Seminyak boutiques, then escort the guy to a brothel.

It's money, it's my work, it's good. I take the wife shopping, drop her off and then the man, husband, goes to massage. Happy ending. Massage just one hour. The girl shopping is normally two, three hours, so the husband already has massage, happy ending and go. After, she ask, 'Where you been?' He says, 'Bintang (supermarket), restaurant.'

– Ricky, taxi driver

One night, pimp Nyoman's girls were all busy with customers, except for pretty 21-year-old Linda. They were parked at the edge of the beach in front of the Padma Hotel. It was a full moon – a beautiful Bali night when all Balinese across the island went to full moon ceremonies to give thanks to their gods. Nyoman had dressed in his traditional Balinese clothes, a sarong, shirt and head cloth, and prayed at the temple earlier. But tonight he was pimping and stood at the back of his four-wheel-drive overlooking the beach. Shadows of palm trees were swaying on the sand, and the white caps of the waves glowing luminously under the specially cast light – a magical effect that many of the hotels and restaurants used along the beachfront. It was balmy and peaceful, with only the sounds of the ocean, the rustle of trees and the laid-back music of Green Day's '21 Guns' coming from inside the car.

Nyoman was chain-smoking and gazing out to sea, contemplating life. His wife had just had a baby girl. It highlighted the darkness of what he was doing and he only wanted to keep selling girls until he'd made enough cash to start a new business, probably a massage parlour, probably with happy endings. But for now the streets were it.

The sound of his assistant's motorbike coming across the car park snapped him out of his musings. A good-looking guy climbed off the back. He was mid-thirties and Australian. He wanted a girl. All business now, Nyoman opened the front car door to give him a look at the merchandise. Linda sat poker-faced, staring out the windscreen. A second earlier she'd been laughing animatedly on her phone. The guy stood there, slightly edgy, staring, thinking, assessing her fuckability. Yep, he liked her. He slipped Nyoman 200,000 rupiah (about $20), and zoomed off on the back of the assistant's motorbike to a nearby hotel that charged Nyoman 50,000 rupiah ($5), the standard hourly rate. The assistant returned to pick up Linda. It was a quick job – within 20 minutes she was back again, sitting in the battered old Toyota, dabbing perfume. The customer had told her he needed to hurry ... his wife was waiting for him back in their Padma Hotel room.

Nyoman was happy to oblige all requests, so long as his girls were not put in danger, like the group sex in a villa swimming pool, which a bunch of English guys requested. The girls had all strutted in their skimpy, sparkly nylon outfits and high heels down the walkway between the private villas at exclusive bvilla in Seminyak. The concierge had phoned ordering ten girls for his guests. But one by one, or sometimes in twos, the girls did the walk of shame back down the long passage as they were rejected. Only two girls made the final cut but were expected to have sex in the swimming pool. They were scared of a pool orgy getting out of hand, so Nyoman gave the cash back, keeping 100,000 rupiah ($10) as a kill fee.

Lewd requests were fine, though. When a middle-aged Australian husband and wife hired one of Nyoman's girls for a threesome and asked him to come and watch for an extra $100, he thought it was weird but jumped at the cash.

Australians were his favourite customers, usually easy-going and drunk. Another one of the seven official pimps was 27-year-old Ketut, a member of another gang, Baladika. He had a request from an Adelaide guy for a hooker all night. Inside his Bali Garden hotel room, he paid Ketut the 700,000 rupiah ($70) service fee upfront, then slurred a request for Ketut to stay an extra few minutes while he had a quick kip. The guy was blind drunk and quickly asleep on one of the twin beds.

The pimp and his girl sat on the edge of the other bed waiting and watching soft porn on the TV. It made the pimp horny and he turned to his hooker, started kissing her and then gave her a test run, right next to his oblivious, snoring Australian customer.

I see on the TV a lot of the sexy sexy, and then I kiss my staff, because she is a beautiful lady – good body, tall, good smile, friendly, you know. And then I make sex, just one time. She was aggressive too, she liked it because she was new. If she were working for maybe one month, two months, she would not be interested in sex.

Did the Australian guy wake up before you left?
Yeah, I say, 'Wake up, wake up, I want to go.' He says, 'Thank you brother, thank you brother.' Was very funny.
  – Ketut, pimp

Also on the streets were hundreds of fake drug dealers, loitering outside clubs or down lanes, stalking tourists, quickly attaching like clingfish as they hustled a potential sucker down the street, saying, 'You want ephedrine, hashish, *ganja*?', displaying the fake drugs in their hands, or digging into their pockets and magically pulling out whatever drug the person wanted.

Shaking off these dealers was often difficult, as they were poor and desperate to find stupid, preferably drunk, tourists. Wayan, a long-term fake drug dealer, rode around on a metallic green scooter, bought from money he won in an illegal gambling racket, with a boutique of imitation drugs in his pockets.

Every night he trawled the streets for hours, hunting for fools. On a good night, he'd also snare a tourist wanting sex and pass him along to his friend Nyoman – for a cut. He didn't like his job, but it was cash, needed to buy his kids an education and a chance for a better life than his.

Customers sometimes they beat me, kick me, say, 'Fuck you.'

Well, you're ripping them off.
Yeah. I don't want to but I make this point to them: 'Sorry, brother, but it's very hard to live here, to get some money, because my system of the government not so good.'
 – Wayan, fake drug dealer

Wayan had been arrested many times when undercover cops did a sweep of the Kuta beachfront area, scooping up all the dealers, taking them to a police station, testing their drugs, then releasing them the next morning.

There were also plenty of dealers with the real stuff, in clubs and on the streets; often in cahoots with the police so they'd all get a slice of the payoff from a busted tourist – who'd almost always be willing to pay big bucks to eliminate the problem before it went further.

Although the western drug dealers usually had no direct contact with locals working the streets, there was a crossover in the criminal underworlds. Lemon Juice boss Marco would sometimes buy a hooker as a gift for his good horses. 'You want to fuck a girl today?' he'd ask, then relish searching for a hot freelance girl in a club.

Marco was good to find beautiful prostitutes ... everybody was surprised, 'Where did you find this girl?' 'Kuta.' Marco was very good, not shy. If he sits in the plane next to you, he makes friends with you, very social.

    – Rafael

But the Lemon Juice boss always warned his horses of the cardinal rule: never ever use drugs in front of a local hooker, as snitching to police would give her the best payday of her career.

Just fuck and kick out, because they can fuck you.

Was it common for bosses to give their horses a hooker?
I hear a lot do that, but I never do because there's a big chance the horse is going to talk to the prostitute and it's going to come back to me. I don't like to mix prostitutes with drug dealer stuff. I was very careful with this.

    – Rafael

One of Rafael's Peruvian partners, Jose Henrici, nicknamed Borrador, Portuguese for 'smudge', because he was always creating a mess, broke the rule and paid for his mistake.

Borrador gave a line to the prostitute and the day after she came back with her cop friend, but they didn't take him to the police station, they just wanted his money. The policeman says, 'I know you give coke to her.' Borrador says, 'Okay, how much do you want?' 'I want $20,000.' 'No, I don't have.' 'Then let's go to the

office.' 'No, I can pay you here but I have $1,000 only,' and then
in the end he pays.

   – Rafael

The western dealers also sometimes paid Laskar gangsters to
resolve problems. For the right money, there was nothing these
guys wouldn't do, including killing. One afternoon Andre hired
a couple of thugs to frighten a Brazilian guy, who was living in
Bali with his wife and kids and neglecting to pay his drug bill.

The heavily built Laskars burst into his house, threw the
guy onto a chair and stuck a gun in his mouth. His terrified
wife stood helplessly watching. One of the gangsters then
phoned their client Andre. 'Okay, you can talk to the guy,' he
said, then held the phone to the guy's ear. Andre told him to
pay up or die. With a mouth full of metal, he sat wide-eyed,
terrified and unable to reply. But as soon as the thugs extracted
the gun, he bolted upstairs and dug out as much cash as he
could find. He delivered the rest to Andre the next day.

He was a little bit angry with me. He says, 'You send Indone-
sian people to my house, my wife is there, they put the gun inside
my mouth,' and I say, 'Yes, and good luck, hey? If you didn't have
the money, he would have shot you. You rob my drugs, rob my
money, you are asking to be shot. Next time think of your wife
if you don't want her to see your bleeding body on the floor.'

   – Andre

In every line of crime, cash and power were the driving forces
and there were large numbers of westerners willing to step into

the Bali underworld and make their inaugural drug run. Some moved up to be dealers, others invested in legitimate Bali businesses like restaurants, villas, clubs, clothes shops or furniture exporting, and others went straight to Kerobokan Prison.

Was so easy to find the people to do the job. I was surprised how easy. Many people, sometimes people I never expect, come and say, 'You have a job for me?' Fuck, you know, everybody wants to carry this shit ... easy money. Well, they think it's easy, but the consequences can be dead.

– Rafael

CHAPTER FOUR

SNOWING IN BALI

We call them horse, mule, runners, monkeys.

Monkeys?
Yeah. Some people say, 'That's my monkey.' These are guys who do many runs and always come through, and everybody knew, 'Oh, this guy is well trained, never caught, cold-blooded.'
   – Alberto, Bali drug dealer

Rafael, if I fly with cocaine in one of those backpacks, what chance do you think I have of success?
Eighty per cent I think you're going to make it.

Eighty per cent?
Actually, I think 95 per cent.

I think I'd be bad, too nervous, I've seen the consequences . .
Yeah, you know the consequences; you've been to the jail. Most of the horses, they don't know what they are doing. They don't

know the consequences, they're stupid. That's why we call horse mule, burro – donkey, idiot. Anybody who is not very clever is burro, donkey, in English.

  – Rafael

BALI 'THE LAST PARADISE' NOW A HEAVEN FOR DRUGGIES?

The evidence that Bali has become a hub of drug activity is found in Kerobokan prison, where an increasing number of locals and foreigners are serving time for drug offences. As of September, there were 80 foreigners in Kerobokan, most of them there because of narcotics.

  – Jakarta Post, 16 September 1999

There was an endless stream of people flying in to Bali carrying drugs; horses organised by the cartel players, as well as people independently lobbing with a bag of drugs, sometimes with Rafael or Alberto's details. Those without any contacts were taking a bigger gamble, but most would ask around in the surf, at the beach, or at nightclubs for a name. People would often say, 'Call Rafael, he's the man,' and pass on his number, taking a cut for the effort. Few runners were getting busted, even those with unbelievably bad packing. People got through with kilos in their backpack, simply cutting the lining and super-gluing it back, or in their suitcase loosely packed among their clothes, rolled up in sleeping bags, or smaller amounts in their undies, pockets, shoes and up their backsides.

People wanting to carry stuff constantly approached Rafael. 'Fuck off, what are you talking about?' was often his retort, worried about his name becoming too hot. But sometimes, if they were a friend of a friend, he'd get back to them, offering a run. An older Brazilian woman, who'd been living in Bali for 20 years, sidled up to him at parties hustling for a chance to run. 'I need a job. I can do it – nobody is going to stop me because I'm old. Let's do it.'

Rafael regularly used runners who didn't fit any stereotype, such as families with kids, or young couples, but Barbara really blew apart any cliché image. She was in her mid-fifties, with bleached blonde, artificially straightened hair to her shoulders, and a cosmetically tightened face, frozen from habitual Botox shots so that even if she got scared, at least it wouldn't show on her face.

One day Rafael and one of his Peruvian partners decided to give the old mare a run.

She flew out, truly excited to be finally doing a run, carrying the specially designed backpack, so that in Peru, all Rafael's packers had to do was stitch the coke into the back of the bag. A week passed and Barbara flew home to Bali with 2.5 kilos of coke in the bag and a smile on her lips. She loved this gig; an exciting trip, all expenses paid and cash to boot. Rafael was waiting for her in his red Jimny at the airport, very pleased to see his old horse walk out with the bag. It was a goal for him, another nice big bag of cash.

In the airport we were so excited. We put the bag in the car,
'Let's go. Woo hooo. Let's celebrate.'
   – Rafael

Rafael drove to the five-star Nikko Bali Resort in the swanky beach area of Nusa Dua on Bali's southern tip. In the car,

Barbara, always loquacious, was high from adrenalin and prattling excitedly about her trip – how she picked up guys for hot sex, how easily she slipped through the airports. Like so many horses straight after a win, she was flying, already keen to run again. Rafael was buzzing too, but careful as always to keep a sharp eye on his rear-vision mirror for any sign of a tail. Today, they were clear. His instincts were razor sharp, giving him a sixth sense that so far had kept him out of jail.

As usual, he valet-parked the Jimny and then the incongruous-looking pair walked into the majestic foyer of the Nikko, across its polished stone floor, underneath its high arched ceiling and black chandeliers. The Nikko was a stunning hotel built high on a cliff, with sweeping ocean views, the sound of indoor waterfalls, the smell of the ocean and feel of the wind. Couples pushing prams, honeymooners holding hands and rich tourists dressed in cool flowing dresses filled the foyer. But Rafael barely noticed anything as he strode through, past the huge limestone artwork on the walls, with his bag of cocaine. He led the way down one of the corridors, and across a bridge that traversed a gaping chasm. The hotel was designed around the dramatic cliff landscape and they were heading to one of the most expensive suites, built against a cliff.

In this wing, they stepped into a glass-panelled lift with ocean views that shot down the cliff. It was a uniquely beautiful hotel, with large pools, spas and marble bathrooms that smelled divine. Rafael was starting to use it for his trysts as well as his drug deals.

After winding their way along the corridors, bridges and

lifts, they reached their room. Rafael did the code knock – three fast, two slow. His partner on this job was one of a pair of Peruvian siblings, the Diaz brothers; both fat, both in the coke business and using fake passports to come and go from Bali.

Mario was like a kid, big and fat and like a retard.
– Rafael

The other brother, Juan, was Rafael's regular business partner. He was fat and short, so nicknamed Poca, Spanish for 'little', though in Bali the dealers joked it was short for Pocahontas – the Disney Indian princess. Poca was bright, regularly organising horses to bring kilos of coke from Peru, but excessively nervy and paranoid, exacerbated by his copious cocaine use, always expecting the worst. According to Rafael, 'Poca was a pussy.' He was also sporadically ripping Rafael off, pocketing petty cash meant for horses' expenses. Rafael was aware of it, but Poca and Mario had good sources in Peru, and you didn't steal someone's connections. So, for now, Rafael was stuck with using him as a partner despite distrusting him.

A moment after Rafael's knocking, Poca anxiously opened the door, jerking his head from side to side, manically scanning the corridor for cops. 'You sure you weren't followed?'

'Sure,' Rafael sighed, thrusting the backpack at him, then slumping into an armchair.

Poca dashed over to the couch and opened it. A split second later his screams tore across the room. Rafael sprang back to his feet, anxious that Poca might alert hotel security. 'Shut up, man. What's wrong? Are you crazy?' Poca was crazy-mad, and paranoid.

'It's the wrong bag,' he yelled.

Rafael raced across the room to look. 'Fuck! Barbara, what have you done?' he gasped. It was full of men's clothes.

Poca was raging at Rafael. 'Oh *estúpido*, you don't check the bag.'

Rafael was freaked too. 'Fuck, it was the same colour.' Poca was suddenly sure this was a police trap; any second now they would kick in the door. He was hysterical. He ran to the window. Rafael pulled him back, telling him to cool it, as he was 100 per cent sure he hadn't been followed.

Barbara stood smiling, amused by the dramatic outburst. She knew she'd simply grabbed the wrong, similar-looking, bag. She nonchalantly suggested driving back to the airport and switching it. Rafael and Poca turned and looked at her, incredulous. The old mare was nuts. Poca started screaming at Rafael again, 'You are fucking *estúpido*, you didn't check the bag, stupid motherfucker.'

Rafael didn't want to risk going back to the airport, but felt he had no choice. Any second now, Poca's shouting was going to bring hotel security running. 'Calm down, my friend, I'm going to fix this,' he said, grabbing his keys and the backpack. 'Let's go quick, Barbara, let's pick up the fucking bag.' On his way out he turned, snarling at Poca, 'And you shut up, pussy, stay here and shit your pants.'

They sped to the airport, parked the car, and raced to look through the windows into the baggage claim area. It was empty between flights, and the conveyor belts stood still. They briskly walked inside, anxious to find the valuable bag. It was eerily quiet, with only sounds echoing from afar. In the distance they could see one or two people, but the baggage area seemed devoid of life.

'Eh, you're not allowed in here, what are you doing?' a voice snapped out of the blue.

They turned and saw a customs official had materialised behind them. Rafael quickly explained that his friend had picked up the wrong bag.

'Follow me,' he said, leading them to a luggage storeroom where they saw the bag sitting on the floor, under a table. Only at that moment did Rafael realise the stress he'd been suppressing. It turned to exultant relief. Foolishly, neither he nor Barbara masked their sheer delight; their emotional reactions so far over the top for a bag of clothes, that the officer suddenly got suspicious. Now, he wanted to search both bags.

Before, he was smiling and nice, and then this guy gets really angry. His evil eyes look at me and look at her, asking, 'Why did you take this bag?' He wants to search everything. I was like, shit ... I was thinking I'm gonna run, leave Barbara, leave the bag and run. But I looked for the door, then I think, fuck, where am I gonna run?

– Rafael

He searched the bag of men's clothes first, then took the other from underneath the table. Barbara had lost the key to the padlock. Rifling in her pockets and purse, she couldn't find it, so it had to be X-rayed. Rafael was panicking, but kept telling himself that Barbara had made it all the way to Bali because it was X-ray-proof. But nothing was guaranteed and this customs guy was being overly pedantic, clearly sensing they were up to something shifty. Rafael was trembling. This wasn't part of his deal as boss.

My heart tum tum tum, my leg started shake a little bit, and then I take a breath, breathing exercises, try to calm down. We go together to the X-ray machine. I run quick to the screen and look, it was perfect. Nothing. 'Okay, thank you very much. Bye-bye.' And then we go, so happy.

– Rafael

As usual after a big goal they celebrated, ordering French champagne on room service and giving Barbara, on top of her $10,000 fee, two nights at the stunning cliff-top hotel.

But the danger for Rafael had only really just begun. His old mare started dining out on the bag-swap story, and Rafael's name got bandied around in Bali. He quickly realised this was the problem of using horses who lived on the island. Others he could send home fast. Now his fame was growing, many more people, often strangers, were approaching him in clubs, restaurants, even in the surf, about doing runs; it was great for business, but extremely dangerous.

Everybody knew about this because Barbara talked too much. Marco joked, 'Look, your mule doesn't work. Viejo, old mule and this is the result.' She thought this was cool, she tells everybody, 'I was working for Rafael, and I take the wrong bag, I go back and change it because I'm Barbara.' But here is a small place, everyone knows everything. She was my big mistake.

My partner Poca used to take care of mules – but I start to get a little bit famous. And then many people come to me: 'Hi, you Rafael?' 'Yep.' 'I'm a friend of Barbara's. Sorry to disturb you, but Barbara tells me you need somebody to work.' I was like, 'Fuck, what's Barbara doing?' Then I was like, 'Okay, just wait. You don't need to contact me, we'll talk through Barbara and when I have something, she will call you. Does she know your number?' 'Yeah she knows my number.'

And then I start to have people on standby in Bali. Barbara found a way to find horses for me, take commission, and make money without risk. But this was a very bad move, because she talked to many people who didn't need to know ... because, fuck ... you know ... She was one of the big mistakes I made in my career.

– Rafael

Rafael wasn't unused to dramas with his horses. Another who was tricky and loose-lipped was a long-time friend from Rio, Sparrow. He was a tall, skinny, goofy guy, who'd been asking Rafael for a run since holidaying in Bali several months earlier. Potentially, he was a great horse, with an English passport and a lot of travel experience, but being worldly wise meant he was acutely aware he was playing Russian roulette.

After months of hassling, Rafael gave him a run. He sent him cash to buy a flight from Rio to Bali, via Peru to pick up the cocaine. But after nervously biting his nails in Lima for a week, and no sign of the bag of drugs, Sparrow bolted empty-handed back to Rio. Rafael was annoyed but practical and organised a runner, Carlos, to deliver the surfboard bag with 2.4 kilos of cocaine directly to Sparrow's doorstep in Brazil, two days later.

Sparrow was finally off and racing across the skies. He flew via Johannesburg to Bangkok, where he changed airlines. Singapore was the next transit stop and he started to spook again. Now only hours from Bali customs, he kept imagining being busted and executed. To soothe his panic, he went to the smokers' lounge and puffed non-stop for 90 minutes. Then he forced his heavy legs to walk back down the corridors to board his flight to Bali. It was 2 a.m. He was having dark thoughts; these could be his last steps as a free man for a long time, maybe for ever. Suddenly, he was at the departure gate. It knocked him out of his fog of fear. The seats were empty; reality hit – he'd missed the flight. It had left 25 minutes earlier, with his surfboard bag on board. Sparrow knew he was now in deep trouble. He raced to a public phone to call Rafael, waking him up. 'I missed my aeroplane,' he confessed like a naughty kid. The line went blue as Rafael blew expletives down it, but he quickly became practical.

'Okay, let's be calm, calm. We're going to do this. Go to the Garuda desk and rebook on the next flight,' he said evenly, suddenly mindful not to spook Sparrow into bolting again.

Rafael was a little bit fed up with me.
    – Sparrow

Sparrow flew out on the next flight at 7 a.m. For nearly three hours his heart beat hard and fast as he was absorbed by a movie in his head, imagining police with machineguns, a squalid little cell, his life razed, wiped, finished. Terrible visuals were rushing through his brain. He thought about his life. Was his dead father looking down disappointed? What would his mum think if he went to jail? Would he ever see his sister again? He questioned why he was doing this – he was a qualified architect – but he knew it was the lure of $12,000 fast cash. Even in these darkest moments, he didn't think of ditching the bag. All too soon he arrived in Bali, and the bag was sitting on the floor near the conveyor belt. He showed his ticket, grabbed the bag and walked over to customs. He was terrified. This was it, right now, the seconds he'd been dreading; mere seconds but they could wipe out the entire rest of his life. He breezed past. Ordeal over.

Suddenly, he felt like a rag doll that had been flung around interminably by a heavyweight champ. The mind-blowing nervous tension fizzled into limp-limbed exhaustion; the line of adrenalin that had sustained him had been cut. As he walked out, home free, into Bali's bright sunshine and cloying heat, he felt like collapsing. He was happy to see Rafael standing waiting for him among the tourists, vaguely disguised in a sports cap, with his hair scrunched up into it, and sunglasses. The old friends smiled at each other, but when Sparrow discovered Rafael had come on his motorbike and not in his car, he simply slung him the bag and teetered off on his spindly legs into the distance to get a taxi. He was way too wobbly to sit on the back of a bike.

Sparrow may have been a bit flaky, but he'd flashed past the post in the end. He went straight to the Bali Subak Hotel in

Legian, where many runners stayed, and had a bit of a lie-down, daydreaming now of the sunny weeks ahead of surfing and partying.

A few hours later, Rafael picked him up in his Jimny, swung via Fabio's house – he was also an investor in this run – and went to a party where Sparrow met the island's big buyers, the Indonesians. It was rare that a horse got to meet them, but Sparrow was a friend of Rafael's.

Barbara had also met them, but she wasn't ever going to deal directly with them. That was no risk; she was a disaster. She turned up at Rafael's house one day wanting to buy some coke to use, but he was rushing out to a party at a big Indonesian boss's villa. She tagged along.

It was sophisticated and posh, with the rich Indonesians smoking cigars and bringing out a silver tray to serve up lines of coke for everyone in the room. They gave it to their trustable man, Rafael, first but he gestured to Barbara, saying, 'Ladies first.' Barbara picked up the little straw and bent over the silver tray, but was finishing a mouthful of chips. She sneezed, spitting bits of chip all over the plate and blowing the coke to smithereens. Rafael was embarrassed and apologised profusely, then pulled out his own coke to make new lines, after cleaning off Barbara's soggy chip bits.

> *I say, fuck, I cannot take this bitch any more. She's too much. I was so embarrassed in front of the big boss at the table. I say, 'Barbara, look what you did.' She says, 'Sorry, sorry.'*
>
> *The coke disappeared, flew, potato spit everywhere. I take care of the situation ... I say, 'Oh sorry, sorry,' and then run*

to the toilet, wash the thing. She was apologising but people were a little bit stressed. And then I make the plate dry, heat it up and take my own coke and make lines.

'Sorry guys, she's a little bit too much. Barbara, don't come close, please.' I make it funny, but they were pissed off with her.
 – Rafael

The night Sparrow met the buyers was also a glamorous party. These guys were the bosses in Bali. They tried to control the island, wanting the cartel players to sell solely and directly to them, so they could sell on to the many big international buyers coming to the island and the local gangs, particularly Laskar, who sold drugs with impunity inside some of the clubs where they did security. These bosses were now filthy rich and didn't only sell drugs but owned villas, restaurants, shops, bars and houses.

These guys . . . before they sell shells on the beach and now they have properties.
 – Rafael

At this point, three of the top Indonesian buyers in Bali were Singapore Edy, Sumatran Nanang, and Taylor. Sumatran Nanang was an aggressive, pudgy-faced, overweight guy with wavy hair that hung past his ears. He usually dressed in tennis shoes, jeans and T-shirt. He was notorious for practising black magic against his enemies – usually with great effect, as the Balinese believed in it totally.

Taylor always dressed in expensive outfits, tailored pants

and long-sleeved Italian designer shirts. He now owned a restaurant on the beach near Fabio's. Singapore Edy was always sharply dressed too – shirt, tie, leather shoes, Rolex. He'd once done a stint in prison for possession of a range of drugs.

Another big case involved Edy Kusyanto – the owner of Ibiza restaurant in Kuta. He was caught in 1995 for possession of drugs, including 307 grams of hashish, 100 grams of cocaine, 9.8 grams of marijuana and 17.9 grams of ecstasy.
  – Jakarta Post, 16 September 1999

I think he got three years. Not so much, because he paid to get out and came back.
  – Rafael

Rafael had met Edy in his pizzeria one day as he sat eating lunch with Fabio, who was already working with him. Fabio pointed across and said, 'You want drugs, that's the boss.' Rafael was keen to meet him, and they soon went upstairs to his office, where Edy sat down at his desk and placed his briefcase on it. 'Right, what do you want?' he asked. 'What do you have?' Rafael enquired. Edy popped the locks and flipped up the lid. It was a pharmacy. 'Everything: ecstasy, *ganja*, coke, heroin.'

Rafael asked if he was interested in buying. 'Oh yeah, why, you have some?'

'Not right now but soon. I can bring you a sample.' Edy was keen. Meanwhile, that afternoon Rafael bought a gram for $100, and the connection was made. But they didn't deal for long, as Rafael liked professionalism.

He says I pay you next week, and then next week, tomorrow, tomorrow, and I was, like, crazy about that.

Selling to the Indonesians was a win win usually. For the westerners, it was safer than trafficking it further, or selling locally, which these bosses didn't like anyway. For the Indonesian bosses, they relied on the South Americans for the cocaine, as it was ubiquitous and cheap in their backyard and they had the contacts.

The Brazilians were the perfect suppliers, as it was safest to move the drugs across the border from the notorious coke countries – Peru, Colombia and Bolivia – to Brazil, and then fly out of one of its many bustling airports, easily camouflaged among the ceaseless throng of tourists. To buy coke in the three coke-producing countries was dirt cheap, usually $1000 a kilo.

In Peru and Brazil, cocaine is like sand in the Sahara, it's everywhere. There are a million places where you can buy a kilo of coke, it's like buying a kilo of sugar in the market.
– Alberto

Every time cocaine crossed a border, its price jumped. Across a single border to Brazil, a kilo cost $5000, and by the time it reached faraway party island Bali, prices hiked up to anything from $20,000 to $90,000 a kilo. The going rate was dictated by how much coke was on the island – that is, whether or not it was snowing in Bali. The cartels, like the Diaz brothers and Rafael, protected their sources, so the Indonesians had to rely on them to get the stuff.

If foreign dealers didn't play by their rules, the Indonesians got angry, as an Aussie rookie learnt. After months of partying on the club circuit, he came to know a couple of the Indonesian bosses. So when he met someone in the surf who'd arrived with 2 kilos in his bag, he acted as sales agent, offering it to Nanang first. Nanang was keen but overstocked and asked him to wait a few days. But the Aussie didn't, he sold it.

As soon as Nanang learnt of the treachery, he sent two of his men to deliver an ultimatum: leave Bali or die. The surfer went into hiding for six months, avoiding clubs and restaurants, until one of his Peruvian drug-dealer friends offered Nanang a sweet coke deal as a peace offering for him, which was accepted.

Dealer Alberto refused to live by the rules. As an agent juggling sellers and buyers, he usually couldn't sit on the stuff or the sellers grew impatient and angry. Most sellers pushed him to offload it fast and in Bali there were always big buyers arriving from France, Italy, Australia, New Zealand, Japan and many other countries, with endless cash and runners ready to go. It was a frenetic business and Alberto was always keen to avoid sitting on coke.

You have to spend money on a hotel and it's a risk because you're sitting on a bomb, it can explode at any time.
– Alberto

One afternoon he offered Nanang a kilo of coke, but the boss needed time to organise cash. Alberto prevaricated, not promising to keep it, and when an Australian turned up with a briefcase full of cash, he sold it. A few days too late, Nanang rang to say he was ready. Alberto broke the news; it was gone. Nanang asked him to come to his shop.

As soon as Alberto walked into Nanang's office, he copped a fist in the face so hard that he reeled back into the wall. It hurt like hell, but he didn't retaliate. He couldn't forget it was their country, especially as Nanang's soldiers were now surrounding him. But fury blazed in his eyes. Nanang saw it and his temper blew. He grabbed a chair, lifted it above his head, set to smash it down on Alberto. Two of his men stepped in between them.

It gave Alberto a second to interject. 'Hey, wait a second. It's not my fault, you know, it wasn't me calling the shots.'

Nanang was trembling with rage. 'I don't give a fuck.'

Alberto grabbed his phone, saying, 'Hold on one second, I'm going to put you on the phone to my friend.' Alberto called the seller. 'Man, this is fucked up; the guy just punched me in the face. Now you fucking sort something out.'

The seller located another kilo of coke for Nanang at the same price. All the dealers knew the Indonesians were volatile – charming one minute, ready to kill you the next – and Nanang was the worst.

There were also fractious tensions between the cartels that flared up when tentative rules of business were violated. The cartels wanted to keep the price as buoyant as possible, but sometimes it collapsed when a Peruvian undercut, sabotaging the market for self-interest. It was easy for them to sell it dirt cheap, as they bought it for so little at home, and had minimal outlay if they carried it themselves. It was fine if they sold it cheap to the cartels, but not to the Indonesian bosses or other international buyers. The rate was usually around $50,000 a kilo, but if supply was weak it shot up to $90,000 or if strong could drop to $20,000. These were Bali's market trends.

Their drug businesses were volatile enough, with busts constantly blowing the bottom line, so when it was one of their own sabotaging the market, it exacerbated the fury.

Jose Henrici, aka Borrador, was living between Peru, where he had a son, and Bali. His expertise was stitching the bags, often working for Rafael packing coke in Peru or Bali into backpacks and surfboard bags. He'd worked with Rafael on Sparrow's second run, meeting the horse in Cuzco, Peru, to give him the bag. Borrador was part of the business, but a soldier not a boss. He'd started getting constantly high, sweating profusely from overuse. Now he'd brought in some coke he bought for $1000 at home, packed and trafficked it himself, and was undercutting everyone.

The Peruvians were putting down the price; that was big fight sometimes with them. We say, 'What the fuck, you fuck the business.' We were selling a kilo here for $50,000, $48,000 and in the end they sell for less than $20,000.

Good quality?

The best. And they start to fuck us, and then we catch one, one time, and tell him get out of the island, motherfucker.
– Rafael

Rafael went out hunting for Borrador the night he discovered his crime. Nanang had been asking Rafael to alert him as soon as he got more coke, but when Rafael offered it to him for the low price of $25,000, as supply was strong, Nanang declined. The boss was now stocked up because Borrador had just sold a few kilos to him for $18,000 each.

Rafael was apoplectic. It was vital for the Bali cartels to keep the prices above at least $25,000 a kilo. Random tourists who lobbed with stuff often naively sold for crazy low prices to the cartels or professional agents like Alberto, but they didn't know the big Indonesian buyers, so it was usually only each other they had to watch.

That night Rafael and his friend and self-appointed body-guard Jando, a purple belt in Jiu-Jitsu, jumped in the car and went out hunting Borrador. As they drove along a dark narrow road in Canggu, they spotted him going in the opposite direction on his motorbike.

Rafael did a fast U-turn, tore after the bike, quickly over-took it and swerved in front, forcing Borrador to slam to a stop. 'Hey, Rafael,' he waved uncertainly.

'Fuck you, man,' Rafael yelled out the window as Jando burst out of the passenger door, rounding on the bike, kick-ing it over and propelling Borrador to the ground. The Peru-vian had no chance to react. Jando grabbed his hand and snapped his thumb back in the Jiu-Jitsu cowhand technique. Borrador writhed in agony with his arm up in the air as Jando snarled, 'What the fuck do you think you're doing, motherfucker?'

Rafael stayed in the driver's seat keeping an eye on pass-ing traffic. He'd told Jando to scare the guy to death, not actually kill him, but to let him think tonight they were going to dump his corpse into one of the surrounding rice paddies.

Out the window Rafael taunted, 'You can't call your mamma now, you're going to die out here, my friend.' The Peruvian, now on his knees with his hands clasped in prayer, begged, 'Please don't kill me.'

Jando kicked him hard in the chest. 'You pussy, stand up and fight.' Sprawled on the ground, Borrador sobbed, 'I don't want to fight.' Jando whacked him several times in the back of the head. 'Why do you want to fuck our business, motherfucker?' he blasted, hauling him up by a clump of hair.

'I didn't do nothing, it was my friend.'

'Bullshit,' Rafael interjected.

'I need money, quick, that's why we sold like that. Sorry,' he sobbed.

To scare him more, Jando whipped a knife out of his pocket and held its blade against his throat. 'Motherfucker, we aren't going to kill you tonight, but leave Bali now. And if you ever come back and sell this shit for less than $25,000, I will slit your throat.'

In the car, Rafael was starting to get antsy, worried a passing car might stop. 'Jando, let's go quick, let's go.' Jando bent down menacingly close to Borrador's face, warning him not to breathe a word of this tête à tête to Nanang or else, slashing his finger across his throat for emphasis.

'I won't say nothing, sorry, sorry,' Borrador whimpered.

In the next few days Rafael heard from the other Peruvians that Borrador had gone back home to the communal house several dealers shared near Kerobokan, whining that Rafael was going to kill him. No one sympathised. They were grateful Rafael had dealt with him, angry too that he'd been undercutting their businesses.

Borrador flew out to Peru the next day and didn't return for six months, when his problems would become insurmountable with the disappearance of his English girlfriend Kate Osborne, in a case that would make global headlines.

Drug dealer justice wasn't always a heated beating – it could be cold and calculated. Paranoid Poca, in the habit of ripping Rafael off and probably others, had organised a horse to run from Peru to Bali with 2 kilos of cocaine. Without a hitch, the horse flew past the post. But when Poca collected and opened the bag, it was a stinging blow.

'Ah fuck, I have some really bad news,' he sighed to Alberto and another dealer who'd been hired to work on this delivery, babysitting the coke and finding a buyer. They were sitting at a restaurant, waiting for instructions, but instead got the news flash – the job was off, there was no coke. Poca had been sent perfectly packed ... bags of sand.

I asked him, 'What the fuck did you do wrong, man?' For sure, he fucked up somehow. Maybe he didn't pay last time, so this was someone in Peru saying, 'Fuck you'. He still had to pay $10,000 for the horse and for hotels and flight.

Did you see a funny side?

Yeah, for sure. We were laughing and joking like, 'Which beach is it from?' and, 'Okay, so how much can we sell Peruvian sand for in Bali, maybe $100 a kilo?'

Was Poca laughing too?

> No, he wasn't laughing, for sure he wasn't.
> – Alberto

CHAPTER FIVE

M3, THE SUNSET CAR WASH

Many people in Peru dream about getting a job like that – to come to Bali, get $10,000.
– Rafael

Bali's M3 Car Wash Café in Sunset Road was set in a unique building, prominent on the four-lane highway that stretched along the spine of Kuta, Legian and Seminyak. It was a concrete shed the size of a soccer pitch. Its unusual aesthetics stood out even among the oddly eclectic architecture in Bali, with round holes cut into a metal façade. Drug dealers, musicians, politicians and journalists all came to sports nights there; stories were written about the refined water M3 used to wash luxury cars, but never the fact that M3 was a giant money laundry. Its owner, nicknamed Chino from his Chinese heritage, was Bali's biggest drug boss, and regarded as the island's Chinese mafioso.

In Sunset Road, this guy had a fucking big place for tuning cars, you know pimping cars, Porsches, Mercedes, to make them more

fast and furious. Chino was a champion of tuning cars, Indonesia champion five time, they take Porsche and pimp you know . . . neon lights, big wheels.
   – Andre

That place was only to wash money, make clean; his ecstasy factory was in Java.
   – Rafael

Chino and Rafael had clicked as soon as they met and quickly forged a business relationship, with Chino insisting Rafael sell exclusively to him. Their preferred place to talk was at sea. The two would meet at Chino's beachfront jet-ski rental spot in Nusa Dua, jump onto powerful jet-skis and tear way out, then spin to an abrupt stop, inches apart. They'd cut the motors, leaving only the sounds of water slapping against the hulls.

In the distance they could see the curved stretch of Nusa Dua beach, with its many hotels and crowds of tourists. Out here, the water gave them privacy, creating the ideal boardroom – quiet with no bugs or risk of anything but fish overhearing. Using the sand and surf as his office had earned Rafael his nickname 'Beach Boy' among the island's drug dealers.

This day, exhilarated after their wild dash out, they were ready to talk tactics, and figure out the best way of using Chino's Porsche to traffic a few kilos of blow to Australia. His car had just won a tuning competition in Jakarta and was being sent to a motor show in Sydney. This was a slam-dunk for a creative drug trafficker – a waste not to use it. Rafael's creative brain lit up with ideas. Undulating on their jet-skis, they agreed the best strategy was to fill the Porsche's spoiler with coke and cover it in resin, ensuring it would emit no smell.

It worked without a hitch. Chino flew to Sydney with his team and a spare spoiler and simply switched them, selling the 3 kilos of coke to one of his many connections and earning a quick $450,000.

Known as the world's multi-billion-dollar glamour drug, coke's array of euphemisms included snow, blow, Charlie, white dust and nose candy. Given the many borders it had to cross to get to Sydney, prices often skyrocketed to $250,000 a kilo. And using the police method for working out the value of a bust to trumpet it to the press, Chino's 3 kilos in Sydney would be worth well over a million dollars in 'street value' – assuming each gram sold for about $350 and the 3 kilos would be cut and mixed into 6 kilos.

Chino was au fait with Sydney, given it was a drug bosses' mecca on his doorstep, and often spent months at a time there, slinging cash to an Australian consulate official to give him visas in his rotating false passports. He set up an ecstasy factory in Sydney's beachside suburb of Maroubra so he could feed the voracious Australian market without crossing international borders. An Australian car wash café chain gave him the inspiration for his Bali car wash.

Chino's life in drugs started in Bali in the early 1990s when he was invited by a friend to join a rock band. He was in his early twenties and moved from Java to Bali, making $15 a night playing keyboards to tourists in pubs and private clubs. He played alongside guitarist Manto and bassist Putu Indrawan, once both stars in the Bali band, Harley Angel, critiqued by the *Jakarta Post* as 'arguably the best rock band Bali has ever produced'. The guys covered songs by bands like Pink Floyd, Led Zeppelin and Deep Purple. Chino's favourite was Pink Floyd's 'Comfortably Numb' – an omen, perhaps, for a state he'd one day need to get used to.

His life seemed as simple as his signature clothes – a baseball cap, sunglasses, sandals, T-shirt and Capri pants – but at this point Chino was sizzling with ambition. He bought a two-door Honda Civic, rented a house in Kuta, and started a T-shirt business, while covertly moving into ecstasy. When the band split after two years, they lost touch until one day, many years later, Chino rocked up at bassist Putu's unsophisticated family restaurant in a back street of Denpasar in a shiny new green Porsche.

One day he came to my warung [restaurant] by Porsche and told me, 'I'm rich now.' 'What?' 'Yes, I'm rich.' I hadn't seen him for a long time, and suddenly he comes here with a fancy car and I'm wondering, 'Why are you rich now?'

Did you ask him?
Yes. He just smiles, so I didn't ask deeper. I was just happy to have a rich friend who still remembers me.

But were you surprised?
Yeah, very, very surprised. Basically, I didn't know for a long time why this guy was rich.
*   – Putu*

Despite the new Porsche, Putu noticed Chino still wore the same simple clothes; the only subtle difference was his sandals were now Louis Vuitton.

Chino invited Putu to bring in his car for a wash at M3. Putu drove a 1977 Toyota Hilux, so he declined, but he did accept invitations to lunch at the M3 café, where Chino would slip him 400 or 500 thousand rupiah [$40 or $50] from his wallet – for most Balinese, about half their monthly salary.

For me he's Robin Hood but for other people he is evil, and I don't care.

Why?
It's his own business, not my business.
  – Putu

He also invited Putu to the grand opening party of M3, held months after it was operating. People from many walks of Chino's life turned up that night, from musicians and local journalists to drug dealers, including Rafael. If the journalists were aware M3 was a giant laundry, they didn't write it. There were many nights when Chino threw open the doors for parties. The glassed-off café would come alive with music, sometimes with ex–band members Putu and Manto jamming, or large screens erected to broadcast international sports events, while kids, including his own son, played video games.

The drug boss had created a grand Bali life, with status, close ties to politicians and cops, real estate and ritzy toys. He owned a large property on the river in the heart of Legian, with a house, swimming pool and huge parking area for his favourite toys – a fleet of prestige cars and motorbikes. The jet-ski rental business comprised a pier and racks on the sand to stack his 20 machines. He was also building a go-kart race-track, and dreamt of one day hosting the world go-kart championships in Bali.

To stay safe, Chino flew high on the radar with his legitimate businesses, or laundries, but was able to use his smarts, connections and cash to switch any radar off the true source of his immense wealth. There was no better place for the slinging of bribes than Bali and Chino had a number of police on his payroll, with local papers reporting he was 'a close friend of some high-rank government officials'. Police officers working for him would sometimes even pass over envelopes filled with cash to the island's drug dealers.

Sometimes I go to Chino's place, M3, to receive $10,000, or $20,000, and the cop, in uniform, full uniform, gives me the money, says, 'Hey, Andre, Chino left this money for you.' 'Oh, thanks for this.' I would never talk to him about drugs, and he never asked, but for sure the cop knew it's cash for drugs, because he was working for the big boss of cocaine in Bali and moving money for him. The police work for good money to give Chino protection. In a police job in Bali, how much do they get? Two million per month [$200]. Chino pays $2000 per month for the guy just to stay inside and not let the other cops in. Chino is the big boss who works directly with the police.

– Andre

Chino was slightly short, slightly plump, with a round happy face and swollen lips. With his easy laugh, intelligence and quiet nature, he was the sort of person most people liked. To him, what he was doing to make his millions was illegal, but not sinister. It was business. He did it professionally, selling the best quality drugs to voracious markets. He worked hard, making himself and others filthy rich, especially anyone who could help slip drugs past the Australian borders.

Just being a conduit to a pliable customs officer at any Australian sea or air border could turn someone into an overnight millionaire. Corrupt customs officials quickly became obscenely rich. Chino used strategies to ensure they kept their jobs by sporadically 'throwing a load'. Once Chino had a border contact, it was vital to keep him in that position and ensure he didn't incur suspicion for never busting a load. So Chino would send a container especially to bust. To make it look even more legit and successful, he'd sometimes pay someone to do a bit of jail time. Chino could then keep using his guy to clear his drugs. This was a trick used by big drug traffickers across the globe.

For Rafael, working with Chino made things quick, easy and safe. He could just sell the bulk of his coke to someone he liked and trusted; they were friends now, but it was the business that bonded them. The deal was that any coke Rafael got, he'd sell to Chino so that he could try to have some control over Bali's cocaine market, to augment his booming ecstasy business, renowned for its world-class pills.

My pills are the best in the world.
   – Chino

The deal suited Rafael, despite riling the other Indonesian buyers, who were being overshadowed by Chino.

It was hard because they knew each other. They got jealous. It was a buyers' war. They say, 'Why are you selling to him and not to me?'

But Chino wanted to control, he had big eyes. He says, 'You are going to work with me; you cannot sell to Nanang or anybody, only to me. Come to me with everything you bring. Anything that comes from your friends, I want to buy. Just bring it to me and I will give you commission. You don't need to take any risk.'

And I say, 'Okay.'

– Rafael

Chino knew about most of the big loads of coke coming to Bali, with his men instructed to keep an ear to the ground. If he got news it was suddenly snowing and one of Rafael's guys had smuggled it in, he'd get his right-hand man, Bejo, a tall, skinny Indonesian, to go to Rafael's house, collect him and bring him to M3 to explain.

Bejo is a danger guy, fucking danger guy.

Why?

He was in the jail here, Kerobokan, two or three times. He's from Laskar Bali; now he has the biggest security company here, for banks, and this guy always has guns. He's a scary guy.

And he still works for Laskar?
Yeah.

   – Andre

Sometimes I was in my house, doing nothing, and then Bejo comes. 'Rafael, Chino wants to talk to you.' 'About what?' 'I don't know.' I say, 'Okay, let's go.' Then we go and Chino says, 'Do you know that some coke has come in the island?' 'No.' 'Well, my people know, somebody is selling coke here. Find out who this guy is. I hear it is Brazilian.' Sometimes it was French, or Italians, but Chino's soldiers knew when the shit started selling in the street. He says, 'Rafael, find this motherfucker, let's fuck him.' I say, 'We don't need to do anything, they are going to fuck themselves.' It's funny, because sometimes people come, they don't even speak English, they don't have any connections, they just hear it's good to bring coke to Bali, and they bring it. They try to do it themselves. It's hard, you have to have connections to sell 1 kilo. Whoa, if you try to sell coke in the street, gram by gram, it's very dangerous.

They fuck up. Or they cannot sell, and they start using it, getting crazy, and in the end they come to me, 'Please, Rafael, help me to sell the shit.' I say, 'Why didn't you tell me before, did you sell to someone else?' Because I worry about getting a problem with Chino.

   – Rafael

Usually, Rafael and Chino would work it out amicably, but sometimes Chino's temper blew, revealing his cold-blooded side.

Bejo and three Indonesian gorillas came to my house with guns.
Chino ordered them, 'Go to Rafael's house, ask him what the
fuck he's doing, why didn't he sell the shit to me?' But the shit
was not mine.

Bejo says, 'Let's go to Chino to talk to him.'

I say, 'No problem, I can talk to him anytime, but why are
the fucking guys here with guns near my family, my kids?' I got
very pissed off.

– Rafael

At M3, Chino was waiting and angrily flipped a table as Rafael
walked in. 'You wanna fuck with me?' he yelled.

'Man, this shit isn't mine. I don't have anything to hide. If
you want to play hard, I can find out who put it here, then
fuck him very bad, teach him to not fuck you.'

I find out it is this guy, fucking Dimitrius the Greek, who brings
and sells it here. He put my name in the fire. Somebody maybe
asks him, 'Who brings this stuff?' and he says, 'Rafael'. He knows
I am the guy, so why does he try to do this behind my back? He
was going to get the same price with me, and I make a com-
mission too.

I come back to Chino and say, 'This is the guy. What are
you going to do?'

'Let's fuck him.'

I say, 'Beat him, put him out of the island, let's take action.'

Chino tells me, 'Okay, take two guys and give him some shit.'

– Rafael

Rafael was friends with the Greek, who used to do frequent Lemon Juice runs for Marco, and had even asked Rafael about doing coke runs. He was smart and hung out with the crew at the club and their other usual haunts. But now he was starting to invest, and keen to be a boss. Rafael had introduced him to many of his Bali contacts, which made his betrayal even more bitter.

Rafael was fuming as he stormed out of M3 with two of Chino's meanest-looking soldiers. They were hard-faced thugs, with hulked up, tattooed bodies, who could scare the living daylights out of someone by just showing up.

As soon as Dimitrius unwittingly opened the door, Rafael burst into his house shouting, 'Why are you doing this to me, motherfucker? Why are you playing behind my back?'

The Greek shot back, 'What are you doing, Rafael? You can't just come in here.'

It was a mistake. One of the thugs cracked him hard on the back of the skull. The Greek's legs buckled. The thug lifted his shirt to flash Dimitrius a glimpse of his pistol. Rafael's eyes blazed as he looked at the Greek, 'Take your glasses off and look in my eyes. Tell me the truth. Did you put any coke in Bali this week?' Chino's two attack dogs were champing at the bit, waiting for a chance to tear him apart.

The Greek was now a fawning mess. 'Sorry, sorry. Please don't kill me. It was not my project, was my friend's.'

Now it was conclusive. Rafael wasn't interested in pathetic excuses.

'I don't give a shit, my friend; now you are going to pay. You come here, you sell on the island, you think you are the boss. Now the big boss wants to kill me. He thinks I put the shit here behind his back. Now you must come and explain yourself to my boss.'

The Greek fell to his knees sobbing. 'I'm not going anywhere; are you gonna kill me?'

Rafael felt like punching him, but right now this guy was too pathetic to hit, with his hands in prayer position, on his knees, pleading for his life. 'Maybe, depends what you say. If you still have some cocaine, you must give it to us now. I'm supposed to take everything you have and kill you, but I want to just buy what you have, then you have one week to go, otherwise, these are Chino's words, "We gonna fuck him very bad." I believe it's better you leave the island.'

He was pissing his pants, like a chicken, he was so nervous, he was such a puss.
  – Rafael

The Greek quickly confessed to having half a kilo of blow still stashed in a safety deposit box up the road in Legian. He offered to get it later, when it got dark.

'No, now,' Rafael shouted. 'If I come back to Chino's office without the coke, without you, I'm gonna get trouble, so it's better your mother cry than mine. Let's go.'

Dimitrius asked if he could first change out of his wet board shorts. Rafael agreed, trailing him to the bedroom to ensure he didn't try a stunt, like leaping out a window. The thugs came too.

'Only you come,' Dimitrius said to Rafael, creating instant suspicion.

'Why, you have something up there?' Rafael asked, turning to Chino's thugs and ordering, 'Come.' They tore apart the bedroom as the Greek stood in the corner, changing his pants, but found nothing. They jumped on their bikes and rode to the safety deposit boxes, where Dimitrius handed Rafael the half a kilo of coke.

Calmer now that he had sorted this out, Rafael said to his ex-friend, 'You have one week to get out of Bali, my friend.'

The Greek quickly acquiesced. 'Okay, I will fix my ticket. I don't want a problem with you, Rafael.'

'Okay, if you come here again, call me first, we're gonna pay you the same price, but you can't come here and put your stuff in the street. You think you're Al Pacino, Scarface? Well, you're not.'

We pay him only $10,000 for the coke; was good stuff. We kick him out from the island. And everything was okay.
  – Rafael

Several months later, the Greek returned to Bali, often working in a separate clique to Rafael with Italian dealer Carlino. But they didn't conflict with Rafael or Chino, as they sent the coke to Australia on Carlino's luxury catamaran, or sold to international buyers in Bali, but never in the streets. Soon, all of them, including Rafael, would be investors in an audaciously big run that turned deadly for one of their mutual friends.

Rafael was getting so busy he was tossing money into other people's runs, including Marco's Lemon Juice, like a big gambler slinging handfuls of chips onto numbers on the roulette table. Lots of people were investing. Chino had people putting up a million dollars for a container load of drugs, doubling their money in days. The odds were gigantic, and the risk minimal if you knew the secrets of the game.

Chino was a calculated gambler and knew Rafael was trustworthy and smart, so he started investing in his runs, rather than just buying on arrival. Some weeks, they were bringing up to 20 kilos to Bali, using two or three horses on different flights. They were also able to traffic big amounts using Rafael's creative new method of packing the coke into windsurfer booms.

Rafael had pioneered the boom method, after surfboard bags became overused. Always wanting to be a step ahead, and have new options, he'd spent weeks studying sports equipment, pondering what to try next. The first boom he packed was the trickiest. He bought the equipment, then set to work in a beach bungalow with Poca. It took them two full days of figuring it out to ensure it was be X-ray-proof.

It was a complex job to make the coke invisible. First they put it in a blender to make it baby-powder fine, obliterating any rocks, then they used a funnel to fill the boom. Finally, they used a tailor-made metal rod, with a coin welded to its end, to pound the coke down hard into the aluminium tube to compact and cement it, and eliminate any air bubbles. This first time, their technique was imperfect – they lost 2 per cent of the coke, as the fine dust blew all over the room, covering them.

I start punching the coke ... suddenly, poof, the coke shoots out from the tube like a bullet from compression of air; we get coke in the eyes, in the face, and that shit comes in my mouth, on my skin, I start to feel itchy. It mixes with your circulation when you sweat and goes in your pores, makes you high; I was like, 'Man, I don't feel good,' – breathing in all the powder, feeling dizzy, hallucinating from the dust, I start to see two people when I look at Poca ... I say, 'Let's stop this shit, let's go to the beach, close up and come back here tomorrow.'

Fuck, it was a big job. That night my body was so tired, pain in my muscles, my hands full of bubbles, I can't sleep; I was totally fucked.

– Rafael

The next morning, a fine mist of snow had settled on the room, covering everything, and they quickly got high again. But they finished the job, sent the boom with its invisible kilo to Malaysia, made $65,000 and, most importantly, had a new winning method. The pair flew to Peru to teach their packers there how to do it, under strict orders to keep it secret.

Obviously, there were no patents in the drug business, and before long horses would talk, booms would get busted, and other traffickers would become aware of the method, but for the time being it belonged exclusively to Rafael and Poca.

Chino knew of the new method, but he left those details up to Rafael. For Chino, being an investor with Rafael from the get-go meant an extra leg of risk, but he got a low price and it also ensured he knew when and how much blow was coming to the island.

But it wasn't always a win. Chino and Rafael were involved in a run by two attractive Mexicans, Clara Gautrin, 32, and

Vincente Garcia, 29, who came into Denpasar posing as lovers, but with an audacious 15.2 kilos of cocaine in their surfboard bag. As Vincente picked up the bag from the carousel, it was already being watched by Bali customs officers. They'd been faxed a tip from Vincente's ex-drug boss in Mexico, as revenge for being cut out of the loop.

Prosecutors asked for death for Vincente; the second drug trafficker in Bali to face possible execution. But the right palms were greased. Clara got seven years and Vincente got life, with a wink that if he kept quiet he'd get out in years. It had been impossible for the judiciary to give a lesser result without the risk of exposing the bribe, as a French trafficker had just been sentenced to life for carrying a lot less.

Michael Blanc got busted at Denpasar Airport with 3.8 kilos of hashish in his dive tanks. He could have cut a deal, but didn't. His mother Helene had been told a payment of between $330,000 and $420,000 could buy her son a 15-year sentence. But she refused, believing her son was innocent, and threw away the only strategy that had a chance of working.

Clara and Vincente were both sent to Kerobokan Prison, in the heart of Bali's tourist area. By chance, Chino's twin brother Toto, an addict, was also soon busted for using drugs. Doing a few months in Kerobokan meant he could easily be the liaison between the Mexicans and his brother. Chino organised private cells for them, and visiting time together. In the less strict men's block, Vincente got a 26-inch LCD television mounted on the wall, internet and a pump for hot and cold running water – making his cell more luxurious than most Balinese homes.

Vincente became a fitness fanatic and kept a low profile as advised, quickly becoming regarded by other inmates as aloof and arrogant. It was all part of the strategy to one day slip out and go home unnoticed.

Outside, Chino was busy juggling his businesses, and delegating to those he could trust. When he invested in Rafael's runs, he handed over the cash as well as the reins. Rafael by now had his business streamlined – with packing crews in place in Brazil and Peru – so he could call the shots from strategically chosen public phone boxes in Bali.

Things were becoming more easy ... I just call, organise, transfer the money through Western Union, and in Peru and Brazil they pack the bag, send the horse and I pick up here.
– Rafael

But it was always a gamble and a horse could crash from the slightest slip. One of his best horses, who'd done 11 runs, got busted on his twelfth. He was flying out of Buenos Aires with 5 kilos of coke in windsurfer booms. The guy was smart, cool and unflappable. On his past three runs, he'd used the tactic of driving from South Brazil to Buenos Aires, as Argentina's airports were slightly easier to penetrate. This time, an X-ray took him down. Rafael's packers had failed. He paid them a hefty $10,000 fee per bag, as the job was dangerous and vital. But they'd failed to fill the booms completely with cocaine, and plugged the ends with fabric. The X-ray showed different colours, creating suspicion. It was an expensive mistake.

Rafael waited for the guy, but he simply didn't turn up. It was always a risk that a horse would either do a runner, or get busted, which was why Rafael felt an adrenalin rush every single time a horse emerged from the airport doors into the Bali sun. Almost always he went to the airport, either to pick up the horse or to spy on them, shadowing their taxi to the Bali Subak Hotel, to ensure they didn't flee or have a police tail.

Once Rafael picked up the coke from the horse, he'd meet Chino at a small beachfront hotel in Nusa Dua. Chino always turned up in a bland chauffeur-driven Toyota Avanza, non-descript on the outside, with a spruced up red leather interior, never using his attention-attracting sports cars. His soldiers would park jet-skis on the beach so, if necessary, he could sprint across the sand and be in the water in seconds. Safety was his priority and so far his scrupulous attention to detail had kept him out of jail. He always insisted Rafael come alone. Their meetings were quick; he'd efficiently test and weigh the coke, then go.

Chino has soldiers everywhere, local people working for him. They make into small quantities and sell gram by gram in the street.

High quality cocaine?
Oh, but they mix, they do all the shit.

At the clubs?
Yeah, I think they sell in Double Six. At the door of the toilet the guys say, 'Coke, coke, ecstasy?'

And Chino sends it overseas?

He has good connection; he sends it to Singapore, Malaysia, Australia. His main goal was to send it to Australia because it's the best money.

– Rafael

After Chino had left the hotel with the coke, Rafael would clean up the evidence, often giving the black plastic wrapping to one of his friends. They would use a knife to scrape off the oily remains stuck to the plastic. 'My friends were so happy, they could sometimes take 5 grams because the plastic grabs a lot of coke.'

Other times, he'd just burn it. On his way home, he'd buy a litre of petrol in a glass bottle from one of the infinite shanty-style shops along the roads selling to local motorcyclists. He'd ride to the beach or a rice paddy, throw all the plastic bags and evidence down, douse in petrol, flick a match and burn the lot. When the coke was carried in a surfboard bag, he'd get rid of the plastic and wash the bag, simply dunking it in his swimming pool or getting the maid to wash it in the shower, making it safe to re-use: 'The water takes all the coke, kills the coke.'

Rafael's deal with Chino was to get half his cash the following day and the rest a couple of weeks later. It was delivered in the same spot, same way. One of Chino's men would ring, saying, 'Meet me at the petrol station near the Bali Deli, 10 pm.' That night they'd arrive on motorbikes. Chino's guy would give Rafael a plastic shopping bag, often with about $50,000 in it and a sarong loosely tossed on top. It would be a quick, no chitchat exchange. Rafael would then take the bag home, adding it to the copious stash in his safe or wardrobe.

Ostensibly, Rafael was exclusive with Chino, but covertly he broke the rules, operating his own pyramid of sellers – such as Brazilian Ruggiero, or several French, Italian and Australian people, who sold small packets to western customers. Selling gram by gram was riskier, as it required dealing with more people, but the prices were high. It meant that even in times when it was snowing, or a Peruvian was undercutting, Rafael could still easily make $50,000 a kilo by getting his guys to sell grams, mostly to rich expats on the island – professionals, business people, doctors and lawyers – delivering to their villas, luxury homes or sometimes their restaurants. These people often paid $150 to $200 a gram.

Rafael also sold kilos to international buyers, but only if Chino wasn't aware of the coke arriving. Rafael felt this was fair, as Chino was sometimes fully stocked and told him to wait because he'd bought cheaply from a Peruvian.

As much as Chino tried to control the island, it was impossible. Bali was a frenetic drug hub, a transit point to Asia and the Pacific, with the world's biggest drug mafia coming to holiday, mingle, network, and organise deals in luxury hotels, in the sun, in paradise.

Italian drug trafficker Sergio Boeri was friendly with the cartel players, including Rafael, who'd been to parties at his villa. Sergio flew in and out of Bali on false passports often, until the day he flew in to celebrate his gorgeous girlfriend's 33rd birthday. Instead of spending the special day sipping French champagne in a luxurious villa, they both spent it on the concrete floor of Bali's police cells.

The alleged head of an Italian drug smuggling syndicate, Sergio Boeri, accused of trafficking at least 30 tons of cocaine and other narcotics from Brazil to Europe, was extradited from Bali to his homeland on Saturday night.

Under heavy police guard, Boeri, 32, was taken from Bali Police Headquarters to the Ngurah Rai International Airport, where he was transferred into the custody of two Rome-based Interpol officers . . .

Boeri, one of Interpol's most wanted men, was caught by Bali Police on 18 August when he arrived at Ngurah Rai Airport with his girlfriend.

– Jakarta Post, 9 February 2002

CHAPTER SIX

DREAM LIFE

All the people in Bali started to know I was the guy who takes care of the coke business. I was the biggest show-off. Cars, motorbikes . . . I buy a Harley-Davidson, a 1-kilo gold necklace. I go out every night, spend money. I build my house and all the young people come here . . .

They say, 'Fuck, whose house is this? What does he do?' 'Dealing coke.' 'Oh, I wanna do too.' And then they try, but they don't have any connection. In the end they come to me, 'Please help me, I have 10 kilos, 5 kilos, 3 kilos.' And I become an agent for them.

I have a collection – five bikes, Honda, Harley-Davidson . . . Fuck, I was crazy. I have one Kawasaki Ninja. People looked at me and asked, 'Who is this guy with this bike?' 'He's the Brazilian guy who takes care of the coke in Bali.'

– Rafael

Rafael was living a decadent life, working hard and playing harder in a blaze of parties, orgies, surfing and drug dealing, often high from his own copious cocaine use. With horses now bringing up to 20 kilos some weeks, the cash was flying in fast.

He'd built his dream house right in front of a surf beach in Bali's Canggu area, paying a customary bribe for permission to erect it within the 100-metre no-build zone. He slung an official $15,000 to set it back just 93 metres from the water. The only catch with the island's endemic corruption was that, within a year, someone else had slung cash to build even closer, directly in front of Rafael's house. He could hardly complain.

Designed by a top architect and featured in magazines, the two-storey mansion was spectacular. It incorporated all Rafael's boyhood fantasies, like the diving board off his bedroom balcony. Most mornings he got up, coming down from a cocaine high, and stumbled bleary-eyed to the board, then dived into the 22-metre pool, racing straight back up his stylish spiral staircase to dive again and again, until he felt fresh.

Anyone entering the high-walled playground through the sliding wooden gate could see it was a labour of love, created by a person with a passion for the ocean. The Beverly Hills-style palm-lined driveway was built with coloured pebbles, shaped in waves. Wave-shaped indents, each with its own lighting, decorated the outside house walls. Beautifying the edge of the pool were four big-breasted mermaids that spouted water strong enough for Rafael to stand under for a hydro massage, usually after a surf. For his more indulgent massages, there was a poolside cabana with its own Bose sound system, and a limestone deck for sunbaking.

Inside the house, large twin feature doors were inlaid with mother-of-pearl flower designs and the floor was recycled teak. The jacuzzi on the deck – for champagne parties – had an expansive view of the surrounding paddy fields.

Next to the pool was a 12-metre high water tower, which Rafael climbed up daily to check the swell. It was also an ideal vantage point to spy on police spying on him.

I think I am the king of the world. I think nothing is going to happen, I always say this in my mind, 'I am never going to get caught.' Sometimes my friends say, 'Hey man, you have to put some money away in case one day you have problems.' I say, 'Fuck off, man, I'm never gonna get caught. Never.'
– Rafael

Rafael refused to think negatively, but wasn't oblivious to the constant threats to his freedom. For protection, he put shards of glass along the top of the concrete walls, kept three large dogs roaming and installed state-of-the-art cameras, infrared laser sensors and intercoms bought in Singapore. His elaborate security wasn't to stop thieves, but to prevent Bali cops scrambling over the wall and planting drugs.

But most of the time he was lax anyway, keeping evidence inside his house.

When you do this shit for a long time, you think it's normal. Sometimes I sit with 5 kilos of coke in my house. I know I am doing something wrong, breaking all the rules.
– Rafael

He was also keeping up to half a million dollars at home, which could be used as evidence against him in a drugs case. After a run or two, the whole house would be billowing with cash – bursting from his Bose speakers, the wardrobes and his capacious safety deposit box, which was sometimes so overstuffed with money he had to bang it shut with his feet.

To help solve the problem, he hired a Frenchman who specialised in designing magician-like hiding places, and whose ingenuity was a godsend to Bali's drug dealers. He built Rafael a TV cabinet with invisible drawers, towel racks with large hollow tubes and a vacuous Buddha head that opened with an undetectable screw.

> *I have so many secret spots but I still have too much money. I have half a million dollars in my hand, in my safe. Money was not a problem at all. I have plenty of problems, but money was not one. The only problem was this: where am I gonna put these fucking bags of money because I don't have any more space? It was totally crazy.*
> – Rafael

Early on, Rafael had accepted payments in rupiah, creating impossibly bulky stashes, given that $100 converted to about 1 million rupiah. Some nights he drove around delivering deals of 5, 10, 20, even 100 grams, to friends; he started out filling his pockets with the cash, then moved to the glove box, then shoved it under the seats and in the door pockets. By the end of the drive, cash would be spilling out everywhere. At home he'd gather it all up, shoving fistfuls into plastic bags, then toss the bags up onto a shelf in his wardrobe, throwing clothes on top. Soon, he started accepting payment only in dollars or euros.

Although his fortune did go up and down, most of the time he was so flush that he lost count of his bags of cash. One afternoon he grabbed a plastic bag stuffed with $50,000 out of his safe to take some to buy a motorbike. Not wanting to expose the cash in his fishbowl upstairs bedroom, in case police were spying with binoculars, he nipped into his en-suite. When there was a knock on the door, high on coke and paranoid, he flung the bag under the sink, but left a stray US$10,000 out. He saw it and stashed it into a toilet bag. At the door, it was only a friend. But it wasn't until six months later, on the first night of a live-aboard surf trip, that he went to brush his teeth and found, mixed among his condoms, toothpaste and cologne, the US$10,000.

I totally forgot about it. I was like, 'What?' And then I didn't have a place to hide it in the boat. I was, 'Shit, why did I bring this sort of money?' But I made a hole in the surfboard cover and kept it there.

– Rafael

Rafael was flinging cash around like it would snow for ever. With a young family, he now employed a staff of four maids, a driver and a gardener, who were paid double the average US$80 monthly wage and given bonuses, like their kids' school fees or new motorbikes. In return they were loyal, and Rafael got them to do little tasks, like changing bags of rupiah to dollars at the money changer, or unwittingly delivering drugs to customers, usually rolled up in a magazine or somehow hidden. If friends needed cash, he often gave them a bundle. He also sponsored Balinese kids to surf at the beach in front of his house, buying them new boards, clothes and equipment.

> *Before, they looked after cows in the paddock. Now they are professional surfers, sponsored by Volcom. Now they are champions. That money was not so clean, but I used some for good things.*
> – Rafael

He was known for his largesse, tipping like a titan at restaurants and hosting sumptuous weekend barbecues open to all his friends, mostly the island's drug dealers. They all turned up for the endless free beer, wine and French champagne – which his wife got cheap from a Garuda employee who stole it from the airline's stock. Fresh fish and lobster was delivered to his door in the morning still flapping in a bucket – only the best and freshest would do. It would always be a lively feast of food and nose candy around the pool.

> *Fuck, I don't have peace, I have so many friends. My fridge was always full of Heineken; I have a fridge only for beer, only for wine, barbecue every weekend. I buy 5 kilos of meat, tenderloin, three boxes of beer ... Door open, I don't care who comes. I refused to accept anything from anybody. My house was a club every weekend. It was like a king's life. The money looked like it's never going to finish.*
> – Rafael

He easily spent US$20,000 a month on extravagant living expenses, splurging US$500 a day on groceries at the western food supermarket, Bali Deli, or out at restaurants. He relished the power kick of slipping off and fixing the entire table's bill, usually exorbitant given his group's penchant for top restaurants and French champagne. He also used at least US$3000 worth of cocaine a month. 'I really fucking love this shit.'

After a successful run and surge of cash, sometimes he'd lighten the load by paying his three young kids' school fees or his Canggu Club membership two years early or he and his Swedish wife, Anna, would fly to shopping mecca Singapore with $30,000 to blow on anything their hearts desired – usually designer clothes, sunglasses, face creams, shoes, toys, computers and cameras.

He also regularly shopped on his way back from jobs when his pockets, wallets, shoes and bags and were stuffed with cash. He'd gather up armfuls of Armani T-shirts, a clutch of Gucci sunglasses or five or six pairs of Diesel jeans and take the lot, rarely asking prices. These were the essentials. In Amsterdam, he stocked up on his favourite Prada shoes at €600 a pair.

I love those shoes. I love to shop in Amsterdam. Prada T-shirts, Armani T-shirts. I wore them tight, so they stretch a little bit and can show my body. Normally white or bright colours, because I have dark skin.

– Rafael

Although, like most men, he wasn't a natural-born shopper, he was lured into shops by something catching his eye in a magazine or a shop window. In Singapore one day, on the way home from a trip to pick up cash with his friend Jando, they went hunting for a Rolex he'd spotted in a magazine and had to have – the huge price tag only increasing its allure.

I got crazy when I saw it in a magazine. I wanna have this shit, I'm gonna buy one. A big, beautiful piece; this model is hard to find but I see the price. What? . . . €25,000.
  – Rafael

The moment he found it in a Singapore shop he unclasped his US$3000 brushed-gold limited edition TAG Heuer and sold it to Jando, who'd shamelessly coveted it, for US$1000. Rafael paid cash for the Rolex, avoiding credit cards and traceable records, and strapped it straight onto his wrist.

Back in Bali he relished flaunting his Rolex, even risking wearing it in the surf.

My friends say, 'You crazy if you use it to surf, what if you lose it?' 'I don't care, I'll buy another one.' I like to show off.
  – Rafael

Despite his pockets bulging with more cash than most of the more distinguished-looking customers could ever afford to spend, the tattooed Brazilian didn't always cut it with snooty shop assistants in high-end stores. They gave him plenty of *Pretty Woman* moments, looking down their noses, assuming he couldn't pay and treating him rudely.

Once, passing through Amsterdam loaded with tens of thousands of euros, he went to look for a leather jacket. Casually dressed in jeans and a pair of flip-flops, with stubble on his chin and the tattoos on his arms exposed, he picked up a jacket and asked the price. It should have been a simple conversation – he didn't really even care. But the sales girl insulted him, insisting she could only give the price to buyers and she felt he was just browsing.

Rafael saw red. She'd pricked his ego. He lashed out in a tirade: 'Fuck you, bitch, who do you think you're talking to?' Rifling in his pockets, he pulled out a wad of €500 notes, waving them under her nose and shouting, 'Do you know what these are? These are each worth US$600. See how many I have. You are really stupid. I come here to buy; your job is to sell. Now, I wanna talk to your manager.'

She was losing her poise, close to tears now. 'Please don't say anything, I'll get fired.'

'Yes, you're gonna get fired. You fuck with me, now I'm gonna fuck with you.'

When the manager came and tried to cool the situation, Rafael ranted, 'This fucking bitch doesn't want to serve me. I don't want to deal with her any more.'

Soon after, he walked out with his new €750 Diesel leather jacket.

Another time, in Stockholm, dressed in a Bob Marley collection adidas tracksuit and new running shoes, he was looking for several pairs of sunglasses. Typically, he knew exactly what he wanted: the latest special edition Ray-Bans with a unique lens and shape that he felt suited his face perfectly; the latest US$600 Dior Biker glasses, for stylishly wearing on his bike; and new Oakleys.

But the sales assistant clearly felt this customer couldn't

afford all the glasses. 'Which pair are you going to take?' he huffed.

'All three,' Rafael replied. The guy raised an arrogant eyebrow. 'Ah, this is going to cost more than US$2000,' he said condescendingly.

Rafael's hackles shot up. 'Fuck you, my friend. What's the problem? I can't buy three pairs of glasses? Should I buy one pair now, come back tomorrow?' Rafael pulled the cash from his pocket. 'This is more cash than you will ever have,' he said, waving it in his face. 'Now I'm gonna buy three, I'm gonna pay cash. Do you have a problem with that or should I go to another shop?'

The sales assistant changed his tune.

I think my face looks like a Brazilian bankrupt. They discriminate a lot against me. Maybe because of the tattoos, they think I'm a criminal or something, or they think I come here just to bullshit, just ask the price and go. And then when I start saying, 'This, this, this, and this', they say, 'How you gonna pay?' and I say, 'Cash'. 'Which ones you gonna take?' and I say 'All'. Fuck, they get crazy.

– Rafael

In Bali, the discrimination was reversed. He was the man, hugely popular and, as a VIP guest at all the most exclusive parties, was given bracelets for free drinks. People would invite him to dinners at the best restaurants, telling him to bring some friends, refusing to let him pay. In return, he'd always bring blow and give friends free lines in the bathrooms.

It was funny because I was very friendly, people loved me because I was a nice guy, I know how to be nice in restaurant, eat properly, good education, but my English a little bit broke, but I think this is funny – they laugh when I say some words.

At the parties they give me the VIP bracelets, I cannot spend money because people call me, 'Hey, Rafael, can you come to Warisan tonight, 10 pm, to have a dinner? I invite you.' It was like this ... 'Come here, you can bring your friends, and bring some stuff.' I say, 'Okay.'

They never let me pay. I just do trips to the toilet, give some lines to people, but sometimes when the bill comes I want to show off ... I hide myself and go pay and when the guy asks for the bill ... 'Oh, it's already paid,' because usually nobody lets me pay for anything.

– Rafael

Rafael's fame was growing exponentially. Because the island was small, people knew he was the coke guy. When he walked into a glamorous party, wearing his tight Armani T-shirt, gold chains, with his blond hair and good looks, heads would turn. People would shout, 'Rafael, Rafael', trying to get his attention. When he went to the toilet, people would race behind him asking to buy some blow.

It was funny because I'm busting to piss, I go to the toilet, everybody boom boom boom on the door: 'Rafael, please give me 1 gram.' 'Stop, I want to piss, man,' but they don't give me peace.

– Rafael

The next night he'd do it all over again – swanky dinner, clubs, private parties, orgies at villas, never wearing the same designer clothes on consecutive nights, but always wearing a pair of his favourite Prada shoes, his Rolex, and a splash of his signature, babe-luring, Paco Rabanne XS. 'Fuck, all the girls like that shit.'

Sometimes he'd be sitting in a restaurant and call for the bill, only to be told another table had fixed it up already. He'd ask the waiter who'd paid, often spotting someone looking slyly at him, trying to establish eye contact. Rafael would avoid it, quickly telling the waiter to give the guy his money back; he'd pay his own bill.

When totally random strangers knew he was a coke dealer, it freaked him out. That was way too dangerous.

At orgies and private villa parties, he'd often pull out 10 grams of coke, warm up a plate and make lines for everyone, showing off; and often creating sales, as tourists on holidays or expats were usually keen to buy more. At parties he'd also meet expats who were buying from one of his own customers, who was cutting and selling. After meeting Rafael, they'd be keen to buy direct and cut out the middleman, to get it purer and cheaper. He'd always keep a stash in the doors of his car outside to sell at night, for top prices, to these people.

When I come to this party, they meet me, they wanna buy straight. 'Oh great, I wanna buy some, can you give me a big quantity?' And then the business blow, you know. Before I sell 5, 10 grams and then people come, 'Can I buy 100 grams? You give me a better price.'

– Rafael

Rafael didn't curb his wild partying, despite now living with Anna, an attractive blonde Swede who he wasn't married to but called his wife. They'd met in a bar in Legian, and soon moved in together. Anna liked using coke, and started helping Rafael with business, usually the accounts, as well as pushing him to be tougher. When she'd fallen pregnant with twins, Rafael was thrilled and they'd had another baby soon afterwards. But creating a family hadn't stopped his promiscuous lifestyle and he knew he was still getting away with it because Anna spent a lot of time drinking and being pretty out of it.

His partying was getting so excessive that he'd drink, use coke and have sex with random girls all night, then get home at dawn and sleep until 3 pm. Usually he'd surf two or three waves, too unfit now to stay in longer, his party lifestyle so frenetic and all-consuming that he was sacrificing the reason he'd come to Bali in the first place. In the afternoon, he'd start snorting a bit of coke, then doing his deliveries, or organising his runs, and be ready to party all over again.

That time, I cannot surf, because I have nightlife. I come tired, I sleep all day, I wake up 3 o'clock, jump in the pool, have a shower, massage. Sometimes I put my phone off, say, 'Today, day off. I don't want to talk to anyone.' And I call to the massage people, they come to my place, massage, I do a little bit of gym. At home I have the equipment to get fit, because when I stop surfing so much, I get skinny, I lose weight, lose weight. I said, 'Fuck, I always had a nice body', and I was like living the dream life.

Sometimes I party for two days, party without sleep, you

know we finish in club, then go to somebody's villa for after party, take all this shit, drugs. And then you see another day, keep partying, sometimes go to the beach, jump in the water without sleeping, surf three or four waves just to put out the toxin, breathe a little bit of oxygen. But finish the session – straight away take a line to keep going. What you going to do tonight? Let's go to the party ... Always we meet new people. Let's go to that girl's villa ... It was very crazy.
– Rafael

Every so often, he'd cut the partying and spend 10 days on a yacht for a live-aboard surf trip. He'd take no coke, eat fresh fish, and surf for hours every day, getting fit. It gave him a break from the party scene, especially during the high season, when it was very dangerous to deal drugs, with undercover cops from Jakarta starting to infiltrate and circulate at parties. Sometimes Marco came on these trips, and Rafael's Peruvian partner Poca, who arranged gorgeous hookers from Brazil to come.

A surf trip was like paradise for me, it was my escape. Go to Sumatra. The yacht worth $2 million, with a nice girl, a beautiful model, or sometimes we bring prostitutes from Brazil; import the girls. Pay for their tickets and give them $2000. They do a good job.

A good job?
They fuck very good and don't complain about anything. Very beautiful and fun too.

Do you share the girls?

Yeah, sometimes, not everyone, but the bosses. Poca, he say let's bring two prostitutes I met in Brazil. They stay with us, but we share sometimes. I take his, he takes mine. But we don't share the girls with everybody, only me and Poca.

What would your wife do if she found out you had a prostitute on the boat?

I think she's gonna be pissed off, but she never found out.

And then, come back from the trip, back to Bali ... beard grow, blond hair burned from the sun, dark skin, fit, ready to rock. Bam. And then, 'Where is the party tonight?'

Normally Ku De Ta has four parties in August – the best ones, I can't miss those. They had a white party same day we got back, because I remember we arrived in the airport at seven o'clock, and I have time to come home, shave, shower, put my best clothes, take my 10 grams, put in the pocket, go whaaaah, look for girls.

Was amazing, because everybody miss me ... 'Where've you been, Rafael? Rafael, Rafael, Rafael ...'

– Rafael

CHAPTER SEVEN

ALL'S FAIR IN LOVE AND WAR

Fuck this guy's crazy, like VIP movie star.
  – Rafael

Filthy rich Hells Angels boss, Tota, from Rio, regularly flew to Bali to play for months at a time in party paradise with his drug dealer friends, and gamble at illegal casinos and cock-fights in the backstreets of up-market Seminyak. He was also a fixture at Fabio's beach bar, an unmissable sight with his side-kicks – two young, beautiful, silicone-breasted girls. He threw cash at them to come to Bali, to accompany him everywhere, have sex on call and be centrepieces in his many hotel-room orgies, which he liked to direct and film.

He's a little bit sexy psycho, this guy. Sometimes I come from surfing in Uluwatu, Tota was already at the bar, sitting with the two beautiful girls, sometimes with five girls, him in the middle.
  – Rafael

He was a Hells Angel biker straight out of Hollywood Central Casting's books. He lavished diamonds on the girls, and used them to create a spectacle. It wasn't hard, they were bombshells – a prerequisite to being his travel babes. They dressed to bring men to their knees, bursting out of tiny bikini tops, minis so micro their underwear flashed. Whenever they threw a long bare leg with a 3-inch spiky heel over the back of Tota's bike, tourists, both men and women, stopped and gaped.

He brings those two girls to show off. They have silicone in the tits, big ones, amazing bodies, not one gram of fat, full of tattoos, long hair. Everybody thinks, 'Wow, beautiful, beautiful girls.' They wear skirts, but so fucking short you can see their underwear easy. They make many orgies, the girls with Tota. He was such a pervert, this guy, he loved to do orgies. But a glamour guy, too. Like, if he has a party at Ku De Ta, he pays for the whole table . . . champagne, dinner. He spends a lot of money. He was addicted to gambling too.

– Rafael

Tota had dark curly hair hanging to his shoulders and tattoos covering his whole body, running up and around his neck, and was contemplating getting a Mike Tyson-style tattoo on his face, even sometimes getting henna swirls around his eyes and temples to test it out. Several times Rafael arrived at Tota's hotel, and found him with henna tattoos all over his face. Rafael would laugh when Tota insisted they were real, but a couple of days later they would be gone, until the next time.

Adding to his dark looks, Tota wore a thick beard and moustache shaved to a sharp point at the corner of his jawbone. And his signature outfit, sacrilege to Armani and Gucci-obsessed

Rafael, was a mesh singlet, jeans and bulky sneakers, for his absurdly tiny feet. He accessorised with chunky gold rings and a heavy gold chain that hung to his navel, dangling a gaudy circle pendant with a large number 13 in the centre.

> *He looks evil, he's the guy you don't want to meet in the night.*
> – Rafael

The master of spectacle loved turning heads and being in the spotlight. He'd enter a super-chic bar with the two babes, barely clothed, draped on either side of him, turning to passionately kiss one and then the other. People always stopped to look, curious about who this huge, muscular, tattooed guy with small sneakered feet – and two gorgeous goddesses all over him – could be.

Seminyak's coolest beachfront bar, Ku De Ta, was his favourite place to create a scene among the voguish set.

> *Any nightclub he comes to with these two girls, it's big trouble for girls with boyfriends because the boys get crazy looking at the girls, crazy, because they are a dream for any man. The kind of body, the sex appeal, the way they dance, the way they talk, like professional porno movie stars. Beautiful. Beautiful, young and very well dressed.*
>
> *Tota was very generous ... gives nice jewellery, diamonds, he likes to pay everything. They have a kind of deal: you come to Bali with me, I'm gonna give you $10,000, but you have to stay in the hotel with me and you have to fuck with who I point to.*

High-class prostitutes?

Exactly. They speak good English. And they get attention wherever they go. His English was very broken but he can communicate, his extravagance makes people want to meet him.

He plays like he has two wives, when people introduce him. 'Hi, my name is Tota. This is my wife number one, this my wife number two, we live together.' And people, 'What?' And sometimes he put them out to dance. 'Go there and make a dance, just to show my friends how hot you are.' And they give a performance.

– Rafael

Years earlier, as a teenager in Brazil, Rafael had seen Tota several times rock up at Rio clubs on his Harley-Davidson with a big group of Hells Angels bikers, so meeting him in Bali was like meeting a legend. But with Tota's sense of humour, and naughty nature, the two quickly bonded. Tota was so impressed with Rafael's tattoos that he went to get more ink at the same Bali tattooist. 'We became very close friends.'

Tota knew Rafael was also a conduit to the biggest drug bosses on the island, and the pair struck a deal for Rafael to organise tens of thousands of ecstasy pills from Chino for Tota to sell in Brazil. And, he'd sell Tota's cocaine in Bali for a 20 per cent cut. It should have been simple, but the game was dicey and their first deal was a disaster.

Tota soon had a horse running with 3 kilos of cocaine. Rafael told Chino to prepare the cash. The island was dry and prices were hiked up to $50,000 a kilo. When the stuff arrived, Rafael went to the Brazilian girls' room, where it was kept, to test it.

It was bad coke, yellowy brown, with a strong kerosene smell and when Rafael used some, his nose bled. He guessed it was mixed with glass shavings to give it a bit of a pearly sheen and fool rookies into thinking it was pure. He scooped a bit onto a spoon, and heated it up, to do a proper quality test by weighing the rock left after burning. The original gram crystallised to only 0.7 gram, proving it was only 70 per cent pure, not 100 per cent, which Chino demanded.

Tota went ballistic, screaming obscenities and threats to kill the guy who'd sent it. Against his instincts, Rafael offered to show it to Chino anyway. Chino was incredulous. 'What! Come on, man, what's wrong with you? Why do you even bring this shit here? . . . Take it away,' he snapped, with a dismissive wave.

Tota planned to throw the lot in the ocean and organise a revenge hit on the guy in Rio. Rafael suggested that instead they should just cut the price and hunt for a new buyer. Out of the blue, Fabio turned up a mysterious buyer from Jakarta, who'd apparently agreed to pay $45,000 a kilo. He wanted 1 kilo the following day, and two more in a week. Tota asked Rafael to do the exchange for a $10,000 fee, unwilling to risk it himself.

Tota was a big guy, big biceps, fit, goes to the gym, but was just showing off because he was really a chicken. This guy was not afraid to die, he don't give a shit, but sometimes so fucking pussy to do anything.
– Rafael

Rafael would have liked a fast $10,000, but he didn't have time. He was going overnight to Singapore with his family to do a shopping and visa run, something expats did to continue living in Bali by renewing their visas out of the country. So he passed the job to Jando.

And it quickly went to hell.

Rafael sensed something was wrong as soon as he flew back to Bali and spoke to Tota. His words said everything was okay, but his tone didn't. He asked Rafael to come to his hotel. One of Tota's hookers answered the door, stark naked, saying 'Hi', strutting back and draping herself on an armchair. Tota was sprawled on the couch with his knees spread wide, wearing only a sarong around his waist, covering little, exposing a lot.

Rafael hesitated awkwardly at the door, a little stunned to see this kind of X-rated scene sober, despite having seen a hell of a lot more in this room during Tota's cocaine-fuelled orgies. 'Come in, Rafael, come in,' Tota sang out. Noticing his discomfort, the lewd biker started toying with him. 'Come on, Rafael, come in, take your clothes off too, you can fuck her if you want. No problem if you don't want, but please come in.'

Inside, things didn't get any less out of kilter. Scattered across the coffee table were hundreds of $100 notes, some still in bunches bound by rubber bands. Tota stretched over, took a note and rolled it into a tube. Rafael stood watching, slightly bemused; the naked girl was totally uninterested. Tota used a lighter and lit the end of the rolled-up $100 note, then used the flame to light a Marlboro Red. As a finale to this weird little act, he flourished the flaming note in the air and stubbed it out in the ashtray before it burnt his fingers.

Rafael thought the guy had lost his mind.

'What the fuck are you doing burning money? Now I know

you're crazy, man. If you don't want it, you can give it to me.'

Tota sat back smoking his Marlboro. 'You can take all this shit. Have a look at it.'

Rafael picked up a bunch to flick through and find out the problem. But he didn't have to. It was obvious at first glance. Benjamin Franklin's face looked as if it had melted.

'Fuck, this is fake, man. Why did you take this shit?' Rafael asked, aghast.

Now, it was clear that Tota was seething. His odd mood had been masking his fury. 'Ask your friend Jando,' he said darkly. Immediately, Rafael knew that tonight there was going to be big strife. Undoubtedly, somebody was going to pay for this before sunup. It was the second insult to Tota's ego in two days.

Rafael phoned Jando, telling him to come to Tota's hotel room pronto. Tota suspected Jando of deceit. Rafael didn't. They sat and waited; the girl still draped on the chair stark naked. When Jando arrived, they showed him the money. Jando was shocked, but accepted no blame. He explained that the buyer, who'd dressed like an executive, had called the shots; insisting Jando pick him up at Denpasar Airport, drive to Uluwatu and pull over in some dark spot. Then, in the dimly lit privacy of the rental car, they exchanged cash and coke. Jando had flicked through the cash, checking for blanks, while the buyer sniffed a bit of the coke. Then, deal done, Jando took him back to the airport. Job done, Tota was a happy man. Jando left, unaware of the Benjamin's facial problems until Rafael called.

The next person on Tota's blame list was his close friend Fabio. All was fair in love and war, and this was war. He grabbed

Marco holds a bag of cocaine at a press conference after his arrest – he was captured after two weeks on the run. He'd fled Jakarta Airport as customs officers were about to find the cocaine in his hang-glider frame. When asked by reporters how he'd escaped, in typical fashion he replied: 'I'm David Copperfield.'

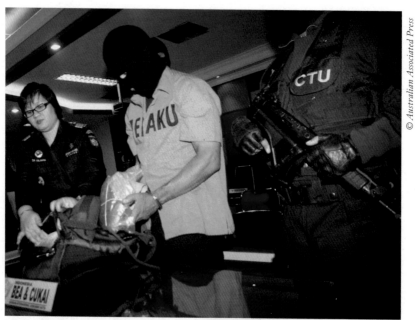

Above: A Brazilian drug dealer holds up the cocaine that took him down in Bali in June 2012. He was busted in dramatic style, with police ambushing him and using guns and fists outside some surf bungalows in Canggu, when he arrived to collect 990 grams of cocaine in a backpack. His arrest sent Bali's dealers fleeing the island.

Right: American big-wave surfer Gabriel languishing in a jail cell in Kerobokan Prison – he'd watched his drug dealing friends get busted like it was a bad movie, then he went down after the police set him up.

British drug trafficker Lindsay Sandiford, a seemingly unlikely courier, was busted in May 2012 at Bali's Denpasar Airport with 4.7 kilos of cocaine in her suitcase. She snitched and set up people for the Bali police. Many dealers fled the island. Andre had previously bought hashish from her.

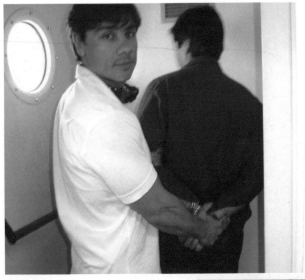

Above: Police Chief Fernando Caieron handcuffs Dimitrius at São Paulo airport, the moment he steps off the plane from Bali: 'When I was handcuffing him, he turned his neck, looked at me and asked, "Why are you doing this? What did I do?" I put my hand on his shoulder and said, "Think it over, my friend!"' – Chief Caieron. After a tip-off, the Operation Playboy cop had spent days laying in wait for Dimitrius.

Right: Dimitrius is made to wear handcuffs and a flak jacket during his transfer by private plane from São Paulo to Florianópolis, the Operation Playboy base. 'They made him out to be the biggest mafia. Bullshit, he was just a playboy.' – Rafael.

After a poolside ambush, police searched Andre's house and found a pile of nearly 80 ziploc bags with a green stripe across the top. Andre had tried to discredit the 'evidence', but it was used against him when one of his horses was busted with 6000 ecstasy pills stashed in an identical green striped bag.

This sports equipment was confiscated from Andre's house. He was using kitesurfing kites, paraglider sails, surfboard bags, windsurfer booms and backpacks to smuggle drugs. Many young and fit-looking traffickers use these methods. 'We don't find any drugs inside, but we already knew [Andre] used that kind of equipment to send and smuggle cocaine abroad.' – Chief Fernando Caieron, Operation Playboy boss.

This is the symbol that distinguishes a Laskar Bali gangster. Many members have it either tattooed on their hand or arm. Laskar Bali is the holiday island's most notorious and violent gang. It has the majority of the lucrative security contacts in the tourist areas – the men in black at the front door of most clubs, bars and restaurants are usually with Laskar. There are at least five big gangs in Bali.

It's from this vantage point, on the bridge high above Padang Padang beach, that Rafael spotted Marco on the sand, before running down to threaten him with a knife after the Japan ecstasy con.

Rafael's fantasy house with a diving board off his bedroom balcony, and his large-breasted mermaid statues. The fourth statue is hidden behind the cabana.

'You want ephedrine, hashish, *ganja*?' The fake drug dealers roaming the streets are always ready to pull any drug you desire from their pockets.

Fake drug dealer Wayan, who didn't want to show his face, spends the balmy nights riding his scooter around, hunting for a tourist to dupe. After a sale, he doesn't go back to that spot for several days to avoid bumping into an angry customer, though he has been bashed many times – it's a hazard of the job.

a vicious-looking scuba diving knife out of a drawer, telling Rafael, 'This is for Fabio. I'm gonna kill this motherfucker tonight.' Tota was suddenly now sure Fabio was involved.

Again, Rafael didn't think so, but this night wouldn't end until Tota exacted revenge on someone. 'He fucked me with this shit, let's go there now, come on, Rafael. I want to fix this, do you know where his villa is?' Rafael insisted he didn't, anxious that Tota's years of Rio shootouts and knife fights would make it easy for him to slaughter their friend Fabio.

I say noooo, I don't go anywhere. I have to go home. I don't know where he lives.
   – Rafael

Then Tota remembered that his horse had delivered the coke to Fabio's new Canggu villa. Rafael left, desperately trying to call Fabio. But his phone was off.

Tota and the horse soon found Fabio's villa. Tota tried the front door, but got no answer. He decided to jump over the wall, parking close enough to it to use the car as a leg-up. Inside, the lights were on and music was playing, but there was no sign of movement. Tota walked towards the glass doors of the master bedroom. He spotted Fabio asleep on the bed alongside one of his hookers. That didn't worry Tota. He loved to share the girls, but his friend was about to get a trip to hell.

Awake and shocked, Fabio was being dragged out of his bedroom, feet first, then thumping down the marble steps to his swimming pool. Tota hurled him into the water and stood yelling obscenities and flinging fistfuls of the fake $100 notes at him. Then he jumped in, putting Fabio in a headlock and pushing him under. 'Why did you rip me off, motherfucker?' he yelled. Every so often he let Fabio up, gasping for air and spluttering, then dunked him again, holding him down longer and longer each time.

The horse, also a Hells Angel, was standing on the car peering over the wall. He'd done a lot of bad stuff in Brazil too, many rumoured brutal murders, and he could see that Tota was close to drowning Fabio. He yelled out, 'Tota, no, don't kill him, that's enough.' But Tota was now so crazed the horse had to jump over the wall and into the pool to drag Tota off.

Fabio was almost unconscious. They left him on the edge of the pool, giving him an ultimatum: 'You have two days to give me back my stuff or the money, otherwise you're dead.' Tota didn't know if Fabio was in on the scam or not. He wasn't, but Fabio knew it was live or die, depending on whether he got the money or not. He was scared, desperately asking his friends, other drug dealers, for help, pleading, 'He's gonna kill me, man. Help me please, man.' He thought about selling his villa, but he only had 48 hours. In the nick of time, he borrowed the $45,000 from the rich Indonesian who owned the bar Fabio ran, as well as being a buyer in the game. Fabio promised to pay it back with interest.

Fabio called me and says, 'Oh fuck, very good, I get the money.'
   – Rafael

Before long, Tota and Fabio were friends again, with the gangster throwing an orgy to wipe out any traces of bad blood between them. Ultimately, he believed Fabio had nothing to do with the scam, but had simply been so desperate to get his hands on some coke to snort that he'd been careless and hadn't sussed out the new buyer – who they never saw again.

The day Fabio handed Tota the cash, they shook hands and went out for dinner, with his two babes and a new addition to the clique – a stunning blonde Swede who was keenly partic-ipating in Tota's orgies, and also relished helping them hunt the night for more girls. Tota loved using his hot babes to lure more hot babes, and with his penchant for paying the bills, and providing free coke, he and his crew usually snared the sexiest girls holidaying in Bali.

They get so many girls, beautiful girls, because they were all so beautiful, and Tota was kind of exotic-looking. The western girls like, you know, a strong, macho Latin man. He had a good bite with the girls. The Swedish girl talks bullshit too, because they hunt together; because the girls attract the other girls. The pros-titutes, the Swedish girl ... he has a crew to catch the girls and the coke helps.

– Rafael

This night they'd been out to Zanzibar Restaurant on the beach-front in Legian and picked up an English porn star. She was perfect, as she wouldn't mind Tota filming the orgy. When they got back to his hotel, the Swede refused to start without Tota's hot friend Rafael. Tota called him. He was at home with his wife and kids, but as soon as they were asleep, he raced over to Tota's hotel room.

I come, knock on the door, and fuck, it was very crazy already, coke on the table, two bottles of champagne. Cigarette smoke everywhere, loud music. It was like big shit, a big orgy.
   – Rafael

As soon as he stepped inside, the girls ripped off his clothes, pre-directed by Tota to do so. Fabio and Tota stood watching and laughing, then Tota interrupted, shouting, 'Wait, wait, wait, I'm gonna film it.' Tota was a frustrated porn director and loved making his explicit dirty films. But he was baiting Rafael, aware his friend was always happy to join in the orgies, even be directed into crude, kinky positions, but point blank refused to be filmed.

Tota was such a pervert! He had it all planned. He knows exactly how he is going to do it.
   – Rafael

The orgy went on for a couple of hours, with the girls sporadically running to the table to use some of the left-over 2 kilos of bad quality blow. With his nose hypersensitive from overuse, Rafael couldn't touch it; so he gulped champagne between the hot and weird sex scenes that Tota was manipulating him into. 'Lift that leg, you go here, spread your legs, bend over,' he'd direct brusquely, actually moving body parts, sometimes touching Rafael where he wanted no man to touch. One of Tota's favourite scenes was his sex sandwich, where he got the girls to lie on top of each other with their legs spread, and Rafael to alternate between them.

Fabio, in his usual night attire of black shirt with black jeans, wasn't interested in joining in, and spent his time sniffing coke, laughing and making quips. 'Hey, Rafael, you're doing good, man.' Now and then Tota tore off his sarong and joined in, using his penis pump to make himself huge. Mostly he preferred slapping the girls' backsides, yelling, '*Rebola rebola*, shake, shake, move your hips,' and using his bag of tricks, like a black vibrating dildo and a small vibrating metal egg.

I don't know how he has the imagination to make this sort of scenario.
  – Rafael

The night finished with Rafael pulling on his clothes, exhausted, and staggering out into the street with Tota's voice fading into the distance, 'Come back, we've still got two bottles of champagne, come on, *bencong*, come back.'

Tota was known for his irrepressible energy for sex, gambling, partying and crazy antics. Rumour had it that in Brazil he'd once arranged to surprise his girlfriend. She was sunbaking with a bunch of friends on Rio's popular Ipanema Beach, when a chopper landed nearby on the sand. Below the rotating blades, two waiters in black tie climbed out and ran over to her, balancing plates of sushi, a bottle of Veuve Clicquot, a bunch of flowers and a short note, 'From your love, Tota.' As the chopper flew off, it rained flower petals down on her. The master of spectacle had done it again, although the relationship didn't last.

There were times when Rafael would arrive at Tota's Bali

hotel room, knock and, after hearing Tota yelling, 'Come in, it's open', walk in to find him in the middle of sex. Rafael would quickly turn to leave, calling, 'I'll come back later', with Tota singing out, 'No, stay, come on, *bencong*, come in here, it's no worries, we can play together.'

'No, no, no.'

The two often went out to clubs together, with Tota getting a kick out of pushing his hot friend Rafael to pick up girls; not that he needed persuasion or help. Tota would create stories, like Rafael was a famous TV star in Brazil, endlessly urging him to go for this hot Australian girl, or that French babe. Rafael usually liked Tota's taste in eye candy and played along. Tota's plan was always to get an orgy going back in his hotel room, and with his crew often got their prey to acquiesce to almost anything. One night, Tota was pushing Rafael to talk to an Italian girl.

Tota says to me, 'Her tits point to the moon.' She was beautiful – dark hair, green eyes, beautiful, beautiful. Tota makes all these jokes and he was so dirty, the way he talks, he says like, 'You already have sex with two guys at the same time? I can do very good performance – me and Rafael, it's the best.'

I say, 'Shut up, man', and he says, 'You like to have sex with Rafael in front of us?', and she was like, 'Come on.' He says, 'I'm just joking, I just want to test you. Because all the Italian girls play like the angel but they have the devil inside.' She says, 'I already have sex with two guys, it was very good,' and he says, 'You like girls?' and she says, 'Yes.' Whoa ... Tota was happy.

The Swedish girl was talking bullshit too, because they hunt

*together, because they have a prey – a beautiful duck. Then we
go to a small club, was loud music, and Tota and the Swedish
girl do a sexy dance. She pretends to give him a blow job. And
he's like a Carioca dancer from Rio – all the Carioca guys they
know how to Samba – and he does the moves.*

*He says, 'You want a drink?' And the Italian says, 'Oh, I'm
starting to get drunk.' And I say, 'Oh, drunk is no problem, I
have some medicine.' And then she was like, 'What?' 'Oh, you
wanna have some coke?' She says, 'Oh, I really need just a little
bit. I can give you some money.' 'No, keep your money.'*

*Tota looks at me, winks, time to go ... he says, 'Let's go to
my home, I don't bring coke here because I'm afraid of the cops,
because Bali's very dangerous, but we can go, take a couple of
lines and then come back.' But bullshit, he just wants to take
the girl.*

– Rafael

Once back at Tota's rooms – with French champagne, copious
coke and Carioca dancing – his harem of girls stripped to their
G-strings, saying, 'Oh, I'm too hot.' Tota ripped his shirt off,
telling Rafael, 'Take your shirt off, man, show her your muscles.' He replied, 'Leave me be', but soon Tota's dirty dancing
and talking, generous lines of coke, and his naked harem,
worked like magic. The new girl was looking at Rafael with
hungry eyes and the room erupted into a heaving orgy, with
Tota directing and Rafael taking time out sometimes to just
watch the girls together. This was a typical night out with Tota.

Rafael realised it was the cocaine that was mostly respon-
sible for these girls participating in the kinky sex scenes; their

behaviour was largely a product of being on holiday in Bali and they were not like that at home.

> *Sometimes I get their number, and when I'm in Holland or some-where for business, I meet them and they are totally different. They are snobby. They don't even give attention to me. In Bali it was, 'Wow, Rafael, you are the man' – they do anything to be with me.*
>
> *When I come to their country, they have normal life, they work, sometimes have a husband. I call, they say, 'Oh, where are you?' 'Amsterdam.' 'Oh my god! Let's meet in the coffee shop . . . oh, Rafael, I have to tell you something. I am mar-ried.'*
>
> *'Oh, no problem . . . me too.' But I never lie when I meet a girl, I say straight away, 'I am married with kids,' because I just wanna fuck, I don't want a relationship or romance. And I say, 'I have a wife, kids.' And if they continue they know I'm just gonna jiggy jig and ciao.*
>
> *Sometimes I think of lying . . . 'Oh, I'm single,' but that's not the way I prefer.*
>
> *– Rafael*

In Bali, Rafael would pick up girls, meeting them at bars, clubs, or private parties, and whisk them away, sometimes to a villa in Ubud for a couple of nights, or to his favourite Nikko Bali Resort. The staff were so familiar with him there they'd call out, 'Hello, Mr Rafael', sometimes putting their foot in it, saying, 'Oh, where's your girlfriend?' when he'd already moved to the next girl.

Mostly the girls were European ... French, Italian or Swedish a lot, Finnish, Norwegian, the Nordic girls ... They come here to spend one week, they want to fuck. I go to the party, take the girl, go to the Nikko, check in, spend the night, I always have some coke on me, and we have some wild sex, drink, use drugs and the day after I put her in her hotel and go home.

Big shit at home, my wife, 'Where you been?' 'I was at party, shut up.' Or, 'I've been doing some business in a hotel' ... make some story you know ... was easy for me.

Did your wife suspect you were seeing other women?

Little bit ... she was very jealous. She never caught me. Sometimes I would have my secret girlfriend too ... just for fucking, nothing else. Brazilian, Australian, you know, sometimes Swedish.

It was a dream life; and then all the other guys see me doing this, they were jealous. 'Fuck, Rafael, I saw you yesterday with a blonde girl ... my god, where is she from? How did you get this girl?' They were curious why it was so easy for me to change the girls every night like this.

Sometimes I'm busy with one girl and then some other beautiful girl comes looking for me, asking my friends, 'Are you Brazilian? Do you know Rafael with long hair? Where is he, I'm looking for him, you know him?' And then they say, 'No ... Rafael's not here,' but I am already with another girl and she come too late.

So there was a queue waiting for you?

Exactly. Sometimes I get in trouble, because I have two or three girls ... Rafael, Rafael, Rafael. Shit, which one am I gonna take?

I always choose one, you know, and say, 'Please can you go and wait for me in the corner of Circle K. I will pick you up in five minutes because my girlfriend is here ... we're finished but still, it's better if you go there.' 'Okay,' they go. I say shit easy, you know. And then she walks out by herself. I go to the toilet, and then pick up the girl on the bike, escape.

Did you ever take more than one then?

Yes, sometimes it was funny because normally the Nordic girls like it. I come with two girls, and then I start to kiss one and then the other one wants to kiss together. I have one here and one there. All the Brazilian guys, my friends, were like, 'Ah, Rafael, come here, introduce me.' And then I say please let's go somewhere and it was hard because the guys follow me on the bike. I have to stop, 'Hey, go away.' Because the girls always say, 'No, no, only you, we don't want anybody, only you.'

CHAPTER EIGHT

LEMON JUICE KING

Rafael's lifestyle sparked jealousy from others, even his so-called friends. Out of the blue one day, he got a call from Lemon Juice boss Marco with a business proposal. Marco explained he was in Amsterdam with the perfect horse, a 140-kilo Jiu-Jitsu prizefighter. The guy was flying to Tokyo to compete in the high-profile Pride Fighting Championships. There, Brazilian fighters were like gods and breezed unchecked through airports.

> *They love Brazilian fighters in Japan. At the airport, they put out the red carpet, they don't check anything.*
> – Rafael

Marco had decided to pack the fighter with 20,000 ecstasy pills, and despite the fighter wanting to buy them in Amsterdam, Marco knew Chino's were the best, and also that Bali customs was easier to penetrate than Dutch, and closer to Japan. As Chino wouldn't deal directly with Marco, he asked Rafael to arrange it, for a commission.

As soon as they flew into Bali, they met with Rafael at Marco's place in Bali Village. Rafael was a little dubious already, as Marco had a reputation for being unreliable and paying late.

'Do you have ecstasy?' the fighter asked.

'Yeah, but cash upfront.'

He didn't have it. He wanted to pay after the run, assuring Rafael it would work. 'It's easy, they don't check me at all because I'm a fighter,' he said, macho-posturing slightly.

Rafael sensed the veiled threat, but chose to ignore it. 'Thanks, but no deal,' he said, standing up to leave. 'If they catch you, or if you die, who is going to pay Chino?'

Marco quickly interjected, desperate not to lose the deal. 'Rafael, come on, please, man, I guarantee your money.' He knew Rafael could be a soft touch, as by now he'd invested in many of his dope runs. 'I'll pay you $1 profit per pill – the easiest $20,000 in your life. Please, I guarantee, I guarantee.'

> *And then I was stupid. I say okay.*
> – Rafael

Rafael rang Chino, and told him the new play. 'No problem,' Chino said, 'you have credit with me anyway.' Awash with cash, Rafael had untypically left a kilo of coke on standby with Chino, and was waiting to be paid in two jet-skis. Chino asked who was organising this run.

'Marco.'

'The Lemon Juice guy?'

'Yeah.'

Chino was well aware of the famous dope dealer's reckless reputation. 'This guy is a bullshit man, I don't have a good feeling.'

Rafael told him he'd made up his mind. 'I'm gonna help the guy, he's my friend.'

'Okay, I'll give you the pills, but if they fuck it up, I'll take the cash out of your kilo here.' Chino couldn't lose, but Rafael could.

A couple of days later, one of Chino's soldiers met with Rafael on the busy beach esplanade in Legian. Surrounded by tourists, sunbaking and strolling, they did the exchange, quick and slick. Their bikes were side-by-side, engines still running, as Chino's man passed Rafael the benign-looking bag of 20,000 ecstasy pills. Rafael quickly slipped it into the storage space under his seat and tore off to Marco's room at Bali Village, just around the corner.

They didn't have long. The fighter was leaving that night and wanted to pack it himself. But his method was slapdash and dangerous. Rafael and Marco watched him haphazardly stuff the plastic bags of pills into his Lycra bike shorts, then pull a pair of shorts over the top. 'I don't think it's good, do you?' the fighter asked.

Rafael jumped up, patting down the fighter's naturally big thighs, now resembling gigantic balloons. 'You're right. You're going to go straight to jail.'

Drug dealer Andre soon arrived. He wasn't part of this deal, but offered to help. The fighter asked his opinion. 'Are you crazy, man? You think this is a kid's game?' Andre knelt down, pulling down the fighter's pants, and quickly started repacking his legs. But the beefy prizefighter was now losing his nerve.

I start to tape the plastic bags of ecstasy on his leg and the guy starts to shake and sweat. Totally scared. Totally. Marco says to him, 'Look, motherfucker, in the ring you look like a lion, now you look like a kid about to pee your pants, you are shaking like a chicken.'

   – Andre

Marco's taunts only exacerbated the fighter's nerves. Now he didn't want to go. Trying to get him to man up, Andre blasted him. 'Brother, you need to listen to me. You called us for this job. We didn't come here with 20,000 ecstasy pills for you to get scared. Now we have the Chinese mafia behind us and you don't want to go. Come on. You go.'

Rafael and Andre had already had a horse busted in Australia using Lycra bike shorts. They'd sent an English guy with coke in his pants to deliver to Rafael's famous surfer buyer in Sydney, who was continually asking for more stuff. The horse chose to fly to Brisbane then drive down to Sydney, to avoid the Harbour City's ostensibly more secure airport. But in Brisbane, sniffer dogs took him down.

On the plane, when he goes to piss, he smells the coke and thinks, 'Oh my god, they're going to find it.'

Why didn't he flush it then?
He feels he will get a problem with us.
   – Rafael

Andre had organised the English horse's run in Bali, down to taping his legs and sending him off. As planned, when the horse landed in Brisbane he phoned Andre, who was waiting in the Bali Subak Hotel room, where they'd packed. Andre trained his horses to use his self-created 'step one, step two' method. After getting through customs, they were trained to call and say, 'Step one okay' and after getting the cash, 'Step two okay.' This time, he didn't say it. Warning lights lit up. Andre asked, 'Step one okay?'

'No.' It was a red alert; a drug boss's nightmare. Police would have been listening. Andre flew into crisis mode, slamming down the phone. Moving fast, he hurled everything onto a sheet on the floor, wrapped it up and ran out of there, with no time to spare. Police officers swooped into the room moments later. Andre's tried and trusted two-step method had saved him – just. But his horse went down.

A British man has been jailed for eight years for trying to smuggle more than $1 million worth of cocaine into Australia. The UK-born travel agent was caught with almost 3 kilos of cocaine stuffed between two pairs of bike pants he was wearing on a flight from Bali ... The Brisbane Supreme Court has heard Mark Allan Stables was working in Bali when he agreed to smuggle the drugs for a group of Brazilians in a bid to get out of debt ... Australian Federal Police are yet to find the Brazilian group which Stables claims was behind the smuggling attempt.

    – AAP, 1 October 2001

I remember this Mark got busted because it's a lot of money lost when somebody busts ... was bad for business.

Did you lose contact after he was busted?

Lose contact totally. But two or three years afterwards, he knocked on my door. I remember it was Christmas time, I had Christmas in my house, and he came. When I see him, I think, 'Fuck, maybe he's come here together with Interpol to catch me,' because he was out of jail early. I say, 'Where is Interpol, they come with you, or are they coming later?' But he says, 'No way. I need money.'

This guy is very skinny, my age, but he looked in so bad shape, like he's dying of cancer or something. The white skin, black eyes, we call him 'Ja Morreu', means already dead, like we say, 'Oh, where is the dead guy?' I remember I say, 'What's your hardest time in jail in Australia?' 'Fighting.' He says one time he was talking on the phone and one black guy broke his tooth and his nose.

– Rafael

He was asking for cash, but instead Rafael gave him a job, enlisting him to sell 50,000 ecstasy pills from Chino, and take a commission. Rafael rented a room for him to stay in to babysit the pills and make deliveries whenever he called. For Rafael, it was not only cash but insurance too.

I think now if he wants to fuck me he has a problem too. But he didn't, he did a good job, then he disappeared. I never heard from him again.

– Rafael

Back in Marco's room, Andre, Rafael and Marco knew a horse could get busted despite perfect packing, or being a revered prizefighter. Trafficking was always a risk, but it was minimised if you were a pro and used your skill. These three had vast experience and today they knew the frightened prizefighter was a dead cert to go to jail. A blind man could see his nerves. So, in a last-minute switch of plan, they decided to put the pills in a paraglider sail, so he could check that in, instead of wearing them. Andre had a spare in his room and ran to get it while Rafael raced off to buy carbon paper to wrap up the pills and make them invisible in an X-ray. It was frantic.

I was thinking, how's Andre going to pack this shit, and he just put carbon around, rolling it up, put in the bag. Fuck, it was very unprofessional packing, big hurry.
  – Rafael

Within minutes of his flight closing, they got the fighter, more cool now, to Denpasar Airport. Despite his freak-out, he was a success.

But Rafael had been a patsy. A week later, everyone simply vanished; Marco didn't answer his phone and the prizefighter was gone, immediately after calling Rafael from Tokyo raving it was a success. Two months later, Rafael still hadn't been paid. He was fuming. Anna also stirred his anger by chiding him for being a fool to trust anyone in the first place.

It was big shit. My wife says, 'You're stupid to give credit to these motherfuckers, they gonna fuck you.'
  Tota told me this story afterwards: Marco says to him in Amsterdam, 'Oh, I have one guy in Bali, he thinks he is something

but he is a piece of shit. Let's make some money on him, easy, because he is too nice. He trusts whatever I say to him.'

Tota says, 'Who is the guy?'

'Rafael.'

Tota says, 'Why do you want to fuck him? The guy is nice.' And then Tota asks him, 'How do you want to fuck him?'

He says, 'I have a guy who wants to buy 20,000 ecstasy pills and Rafael knows the guy in Bali with the best ones. Let's buy the ecstasy with Rafael, we take on credit, and we don't need to pay. He's already rich, he doesn't need money, motherfucker.' And then they come here.

Marco was jealous of my success. He became second with his Lemon Juice, doesn't make as much money as coke. He was jealous of all the girls, all my lifestyle, house, car, clothes, like VIP everywhere. I feel he was very unsatisfied. And then he tried to fuck me.

– Rafael

After learning he'd been played, Rafael knew he had to avenge himself, as much for his pride as to demonstrate he was nobody's fool. Marco had flown back to Amsterdam to set up another Lemon Juice run, straight after the Tokyo run, but Rafael heard he was now back in Bali, hiding out at their friend Fernando's house. Rafael called, asking, 'Where's Marco?'

'I don't know,' Fernando replied, in duet with Marco bellowing, 'Tell the motherfucker I'm not here.'

Rafael abruptly cut the call, grabbed a knife and flew out the door.

I was like, 'Fuck, I'm gonna kill him.'

He drove straight to Fernando's house. Another dealer, Paulo, answered the door. He was friendly, but saw the knife in Rafael's back pocket. 'What's that, Rafael?'

'You know what it is, my friend, it's a fucking knife and it's for putting in the neck of Marco. I know he's here. You're a motherfucker too, for hiding him,' Rafael said, striding through the house.

'Rafael, calm down,' Paulo urged.

'No, tell me where he is.'

Sick of pussyfooting around, Rafael grabbed Paulo around the neck, holding the knife to his throat. 'Where is he?'

'He's in Padang, he's gone to Padang.'

Rafael sped off to Padang Padang, a top surf spot that he knew intimately. From the bridge crossing high above the cove, he spotted Marco on the sand below. Rafael sprang down the steps that spiralled inside a canopy of trees and rock, giving him cover for a fast and stealthy entrance to the beach.

A bunch of Marco's horses sat on the sand, facing the water. Marco was a few metres further up the sand, with his head down in his rubber boat. Rafael crept behind them, then sprang at Marco, shouting, 'Hey motherfucker, what do you think you're doing?' Marco shot bolt upright.

He looks like he's seen a ghost when he sees me. And then he tried to be arrogant. 'Why did you come here? If you're gonna punch me, punch me.' I was so angry, I use all my power, I went straight to him, pow! My hand hurt for two days. Marco flies

across to the other side of the boat. And then I take the knife
to his neck ... I say, 'Now you gonna die, motherfucker.'
 – Rafael

Rafael was kneeling on Marco's chest as the horses, now all on
their feet, were circling threateningly. Rafael thought fast. He
turned to look up at the high bridge, packed with locals leaning
on the railings, and waved. Predictably, they all waved back.
'You think I come here alone?' Rafael shouted at Marco's men,
pointing to the bridge. 'Those are Chino's guys and if you touch
me, they're gonna kill you.' They all knew of Chino and immediately backed off. Rafael stood up and planted his foot on
Marco's neck. 'You guys want to try to touch me, come and
touch me.'

Croakily, Marco pleaded, 'Rafael, please.' Rafael slipped his
knife back in his pocket as curious onlookers started coming
in for a closer look. Fernando and another mutual friend came
out of the surf. Looking down at Marco sprawled on the sand,
Fernando said, 'I told you, man, don't do that with Rafael, he's
gonna fuck you. Now see what you do.'

Rafael ignored the chitchat, and crushing his foot harder into
Marco's neck, shouted, 'I want my money now, motherfucker.'
He snatched a camera off the edge of Marco's boat and slung it
around his neck. 'Now, I'm gonna take everything you've got.
What else? Give me your watch.' He ripped the Rolex off his
wrist, saw it was a fake and stuffed it in his pocket anyway.

'I have money, please don't kill me, please.'

Rafael looked down at the Judas. 'I will kill you, fool, but
first I want my money. Now stand up, motherfucker, let's go.'

Marco's men moved aside, clearing a path for the crazed drug boss to pass with his captive.

I get, like, evil.

As they walked, a reckless stranger flew over and snapped a photo. Rafael went beserk, yanking the knife out of his back pocket and pointing it at him, screaming, 'You come here, motherfucker, give me the fucking camera now.' He handed it over instantly.

One of Marco's horses tried to calm him down. 'Rafael, come on, don't do this.'

Rafael spun around with his knife held ready to attack. 'You want to fight me too, motherfucker, come on then, try your luck,' he shouted. He swept around with the knife, slicing the air, daring anyone to make a move, then grabbed Marco, and snapped, 'Marco, come with me, come.'

He came like a chicken.

The atmosphere in the car was tense. 'How're you going to pay me, motherfucker?' Rafael spat tersely. 'I want my $20,000 plus the cost of the pills.'

Marco was obsequious, eager to comply with anything. 'I have $3000 cash now; I'll give it to you. Let's go to my room.'

At Bali Village, Marco gave Rafael $3000 cash, two surfboards and another camera. Rafael did his own sweep, taking anything else of any value, including a paraglider, which he knew Marco needed for Lemon Juice runs, and his passport.

'I don't want this shit, I want my money. I give you two weeks. If you don't pay, first I'm gonna burn your passport just to fuck you. Second, I'm gonna torture you. The rest is secret. You gonna have to wait to see what I do.' Rafael was calmer now, and trying to scare him into submission.

It worked. Marco organised most of the cash within two weeks.

Everybody on the island talked about this. Nobody ever expected me to do that. I was the nicest guy in the world and then I went crazy. But nobody fuck with me after that. Because Marco was the top, famous guy here, and then I made him like a chicken in front of all his guys on the beach. I don't know why nobody had done that before because he was bad, he did bullshit with everybody, small things like he takes money and promises, 'Tomorrow I bring your Lemon Juice,' and then, 'Oh, tomorrow, tomorrow.' But I was the one who give big shit to him.

Afterwards, we become friends again. He say, 'Oh, I never think you're gonna punch me like that.' I say, 'I never think you were gonna fuck me like that. You're lucky I didn't stick the knife in you; I was ready. I was thinking to clean my name, the best way to kill you and then everybody's afraid, nobody going to try to bullshit me any more. Because you know how people talk, everybody will say, "Oh, Rafael killed Marco, don't play with him, because he can kill you."' . . . Like I say to Marco, 'You're going to be my marketing to be a bad boy.' He says, 'I'm sorry. I was too high on coke, and I see you full of money, cars, motor-bike, I get big eyes at that time.'

– Rafael

Marco had been riling a lot of people, paying horses late, not delivering Lemon Juice on time and being generally arrogant.

He was too much of a motherfucker to pay – tomorrow, tomorrow, tomorrow. And then the horse or other people get crazy, want to punch him, but if you punch him, you won't get the money. That's what he wants. Lose your temper, punch him, ah fuck, you're not going to get anything. It was hard to work with him.

– Andre

Being Bali's Lemon Juice boss had given Marco the kudos and power that had eluded him as the underdog growing up. He'd been the poor kid, ingratiating himself into the rich crew by using his big personality and quick wit. His gregarious, sunny personality had been his ticket to the playboy lifestyle since he was a teenager in Brazil.

He was a clown, very funny, always full of jokes, but very arrogant. He really liked to be noticed, very egocentric guy and always liked to be the centre of attention. He was always pretending he was the number one boss in Bali, but he was just dealing marijuana. When you deal marijuana you are nothing compared to people who deal cocaine or ecstasy or heroin, unless you're dealing tonnes of marijuana.

He always thought he was the best, because everybody was always looking for him to get the best marijuana on the island, he was always acting like he was on top of the world ... he walked around full of attitude ... sitting in a restaurant full of arrogance, always with superiority.

In what way?

The way he talked to the people … he always liked to feel
important. There was a time he started to tell people his name
was Max, because he was the 'maximum'. I was like, 'Fucking
Max, give me a break.' Max is minimum, not maximum. But
he was a funny guy.

    – Alberto, drug dealer

The Lemon Juice boss's fortunes had gone up and down ever
since he was a child. Marco had begun life with a silver spoon
in his mouth, but it had quickly tarnished. He was born into
a rich family in Manaus, the Amazon's capital city, to a young
beauty queen whose own father was a wealthy media mogul.
But life turned dark for the young boy when he first saw his
father bash his mother. They moved to Rio, where before long
his mother left behind her two toddler sons.

My mother escaped from the house when I was three years old
because my father beat her. I don't use my father's name because
I'm angry with him. I saw him beat my mother. I was a very
small boy, but even now I can still remember.

    – Marco

There was still money for a while, enough to give Marco ten
years of show jumping lessons – and a nanny and maid in a
nice apartment 50 metres from the beach in Rio's up-market
Ipanema district. When the cash ran out, he became the poor
kid from the Amazon jungle, mixing with Rio's rich kids,
earning him the nickname *Curumim* – or little Indian boy –

which stuck. But he was popular, winning his place in the elite group by being able to make people laugh.

He became a beach boy, with all the rich-kid toys like surfboards, jet-skis and hang-gliders, courtesy of his best friend Beto, Marco's idol, who seemingly had everything: parents who loved him, good looks, money and as many gorgeous girls as a rock star. He was also an exceptional all-round sportsman, with tennis, surfing and hang-gliding his main pursuits. His father was a Rio property mogul. If the family flew to Aspen to snowboard, or Europe for a holiday, they'd take little Marco, paying for everything and slinging him spending money.

Marco was the funny guy in the group, the poor one. And then they go to Aspen to snowboard, and let's bring Marco because he's fun, so funny, makes jokes all the time.

  – Rafael

My friend Beto was always using cocaine, but he was a strong guy, blond guy, much more beautiful than me. I'm nothing compared to him; he's a very beautiful guy and very rich. More than 100 girls want to marry him. But listen, the guy did everything for me. When I turned 16, he gave me a green Volkswagen. I had no licence, but I could drive. I was his driver for two years. I drove Beto up the mountain when he was hang-gliding and after he flew I went to get him on the beach. Beto said if I crashed the car, 'No problem, papa will buy you a new one.' This family brought me to Europe, America, to everywhere, because before I have no money, no money and no family. The problem was like that.

  – Marco

But Beto's largesse came at a heavy cost. Four years younger and indebted, Marco did anything to please his best friend. Beto soon had his hilariously funny, pliable young acolyte, at just 14 years old, running up into Rio's dangerous *favelas* – mountain slums full of criminals and drug dealers – to get him cocaine. The kid did it like a grateful puppy.

I've been playing narcotics in Brazil for a long time. My friend Beto put me in this business when I was a little boy. He pushed me to get cocaine, not for business – he's a user. He would bring me to the bottom of the favela, *stop the car far away, and say, 'Go.' Then I walk up 20 minutes, all the way to the top of the mountain with my schoolbag, past 20 dangerous policemen with guns. At the top they call . . . 'Little boy, what you want? Black or white?' Black is marijuana, white is cocaine. 'I want white.' 'Ooh, good boy.' I say, 'I like cocaine.' Bullshit. I never used the cocaine. I was a little boy, I was a child. I go up with my lunchbox and come down with a stack of cocaine for my friend.*
　– Marco

It wasn't long before Marco was doing much more than filling up his lunchbox. Starting to hang-glide at just 14 years, he quickly realised a natural talent. By 16 years he was competing internationally, with his first overseas trip to Bogotá, Colombia, Pablo Escobar's turf. Marco won and flew home with a gold trophy in his hands and white snow in his pants.

Beto told me, 'Marco, take this.' So I arrive back in Brazil with seven hang-gliding pilots, a trophy and 100 grams of cocaine in my underwear. Nobody checked anything.

    – Marco

To Marco it was the perfect set-up; trafficking drugs gave him the means to fly, and flying gave him the means to traffic. It catapulted him into a playboy lifestyle. On his second overseas trip to America, at 17, his career of commercial trafficking began.

Believe me, when I go to California there is [a man like] Pablo Escobar – a boss, selling drugs around Brazil, around the world – he came to me and says, 'Marco, now listen to me. You go to America. I have many friends in America, international, so you can make more money.' I take 3 kilos the first time, came through easy. There is another Pablo Escobar ... came to my hang-glider.

*   I compete everywhere in the world and always I bring nar-coba [drugs]. I take cocaine to America, to Italy, to Spain, to Portugal, Switzerland, Germany, Australia, everywhere. I'm a Brazilian champion, so when I come, they check but they don't really check.*

    – Marco

The trafficking gave Marco his own cash for the first time. It gave him freedom to fly, and he would often soar in the skies above Rio, sometimes 3000 feet up – so high that the arms of the famous statue of Christ would fade out, then disappear.

Sometimes he'd circle with 10 or 20 others, flying close for a chat, before swooping through the sky like a god – with adrenalin in his veins and peace in his heart. Often, to enhance the bliss and awe, he'd smoke a joint before launching off.

Ooh, it's the best you know; a very good sensation if you smoke a joint to fly. Wow. I always smoke and fly, smoke and fly, you know, like meditation. I have flown many places in your country, you know. I fly everywhere over there: Adelaide, Stanwell Park, Byron Bay, the Gold Coast, I fly everywhere. I fly competition for 12 years, I always carry some cocaine.

– Marco

A near-fatal accident when he was 19 undoubtedly instilled a deep sense of invincibility. It was as if some angel was perched on his shoulder. He crashed his glider into a sheer Rio cliff. Miraculously, his glider clipped a single isolated branch and snagged on it, leaving him precariously dangling 700 metres up. A friend flew his glider close, calling, 'Marco, you okay?' There was no answer, but the friend couldn't risk going closer and getting entangled. Two helicopters flew in to rescue him, but it was a sensitive and complex mission to ensure the wind from the rotating blades didn't blow him off, into a death plunge.

I hang by one tree for four and a half hours. I need two helicopters to help me, because my position in the rock is negative [concave], so they cannot get me. After four hours, a helicopter pilot rescued me. It was like a miracle. I have no injury and they put in television, newspaper and radio.

Straight after his TV interviews, he borrowed a glider, went back up to the top of the cliff and took off again. Those who knew him weren't surprised.

The accident undoubtedly swelled his sense of invincibility, which equipped him well for drug trafficking – never showing any fear – but also making him dangerously reckless.

Blithely, he flew all over the globe with his hang-glider loaded up with blow, even to notoriously tricky countries like Australia. Twice he flew to Sydney for competitions, making double his usual trafficking fee, at $10,000 a kilo – 'Australian people love cocaine so much.' He breezed into Sydney on his first trip with 5 kilos, as part of a 12-pilot Brazilian team. 'There are 20 hang-gliders and only one has stuff – mine. But they don't check at all.' On the second trip to Sydney, he took 7 kilos, tipping a friend to bring some coke too, telling him it was easy. Marco made it in, but his friend, and friend's partners, didn't.

When I came second time I call my other friend in Brazil, I say come over because it's no problem.

I flew Rio–LA, LA–Honolulu, Honolulu–Sydney. My friend came the other way; he flew Rio, Argentina, Auckland, Sydney. But in Auckland, there was this very small dog, and they found the stuff in his hang-glider. They don't arrest him because he was in transit, so they call the Australian police and say, 'There are two Brazilian guys arriving with drugs in their hang-glider.'

Did they go to jail?
Yeah, my friend went to jail for five and a half years in Sydney.
    – Marco

The court was told that 20 packets of cocaine weighing more than 2.6 kilos were brought into Australia from South America compressed inside the struts of the dismantled hang-glider ... In his defence Sonino, a Brazilian hang-gliding champion, said he had come to Australia for a world hang-gliding championship in January.

    – *Sydney Morning Herald*, 13 November 1987

Marco was undeterred by his friends' bad luck. Trafficking was his game; he was brazen, confident and loved it. But he had a penchant for tempting fate. On his way out of Sydney loaded up with drug money, he risked a kamikaze-style joke, crazily baiting an immigration officer. He pulled out a $10,000 wad, waving the notes in the official's face, taunting, 'You are crazy, man, I want to stay here for two, three months, I have $10,000 to spend, all this money here, but you only give me a month visa.'

I was joking with the guy. I'm always joking you know, that's my biggest problem. Always joking. The guy let me go inside the plane, the engine was already on ... and then the door opens again, two officers come and look ... then they say, 'That's him,' then, 'You follow us, let's go.' I follow them to a small room, I take in my backpack, the other US$28,000 I had inside my professional book [containing photos and his CV]. He asked me, 'You have more money?' I say, 'I have.'

    – Marco

Marco had US$38,000, but no Australian dollars. On the advice of his Sydney buyer, he'd spent days traipsing around Kings

Cross, carrying plastic shopping bags stuffed with Aussie dollars to change at banks and money changers. So legally, the cash didn't belong to Australia. It worked.

After 45 minutes, they ask many things, you know, and I start joking, joking, joking. I say to the officer, 'You can say the money is from drugs, you can say whatever you want, but this money belongs to America and not to you, man.' I say, 'Man, you have to kill me to take my money. You have to shoot me. If you want to take my money, I make a big problem here . . . I call my embassy. This money don't belong to you.' It's already 45 minutes, people waiting in the flight. I say, 'What do you want?' And the officer says to me, 'Next time I get you.' And then I say to him, 'Okay, I see you next time, bye-bye.'
    – Marco

Aside from traversing the globe with his glider worth its weight in cocaine, Marco spent time instructing students and also flying ultra-gliders above Rio's beaches with advertisements for companies like McDonald's, Coca-Cola and Pepsi. It wasn't until his late twenties that he first flew to Bali after a close friend urged him to come. He was quickly lured by the lifestyle the tropical isle offered. The azure sparkling oceans and sunny days let him swim, surf, jet-ski, and hang-glide endlessly.

My life was 24 hours – morning surfing, afternoon flying. I love sport, I do sport all the time.
    – Marco

Soon he was travelling between three homes, in Bali, Rio and Amsterdam, quickly getting a profile in Bali as 'the man', or the boss of top-grade dope, selling to rich expats, tourists and surfers. In Amsterdam he had an X-ray machine at home to check the drugs were invisible, before sending his horses to Bali and Brazil.

Marco was the best serving these kind of really rich people; the really high-class, rich people. These people like skunk, the good weed – it's like drinking French champagne. The right level of people, the people who have a big house, these are the customers. No one is smoking Sumatran weed. Bad smell, bad taste. They wanna get the best.

   – Andre

He was the guy to get weed from. Anybody who was anybody who wanted to buy weed would buy it from him. He had a monopoly. He rode around on a motorbike with a fluorescent yellow windbreaker with big block letters saying Lemon Juice. Guys say to him, 'What are you doing, man, why don't you just go to the cops and get the handcuffs on now?' Everyone knew Lemon Juice was weed. The cops I'm sure knew too. And he's like, it's just advertising it, you know.

   – Gabriel, American surfer

Marco was the pioneer of the Lemon Juice dope runs, also introducing his inspired idea of using paragliders to carry dope. It had changed the game, by giving horses the ability to carry up to 12 kilos in one run. Many of the big dealers, like Rafael and Dimitrius, had started out in the business as Marco's horses, and most of his friends were doing runs, even if it was just a little bit in their shoes.

Marco's horses were often educated, middle-class, wealthy and even included one of Brazil's top male models, working for high-end brands, flying between South America, Europe and Bali. With his hot looks and fame, he breezed with only scant checks through customs, easily trafficking kilos of dope. He was a playboy who'd had trysts with international mega-stars, and had once worked with Cindy Crawford, impressing the guys when he sat chatting with her one night in a Bali bar.

He took big amounts, 3 kilos, 6 kilos. All my good friends bring Lemon Juice to Bali. No one touched him because he was famous.
 – Marco

He was one of the most beautiful guys I've met in my life. The motherfucker was beautiful. He's the best friend of Curumim. Curumim liked to hang out with him because he was one of the most famous faces in the world at that time. All the girls kill themselves to fuck him. I was jealous, because every girl wants him. He caught all the rich bitches; he was the man.
 – Rafael

Marco paid his horses around $2000 a kilo to traffic, still making a good profit after deducting hotel and flight costs. He bought a kilo of dope in Amsterdam for $3000 and in Bali sold it for $500 per 25 grams, adding up to $20,000 per kilo.

Most of the guys in Bali start this business working for Marco.
Marco was the first one, and almost all the guys start carrying
drugs for Marco.
  – Andre

Marco was living the high life, doing a chef course in Lausanne, Switzerland – 'I make good food, believe me' – snowboarding in the Austrian Alps, and 'snowboarding' in Bali; another Marco-coined expression that caught on as a euphemism for using cocaine. He shouted friends trips on live-aboard surfboats, and once paid for Rafael to take a trip to Sydney with him. He was always fun, chatting to everyone in a plane or bar, sniffing coke in the plane toilets, shouting rounds of drinks, breaking into Gloria Gaynor's 'Never Can Say Goodbye'. The air was always electric around Marco.

He was always pushing the boundaries, tempting fate. Hang-gliding in Sydney with Rafael, he'd insist on launching from forbidden spots, and end up being chased by police. He'd also always travel with drugs for personal use, once nearly getting busted. 'Inside I had 100 grams of cocaine, 30 grams of Lemon Juice, but this time I make small eggs, I put in my ass.'

Arriving at Sydney Airport with Rafael, Marco was collecting his luggage from the carousel when a little dog started sniffing his backside. It became a running joke among the dealers that he'd passed wind as he picked up his bags. Again, he got away with it.

He was always sniffing inside the aeroplane. All the time he
travel, he put something in the ass just for himself, it's crazy.
  – Andre

His life was a blast – he was living his dream, until the day he crashed a glider in Bali and died. For years he'd been making disparaging jokes about paragliders using 'plastic bags', believing it was a lesser sport than hang-gliding. But one afternoon, untypically flying a 'plastic bag', he lost control and crashed hundreds of metres to earth.

Lying there unconscious, with blood pouring out of his nose and mouth, it looked hopeless. He'd broken his femur, hip and ankle and split his intestines. 'When the doctor in Denpasar come to see me, he says I'm already dead.' But his long-time loyal friend Gui, the guy who'd called out to him on his first crash into the cliff all those years earlier, wasn't giving up without a fight.

Gui organised a plane to take him to Singapore, where he'd get better medical care – in Bali they were already talking about amputating his foot. While waiting for the plane, Marco, who'd lost 3 litres of blood, had a transfusion from a friend with a matching blood type. It took 24 hours to organise the flight, as the pilot insisted on cash upfront. Once he had it, they took off.

Flying over Jakarta, Marco had a heart attack and died, but was resuscitated. With the plane's oxygen then depleted, Gui told the pilot to go down. The plane made a pit stop in Jakarta to fill up on oxygen. Marco was critical, slipping in and out of consciousness. When he finally made it to Singapore General Hospital, he was in bad shape and looked unlikely to make it.

This is the most emotional story ever. When I have the accident, I die. Marco survives again. Oh, you don't believe, you don't believe ... My heart stopped, back again, first time.

Second time, inside a flight, third time in Jakarta. I have three heart attacks. You don't believe ...

In Singapore I'd been in a coma for one month, the doctor says, 'Marco is already dead,' they bring the priest, my mother came, he say, 'Marco is already dead.' And then he make like a prayer, 'Maria, Marco bye-bye', and then the priest says to my mother, 'You have to pay $100.' My mother gives money to the priest. The priest goes away ... after five minutes I open my eyes, 'Mamma mamma.' Then my mother tried to find the priest but he already escaped.

   – Marco

After three months of drifting in and out of comas, Marco recovered well enough to do a runner, escaping Singapore without paying his hospital bill. It was more than $200,000 and even after insurance and friends chipping in, he owed more than $50,000. For the next two years, he was in a wheelchair, but used it to his advantage smuggling Lemon Juice to Bali.

His friends thought that the accident might make him less erratic, reckless and arrogant, but it seemed to exacerbate those traits. He'd fallen from the skies, defied death a second time; now, despite being left with a permanent limp, he truly believed he was invincible. Rafael had been working less and less with him since the accident, and after the ecstasy con, he boycotted any jobs with him, although he would later inadvertently be involved in the most deadly run of all.

After the accident, he talk bullshit about everybody, make gossip. If he knows about some deal, he talks with the wrong people to make shit. He was crazy. Man, I only help this motherfucker, I give coke, I give money, I give girls, I give him everything and then he wants to fuck with me. This guy is trouble walking – he talk too much. I start to keep a distance, because I think he get crazy.

   – Rafael

CHAPTER NINE

THE HORSE WHISPERER

As much as the guys sometimes fell out, they were usually out playing again soon. One night, Rafael invited a bunch to dinner at one of Bali's best restaurants, Warisan. After a 4-kilo win, it was his shout. They sat at a table in an al fresco corner, over-looking rice paddies. A few of them were with pretty young hookers or girlfriends, and it quickly got lively, with champagne flowing at the table and cocaine snowing in the bathroom. But the relaxed ambience was about to turn.

We celebrate, the horse just arrive with 4 kilos. Cash coming. I was very happy.
   – Rafael

A Brazilian man ambled up to one of the dealers, Black Julio, who vaguely knew him, asking if he could take his photo. But it was a ruse. Instead, he spun around and snapped a shot of Marco. Marco saw it and sensed danger, dashing over to Rafael, asking, 'Who's that?' Rafael didn't know, but was blasé until Marco said, 'I think he's a cop.'

'What? Why?' Rafael was suddenly listening. For all Marco's japery, his instincts were red hot. 'We're the only drug dealers here, and the guy has a camera, come on it's a crazy coincidence.' Rafael scrutinised the guy as he was talking to Black Julio, but he noticed Rafael looking.

He moseyed over, said 'Hi', then quick as a flash took a shot of Rafael. Instinctively, Rafael grabbed the camera: 'Hey, why did you take a photo of me?' The guy tussled, yanking his camera back, but he was either naïve or stupid as he didn't stand a chance against these guys.

Bras flew around behind him and, in a Jiu-Jitsu choke move, squeezed his neck, cut the blood to his brain and blacked him out, then lowered him to the ground. Rafael quickly checked his pockets, but found nothing.

The restaurant was large, with tables spread out, so other diners didn't seem to notice the fracas. But a waiter raced straight over, asking, 'What's happened?' A prerequisite for being a good drug dealer was staying cool in a hot spot, and making up stories, so Rafael easily slipped into casual banter. 'Oh, this guy is very drunk, sorry. We'll take him out before he throws up.' Rafael and Bras hauled him off the floor, slung his limp arms around their shoulders and dragged him out.

After dumping him on the concrete, Bras slapped his face to get the blood circulating, and as he came to, gripped him by the throat. Rafael asked, 'Why did you take a photo of me, motherfucker? Who are you?'

He gave a glassy-eyed stare, but didn't speak. Bras tightened his grip. Rafael grabbed the camera, ripped out the film and threw it back onto his chest. 'Motherfucker, we don't want to see you again. If we do, we will kill you. This time we're giving you a chance, but you better run for your life.'

They watched him get up and bolt. The dealers didn't let the incident ruin the rest of the night, but it was unnerving. They suspected he'd been working for bad Brazilian cops, who notoriously kidnapped the children of rich drug bosses for ransom. Whoever he was, they knew he was up to no good.

The playboys needed to be as careful of the Brazilian cops as the Bali cops, with many of them spending several months a year in Brazil and the cops now aware of the runs between Amsterdam, Bali and Brazil. Marco was sharing his apartment in Amsterdam with another trafficker, Andre, to split the cost. Like Marco, Andre lived between Bali, Holland and Brazil. Unlike him, he was scrupulously careful with the cash he made, building an empire, but was already being watched by the cops.

Although Andre spent a lot of time in Bali partying with the others, he was an entrepreneur, with two top restaurants, one nightclub, and a beachfront mansion with a swimming pool and private gym in an exclusive beach resort area, Garopaba, South Brazil. He also had two apartments in São Paulo, and a share in a surf camp in Sumatra, Indonesia. He drove a $100,000 car and flew to Hawaii and Europe at least once a month. He lived in Bali several months a year, during the surf season, which coincided with the winter months in Brazil, when his seaside city virtually closed down and his restaurants shut. He was splurging a fortune on air tickets.

For him, this was why he dealt drugs – to get filthy rich. And it was working.

*Every month, I send cocaine to Europe and get €50,000 profit or
I send every month 2 kilos, 3 kilos and every month come €50,000,
€100,000 profit. In Brazil my life was fucking beautiful.*

– Andre

To Andre, life was about the ability to wake up in Brazil, whimsically fly to Paris for a David Guetta concert and then on to
Hawaii or Bali to surf a few days later. Living moment to
moment made him feel alive. But such an indulgent lifestyle
costs big bucks, and it was a freak incident one dark night,
when he was just 19 years old, that gave him the key to living
his impulsive dreams.

He was smart, educated and polite, from a wealthy upper
middle-class family. His sisters were doctors; he was the black
sheep. As a teenager, he'd sacrificed his family, choosing a fast
life of fast bucks over humdrum routine. He was studying
tourism at university and working casually at his father's fishing
company, selling shrimp to São Paulo's top restaurants, when
overnight it rained money.

*I was in the house and the captain from one of my father's boats
comes and says, 'Hey, Andre, you smoke marijuana, don't you?'
I was surprised. I say, 'Yeah, Master Antonio, you know I like
marijuana. Why?' He says, 'The beach is full of marijuana.' And
he shows me one pineapple can full of really, really good quality
stuff. This was a point in my life when it changed.*

Andre raced down to the beach and saw hundreds of washed
up pineapple tins scattered on the sand. In the moonlight, he

ran around collecting 108 tins, which he stashed in his father's beach house. The next day he saw a newsflash. Police had intercepted and raided a ship passing the Brazilian coastline and two container loads of pineapple tins, stuffed with 20 tonnes of marijuana, had been thrown overboard to evade arrest. For Andre, it was like Christmas and the catalyst to a new, decadent life. Alone.

One day I have an old car, I put shrimps inside it and go to São Paulo to sell them to make money. The next day I have $108,000 in marijuana, I buy a new car and I park it in my house in São Paulo. My dad just looks at me, he looks at the car, he doesn't say anything. We have dinner with the family; afterwards he calls me to his office and says, 'Andre, I know you are a drug dealer. I know you have a lot of cans in the beach house. You have two days to clear them out.'

My father is a harbour man, a hard man. He has three really nice daughters; he doesn't need a crazy guy around. He tells me, 'If you want to live in this house, you can live here. Stop doing this and you can keep your family. But if you want to be a drug dealer, please, get out.' So I'm 19 years old, $100,000 in my pocket, he gives me the option. I go straight to California.

He was soon a busy LA drug dealer, selling cocaine, LSD and marijuana, often roller-skating along the Venice Beach esplanade with a bag of gear. He'd hooked up with a bunch of surfers, mostly Mexicans and Brazilians, who were sharing a condominium. The Mexicans were smuggling drugs across the border from Tijuana, so drugs were on tap. Andre spent his days selling and surfing, with regular trips down to Hawaii to ride the big waves. Before long, he joined the fast flow of surfers to Bali.

At 22, with a backpack slung over his shoulder, packed full of clothes and LSD, he walked into the surfers' haunt, the Aquarius Hotel, situated on the main street in Kuta. This was Andre's first time in Bali and it was the early 1990s, so things were very basic, with few hotels, and stinking open drains flanking the sides of roads. Andre checked into a room, grabbed his board and hit the beach.

Within days he was connected to the island's Peruvian players, who were pioneering the coke scene, easily paying for a life of surfing and partying by bringing blow from their backyard. Andre's LSD didn't sell, but he quickly learnt coke was the drug to play.

I saw these Peruvian guys in Bali, really rich: Poca, Mario, Borrador and Jerome. Big hotels, the best cars, big, big boats, they live like kings. This opened my eyes, this got me interested in smuggling to Bali. These guys introduced me to the buyers of cocaine, to boats, the best waves, many girls, cars, everything. I came here for one month, stayed three months, and went back with my mind really, really running: 'Wow, that place was amazing.' Perfect for me, first because I met the Peruvian guys, and because it felt like paradise. The most friendly people, always smiling. If you have money in Bali, you live like a king. And I started bringing here.

Andre did three coke runs to Bali, stashing one or two kilos into the speakers of a sound system. The first time he sold to Chino and made $40,000, he was hooked. But he was savvy, with the opinion that, if you're smart, you become an investor or boss, avoiding the risk of carrying. He was quickly using a stable of horses to move coke from Brazil to Bali and Amsterdam. And, with his tactic of turning horses around in Amsterdam, repacked with ecstasy and marijuana, his business exploded. Suddenly, the world was his playground ... just the way he'd pictured it.

You get one lifestyle, really high, you know. Going to the airport and taking a flight is as normal as taking a bus.

Andre also sometimes got his horses to bring cash back – up to €300,000, in €500 notes, hidden in secret compartments in their suitcases. 'If the police in Brazil catch you with €200,000, they either kill you or steal your money. The big risk is in Brazil.'

The risk in Europe was having the cash confiscated, as Andre found out one day. Flying out of Holland with €100,000, he was searched. Customs found two packets of €500 bills stashed in a pouch in his underpants. They took the cash, made him sign a document in Dutch, and then let him fly back to Brazil. He immediately called a lawyer, who knew a *sponk* lawyer in Amsterdam, who worked exclusively for drug traffickers.

This guy ask me, 'How much money?' '€100,000.' 'You sign something?' 'Yes.' 'It was Dutch?' 'Yes.' 'You understand Dutch?' 'No.' 'Okay, you can get your money back.' This sponk gets the money and sends it to my lawyer in Brazil. I pay 20 per cent for the two lawyers; I lost €20,000, but better than losing it all.

And only because they made you sign something you couldn't understand?

Yeah. In Holland they are really, really precise with the law.

Andre had invested his megabucks into the businesses only after his father died, using the excuse of an inheritance for suddenly being flush with cash.

When my father passed away, for me it was the big launder for the society. My father was not a rich man, but he had something. I tell my sisters, 'I don't want anything. You can share between you and mamma, I don't need the money.' But I tell everybody else, 'Oh, now is my time because my father passed away and leave for me good, good money.' Now I can realise my dreams, build restaurant, build my house.

He relished the prestige of being the young, sharply dressed, successful man, invariably with a beautiful girl on his arm, but feared one day his cover would be blown.

I really care about my position in the city, in the society. Nobody had any suspicion about me. Everybody was looking at me like a successful business guy. Good lifestyle, come to Bali for six months, live in Brazil for three months, three months in Hawaii. Always working restaurants, people look, 'Oh, this is a successful guy.'

And you liked that image?

Yeah. But I am always afraid of the truth.

His Thai restaurant won Best Oriental Restaurant several times, and his Japanese restaurant, with a Bali corner, was also booming. But he was uncomfortable with accolades, aware that, with the cash he was laundering on everything from imported Bali furniture to Balinese-created uniforms for his staff, even a fool could create a beautiful ambience.

I never like to talk too much like, 'Oh, I'm fucking good, my restaurant is the best.' I never like these titles for me. It's really, really beautiful, but why is my restaurant beautiful, the best restaurant? Because I had support of $1 million a year. If I don't do the best restaurant, I'm stupid. Also, I don't want to call attention on myself. 'Wow … how does this guy have so much money when his restaurant's only open three months a year?'

Seeing his success, and hearing whispers, sometimes young guys or girls approached him, asking to do a run. One day a 22-year-old Frenchman, nicknamed Fox, whose father was working in the French consulate, asked him for a job. Fox's approach was lucky timing, as Andre was about to fly to Bali and always liked to send a few kilos ahead so he'd have cash to play with.

Fox would later meet up with Rafael, work with him, and then double-cross him. But on this first run, like most of his new horses, Andre put him through his paces for three days. Andre's system aimed to reduce the busts by ensuring the horses were fit to run.

Two days, three days before flying are always nervous days for the horse. They're thinking, 'Oh, I can go to jail', their mind never stops. So when I'm in Brazil, I bring the horse to the beach. 'You fly Friday, come here Wednesday.' When they come, they are scared, new horses are always scared. So I put him in the style the guy dreams to be in: the best hotel in front of the beach, I hire a nice car for them for two days. 'Oh you want to do the parties, I know the best place, you will have a VIP pass tonight.' So the guy feels good, feels confident. You need to incorporate this personage – 'Now I'm the man, I'm going to Bali to spend my vacation there. I was in a beautiful place in Brazil, now I'm going to Bali. I'm going to my paradise to have my vacation.' Forget you have cocaine.

Also, normally I ask, 'What are you going to do with the money?' Everyone has a dream; the horse always has one thing they want to buy. I ask them, 'Why you doing this?' 'Ah, I want to buy a car, I want to change my house.' I just ask the horse once, 'Are you sure you want to do this? You know about the risks, the death penalty?' 'Yes.' After they say yes, I don't ask again, just talk about the success. You put the money like 100 per cent in their pocket. 'What sort of car you want to buy?' 'Oh, the black one because it's beautiful,' they start to mentalise, see success. I read The Secret, *it's like that. Mentalisation, this is the big truth of the world; you are what you think; you attract for yourself what you think.*

This is like brainwashing. Two days or three days to wash the brain, to make the guy really confident and then he goes to Bali, no worries.

Andre also bought them a pair of good shoes, clothes – usually a standard Polo shirt, blue or white – and a standard black bag, so they'd just blend in with the thousands of real tourists. He habitually watched shows like *Banged Up Abroad* and *Behind Bars*, to spy clues from others' mistakes, or details of police busts. Teaching his horses as many tips as possible was his goal.

He'd been headhunted to work with Colombian cartels moving tonnes of cocaine, but aside from the draconian penalties if busted trafficking tonnes, he didn't agree with their philosophy of sending dozens of untrained, peasant horses – who usually spoke no English and had never been on a plane – sure that a percentage would crash and burn, but with this simple collateral damage built into their business plan. They were numbers, not lives, and Andre preferred trying to make every horse a winner.

Can I explain a difference between mule and horse. Mules are not like the kind of people who work for me, people who come to Bali to enjoy life; this is a real horse. But mules, not horses, mules are really, really desperate people. Really poor people, don't speak English, and they fall like flies . . . this type of business is like Colombian business, Peruvian business; they send many mules to fly, maybe they send five, they know three will get arrested. But for them, it doesn't matter. It's just one less number in your account business. Who does this is just the big cartels, like Colombians, Peruvians; they have 20 tonnes, they know they will lose 2 tonnes on the way. But still they have big, big money because they send 18 successfully. It's not my way. I have one guy, 5 kilos of cocaine, and if I lose 2, oh it's a big loss.

– Andre

Customs officers at Hato Airport on Curaçao accomplished a record catch in August 2002, when Crown Prince Willem-Alexander and his wife Máxima were on board a flight to Amsterdam following a tour of the Antilles. Ninety-nine smugglers had checked in for the flight, expecting that passengers would not be checked if members of the royal family were on board.

    – Spiegel Online, 11 February 2004

There are 32 of those flights a week [from the Dutch Antilles in the Caribbean – a transshipment point for cocaine – to Amsterdam], with as many as 40 passengers on each plane carrying drugs. Last year 2176 smugglers from the Dutch Antilles were arrested at Schiphol [Amsterdam Airport] and six tonnes of cocaine seized.

    – The Mail on Sunday, London, 15 February 2004

In my business, I send one horse and I put all my energy to have success with this one. I don't put 10 knowing I am to lose five. I don't like to play with the life of other people. Everyone who spends three years, five years, seven years in the jail – doesn't matter Brazil, Europe, Bali – this destroys your life. I don't like that. If this happens, I help, give money, give lawyers, support the family. I don't like to see the horse bust. I play one by one, I like to be a success. I teach them step by step like a kid. Talk for two days about their comportment inside the airport. I have in my house DVDs to teach them about the airport. I went with my girlfriend and recorded everything . . . 'Oh baby, come here,' pretending to film her . . . but I use it to show the horses. 'Look, this is the Federal Police counter, don't stand in front of that, never ever stay in the departure lounge or the lines a long time.' Like ... your flight is 10 pm, don't go to the departure lounge at 8 pm ... go inside the shops, in the Rolex shop and look at watches, inside Nokia and look at all the cellphones, ask questions. Spend your time inside the shops, don't spend your time in public areas. Why? The undercover cops are always looking for something suspicious in the public areas ... the guy reading a newspaper and looking around all the time ... nervous. This is suspicious. They work the line too. But if you are inside a shop, you are a tourist. The cops don't look inside the shops. Just before your flight closes, go to the lounge and straight on the aeroplane. You get only one or two minutes in the risky area. Small, small tips, but they make all the difference between freedom or jail.

   – Andre

Andre made it his business to understand the psyche of a horse, aware it was not only about the cash and adrenalin but about power and status too. Almost always, after a first run, he watched with wry amusement his horses go out to buy expensive designer sunglasses.

This is typical for the horses. This is famous: 90–95 per cent of horses, when they get their first money, they buy something to show, 'Now I am someone, now I am good enough.' And this is really, really stupid. Because the guy puts his life at risk, to buy a $3000 watch. It's more funny in Bali, because sometimes the mule is mule, not fucking intelligent – comes here to Bali and *spends his money on fake glasses, fake watch, because Bali is specialist for fake. And the mule goes ... 'Ah, look what I bought.' I say, 'Oh this is beautiful, but it's fake.' 'Ah, no.' Stupid.*

Despite his training regime, many of Andre's horses were still busted; it was a hazard of the game, sometimes plain bad luck but usually due to small nuances that could have been avoided, such as a horse Dimitrius the Greek had organised to run to Bali with 7.3 kilos inside a surfboard bag. He went down simply because he didn't look the part he was playing.

The pale complexion of a man who tried to check two surf-boards on an international flight aroused the suspicion of Brazilian airport security officials, who said they found nearly 7 kilos of cocaine hidden in a package between the boards. Luis Alberto Faria Cafiero, 27, was arrested Friday in São Paulo before boarding a flight to Johannesburg, South Africa, with a connection to Bali, Indonesia. 'He did not look like a person who's always out on the beach,' said Federal police officer Isaias Santos Vilela.

– AP Worldstream, 11 October 2003

This seemingly small detail of a lack of a suntan would later have explosive consequences for Dimitrius, when his horse turned police informant. 'I know the benefits of the whistle-blower,' he said in his judicial testimony.

How many of your horses have been busted?
Many, more than 10.

In Bali?

No, never ever. In France twice, four horses fall in Amsterdam, in Peru, in Australia ... many. But never in Brazil for my good luck, because Brazil is the worst, the law is hard, the prison is terrible.
– Andre

It was Andre's first real red alert for his own safety when one of his best horses, Rabbit, got busted at Charles de Gaulle Airport in Paris, en route to Amsterdam. It was seen as safer to fly to Paris or Brussels, clear customs there, and fly domestically or drive to Amsterdam, Europe's drug gateway. Rabbit had done 10 runs, knew the game, but became cocky. Foolishly, he carried a silver ashtray in his luggage, which he'd been using to smoke joints. His arrogance coincided with bad luck. On his flight, a bunch of 12 Peruvians, smuggling blow in their stomachs, were busted, sparking an intensive search of everyone on board. After finding the tainted ashtray, they put Rabbit through the wringer, and busted him with 4 kilos of coke in his hang-glider. Rabbit was being pushed to give up his boss, but knowing the dire consequences of snitching, he didn't, claiming he'd trafficked the coke on his own.

He didn't want to lose the life. He say, 'This I buy for myself, I was crazy, totally addicted, I lose my mind and bring this for myself.' This is the best thing to say, because the sentence comes down for addicts anyway.

Rabbit got off with only 11 months jail. But his bust tipped Andre some gut-wrenching news. Rabbit phoned him from jail one day telling him that two officers from America's Drug Enforcement Administration (DEA) had come in asking questions specifically about him.

I say, 'What are you fucking talk about, Rabbit?' 'Two guys come here, one girl and one guy from the DEA, and ask about you by name, say, "Eh, you work for Andre? Give the guy up and you can get less time in the prison."' I say, 'But how do they get connection?' He say, 'I don't know, I'm just telling you about it.' I say, 'Fuck, now I'm fucked up.' After this, I know I'm hot. This is the first red light, bam bam, now the DEA is behind me. I start to think why is the DEA behind me?

It didn't take Andre long to realise how he'd hit the Agency's radar. It was a capricious last-minute change of plan that cursed him. He'd flown to Peru a year earlier to buy 30 kilos of coke with a partner, a white-haired, 65-year-old trafficking veteran. They'd booked three horses to take 10 kilos each, but when one failed to show, the partner, after years of being a boss, decided to carry the stuff. Quickly exhilarated by the idea, he wanted to fly all the way from Lima to São Paulo and on to Amsterdam.

Andre wasn't thrilled. The danger was that Andre had openly hung out with the man for five days in Lima, using his real identity, his real passport, staying in the same hotel, dining together, with CCTV cameras undoubtedly recording it all. If he'd known the man was going to run, Andre would have stayed clear of him in public. With the abrupt last-minute change of plan, Andre packed the paraglider for the other two horses, always preferring to do it himself, precise and careful, and then flew out – leaving four hours ahead of his partner to avoid being on his flight or coming in behind him in case of a bust.

His partner did get busted. The Peruvian airports were tough, with the DEA now working with local cops, and it didn't take much to create suspicion. The man had previously trafficked at least 20 times himself, but this time made an error. He wore a business suit as well as carrying a paraglider, and his incongruous look cast suspicion. The Peru police and DEA took him down for 10 kilos. He didn't snitch, but Andre was sure the DEA would have investigated whether the old man had been seen with anyone in Lima.

That's the start of my problems, because after this I know the DEA know my face, know my passport.

But Andre didn't slow down the game. Aware he was hot, he took extra care, but was still living the high life. Like Marco, and many of the players, Bali was where he'd spend months at a time, broken by occasional trips overseas to fix deals. Sharing the apartment in Amsterdam meant Andre and Marco often worked together through sheer convenience. If Andre was in Amsterdam, Marco would sometimes organise a horse and ask Andre to meet him. No one ever did gratis favours, but Andre would do it for a commission, usually buying some Lemon Juice or ecstasy and sending the horse back to Brazil reloaded.

Despite working with Marco, Andre lamented the Lemon Juice boss's cowboy antics and insouciant attitude to money.

Andre was the antithesis, pedantically precise about cash and ruthlessly capitalistic.

I never like to work with Marco too much, because when I do business I like details. I pay five, I sell for 10, I have five profit, clear like water. Marco is totally different. 'Ah, I buy 2 kilos, I want to give 200 grams to my neighbour, and 200 grams for you, because you have beautiful eyes.' Whaaaa ... I say, 'Hey wait, man, where is your profit?' For me this is stupid. If I put my life at risk, I will not give it away. Marco is crazy.

It was Marco's endless frivolous antics that fazed Andre – like the time Marco had phoned him in Brazil from their flat in Amsterdam, asking if he knew anyone who had 30 grams of coke he could buy to use on the weekend. Andre did and the supplier organised a courier. The courier then vanished. It turned out Marco had invited him in and spent three days sniffing the entire $3000 worth of cocaine with the total stranger. Another time, Andre and Marco invested in a 2 kilo run to Bali. Andre sold the stuff to Chino and later learnt Marco was buying it back at street prices.

I talk to Chino, just talk cos he's my friend, 'Hey Chino, is every-thing okay?' 'I'm okay but I'm fucking angry with Marco – he calls me 10 times a day.' 'Why?' 'To buy cocaine.' 'Are you selling cocaine to Marco ... for how much do you sell?' '$150 a gram.' 'Are you kidding me?' Marco sells to him for $60 a gram, now he buys it back for $150. Fucking good business. This is typical example how stupid he can be in the mind.

CHAPTER TEN

007

Indonesian Police on Tuesday were questioning 13 European tourists arrested on the resort island of Bali during what police have termed a 'drugs party' in their rented villa ... The group includes nine French citizens, three Italians and one Swiss National ... Officers confiscated 2.5 grams of cocaine and 10.2 grams of hashish ... Police in Indonesia, where drug crimes had previously been treated as minor offences, have declared war on drug traffickers and users in the past year ...
– Agence France-Presse, 22 August 2000

Criticised for its futile attempts to curb drug trafficking, the government has now decided to change tack ... The President also voiced her disappointment over the light sentences meted out to convicted drug traffickers ... 'Major offenders, like producers and dealers, should be punished by death. For me, it is better to have a person suffer capital punishment than to see the whole community become addicted to drugs,' she remarked ...

Indonesia has become well known not only as a place of

transit for international traffickers, but also as a producing country.

   – Jakarta Post, 30 October 2001

People used to joke, 'It's snowing in Bali, it's snowing in Bali.' I used to joke with my friends, I'm the only one riding a Jimny that's worth a Ferrari, because I had all the doors stocked up with coke.

   – Alberto

The more it was snowing in Bali, the hotter it got. Undercover police were stalking the nights; infiltrating clubs, bars and restaurants, and raiding luxury villas and expatriates' homes, often after a Balinese dealer or vengeful staff had tipped off the cops for a fee.

It wasn't slowing the dealers down. Peruvian drug dealer Alberto always watched his rear-vision mirror. With the clique of big players overtly partying and splashing cash at the same few top restaurants, bars and clubs nightly, he had no doubt the Intel cops knew exactly who they were. The island was small. But for Alberto, this charged the game with extra zing. He relished outwitting the cops, never letting them catch him red-handed, cleverly using Bali's labyrinth of infinite hotel rooms like a house of mirrors, going in one door and out another, vanishing in a smoke of tourists.

You're always on the edge, always risking your life, no matter how many times you do it. I loved that feeling of a big adrenalin rush. I was addicted to it. More than the money, it was the rush that kept me hooked. Whenever you open a bag with a lot of cocaine, your life can end right there. If the wrong person knocks on your door, your life's finished.

   – Alberto

Ensuring the wrong person didn't knock on his door, Alberto trusted almost no one. One day a Peruvian wanting to sell 2 kilos of blow he'd brought to Bali contacted Alberto to be his sales agent. Alberto quickly found some Italian buyers and set up the deal for 6 pm at the five-star Nikko Bali Resort. Alberto and his client booked into a $350 room so they could use it to party in after they had their bag of cash. The Italians were on the same floor and Alberto was waiting for his contact, who'd found him the buyers, to call so they could all meet, at first without the coke. But when he called, he made the tactical error of using the room phone, instead of his mobile. The deal unravelled fast.

'Eh, why the fuck you calling from the room? Now the guys know which room we're in,' Alberto snapped.

'Yeah, it's okay, they're my friends,' the contact replied. But it wasn't okay; these buyers were new and could be undercover cops. It was vital they didn't know where the coke was until they'd met.

Alberto's client started to panic. 'Fuck, let's get out of here now.' Alberto was feeling paranoid too, but suggested just changing rooms. The client was already bolting out the door, so Alberto raced after him.

We went straight down, got into the car and drove off. He was freaking. We didn't have time to pick up our clothes or anything.

He drove all the way to Jimbaran, and dropped me off at the Inter-Continental Hotel. I told him, 'This is kind of risky and stupid,' because I was in sandals, board shorts, a T-shirt, with a little bag, arriving at night at a five-star hotel to book a $375 room, with no luggage, no passport, looking like a beach boy. I was like something very unusual, strange ... it was all wrong. You don't want to be unusual; you want to blend in to the scene. I always check in to nice hotels in jeans, shoes, a nice collar shirt, put perfume, have a shower, shave, walk in nice. I don't go with a backpack, looking like I can't afford this type of hotel.

I was feeling completely nervous ... so I book into this hotel; I had some story like I always did. 'Oh my luggage just got lost, please can I check in now? Tomorrow I'm going to get my passport and my luggage.' But I was thinking, 'Fuck, man, this is too suspicious, too stupid.'

Alberto went straight up to his room, locked the door and put a chair against it. Then he filled the bath with water, opened the bag of coke and put it on the bathroom floor, ready for the worst.

I went to the toilet maybe five times that night. I had full-on diarrhoea from stress. I had the bag of coke open next to the bathtub, so if they bang on the door, I could just run to the bathroom and throw it in the water – it's gone, in one quick second.

It was an interminable night of broken sleep, drifting off, then jolted wide awake, alert to the littlest noise, listening to hear if cops were assembling outside his door. It was a relief to still be lying in his soft five-star bed at daybreak, not sprawled on the concrete floor of some police cell, as he had visualised many times during the night.

Now it was time to go, so he raced downstairs, jumped in a cab and went straight to the popular four-star Padma Hotel on Legian beach. It was his deal bolthole, the hotel where he felt comfortable and did most of his big deals, sometimes two or three a week.

When I got there I was like, 'Phew'. I loved to do deals there. I knew the hotel and felt safe. There were a lot of escape routes; you could run to the beach, run to the side, and all the rooms had balconies so you could jump, and a big garden too, so a lot of hiding places. And it had a lot of different buildings, so we would always do tricks. I would book into a room and have a friend book into another. Okay now, boom; I would run with the gear to his room, and he would come to my room. So if somebody was following me and they knew the room I booked, I'm not there any more. One step ahead.

This morning he did his 'hey presto incognito' trick, but was still twitchy, and keen to get rid of the blow fast. The deal with the Italians was off, but Alberto found another buyer, offloaded the coke and was safe. This time.

In the time before the deal takes place, you are sitting on a bomb, and you have that edgy feeling, like okay this could be my last deal. You don't want to think about it, but you always have the thoughts in the back of your mind that your life is on the line right here and now, these are the crucial moments. Once it's finished, you have a bag full of money and you have this feeling like, 'Yes, done it again, fuck yeah! Phew ... finished.' You get real happy, it's time to party.

Just like Rafael, Andre and Marco, Alberto had been lured to Bali by the lifestyle. He'd first arrived for a surfing holiday, met an Australian girl and stayed a year, racking up huge debts and visa overstay fines. So when Diaz brother Poca, who he'd met on the night scene, offered him a fast way to wipe his debts by a quick trip to Peru, he decided why not.

I did it because I realised there were a lot of people doing this, and I needed the money. I was with debts, like a lot of bills piling up, so I took my chance. I crossed the globe, picked up this bag with two and a half kilos, put it on my back, and then starts the Midnight Express *movie.*

He'd spent two weeks surfing in Lima to give himself a viable cover. Then, on the final day, Poca's local contact passed him a loaded backpack. From that moment, his muscles were flexed tight, as on every leg of the run he imagined jail, just waiting for the barred door of a cell to slam shut: 'I thought there was a 50:50 chance of going to jail.'

He was on his own, and knew if he got busted no one would come running to help, so he decided to play by his own rules, using his instincts. Instead of risking Lima's airport, as advised, he took the bus to Santiago, Chile. Typically, all bags were offloaded at the border, and searched one by one. Alberto was anxiously watching as sniffer dogs prowled the bags. 'This yours?' an official shouted. 'Yes, that's mine,' Alberto said, acting blasé as the man unzipped his backpack to let a Labrador stick its nose inside. Alberto tensed in a split second of terror, but the dog lost interest fast. The repellent spray had worked.

His next test was a passport check. Alberto reached the front of the line. The customs official was a cliché baddie, laughable if it hadn't been such a scary moment. He had a hulking body, huge hands, big head and face, dominated by a handlebar moustache and mirrored Ray-Bans. Alberto handed him his passport. He lifted his sunglasses – it was night time – stared into Alberto's eyes and asked, 'What's your full name and date of birth?' These were ostensibly benign questions, but clever in their simplicity to catch anyone travelling on a false passport, who at the critical moment blew it on the basics. Alberto was using his real name and had mentally rehearsed on the bus trip for the notorious border quiz.

It was one of the scariest moments of my life. I was freaking out, but I was cold-blooded … my life was depending on it.

He nailed that Chilean inquisition, but for the entire 48 hours was like a kid on a ghost train: sitting on the edge of his seat waiting for the next ghost to lurch out of the shadows. Unlike Marco, he didn't have insouciant confidence, though he was good at masking his terror with a macho nonchalance.

Simple things, that on a non-drug run flight would mean nothing, turned into heart-palpitating moments. Like discovering his bag was checked only as far as Kuala Lumpur, where he'd have to collect and re-check it. If he got busted there, his fate would be mandatory hanging. A voice in his head was now screaming, 'Abort, abort, abort.' By the time his plane hit the tarmac in Argentina, transiting in Buenos Aires, he'd calmed down, and despite possibly creating suspicion, he requested his bag be re-ticketed all the way to Bali. 'No problem, sir,' the girl breezily replied, but a ghost sprang out of the shadows when she radioed to have his bag brought up. She placed it on the counter, right in front of him. 'Is this your bag, sir?'

He took a breath. 'Yeah, that's my luggage.'

I was looking pretty calm, but inside I was shaking. She ripped the sticker off and put a new tag on it to send it all the way to Denpasar. I was like, 'Oh, wow' . . . relief.

But not for long. While standing in line to re-board, his name suddenly blasted out of loudspeakers across the airport; they were calling him to the airline desk. He froze, every muscle rigid, his chest squeezing tight. They'd found the blow. He had to run, but where? He was thinking fast. He frantically looked around for an escape. Maybe the toilet window? No, he was on the second floor, and even if he made the jump, he'd never escape the airport fences. He was stuck, plunged into a nightmare where he was being chased but couldn't run.

I thought, 'This is it. I'm gone. Oh fuck, they found it for sure.'
My heart was banging. I was looking everywhere for somewhere
to run. Then I thought I'm going to just play dumb. I made up
a quick story in my head: 'I exchanged my surfboard for this
bag with a guy, Pablo, and I didn't know the shit was there.' I
would stick with the story to the end.

'Has Mr Alberto Lopez gone through yet? Is he already on the
plane?'

'Not yet.'

'Okay. When he comes, please hold him because we have a
problem.'

Alberto, now third in line, overheard this conversation, but
stuck to his plan. It was his only option; there was no turning
back. With adrenalin coursing though his veins, he showed the
girl his boarding pass, bracing for police to pounce, his eyes
scanning for them, sure these were his last seconds of freedom.
'Thank you, sir,' she said, letting him pass. Now it felt surreal,
as if somebody were playing a sick game, watching him squirm.
Trembling imperceptibly, he walked onto the plane, found his
seat and sat down.

I was getting mentally ready to be tortured. I'd heard that's what
they did. I was just waiting for Federal Police to come. Then
the stewardess comes and says, 'Oh, excuse me, are you Mr
Lopez? We have a little problem, we overbooked the plane, and
sold your seat to a family travelling together, so would you mind
if we moved you to business class?' I was thinking, 'Thank you,
god, I'm never ever going to do this again.'

Finally he arrived in Bali, picked up his bag and, despite a raging pulse, breezed through customs, feeling sheer joy on the other side.

> *I went through like a kiddy arriving in Disneyland, really happy. I walked outside and saw my Aussie friend waiting. I didn't know he'd be there, but he knew the drug dealers and they paid him to pick me up. He didn't say a word, just put a big smile on his face, turned around and started walking to the car park. I just followed him at a distance and we jumped in the car and started celebrating. 'Yeah, I made it ... I thought I was going to be in fucking jail for life, I just fucking made it.' We were just going crazy.*

It had been two days of jangling nerves and dicey moments, but he was back in the black with cash spilling out of his pockets. The trip gave him something else, too – a brand new career. He'd proved cold-blooded in the face of hot spots and quickly became a busy go-to guy, with the Peruvians Poca and Jerome, and Indonesian bosses, hiring him to pick up horses, babysit drugs, find buyers, deliver samples, and do deals. In future, he would operate only inside Bali, without risking airports. The door swung open to the blazing underworld of elegant parties, rich, important people, luxury villas, beautiful girls and more cash some days than most people see in a lifetime.

> *There was a very glamorous side to this business. You'd feel very important; there was all this fantasy surrounding it. Whenever I was going to do business, I set myself in secret agent mode. I*

would become a completely different person, like James Bond or whatever. I have to always be the best, a step ahead, making up stories, checking into hotels, driving around the streets, always watching if I'm being followed. It was like living in a movie, like Tequila Sunrise. I would do that secret agent thing until the deal was done, then go back to my normal life as a surfer, just cruise and surf. So I had like two lives, parallel.

Putting himself into secret agent mode one day, he was meeting a big Indonesian buyer who wanted 4.5 kilos. Alberto felt comfortable with him because he was rich. If he got a problem, he could buy his way out instead of snitching. It was the little Indonesian players who were dangerous, as he'd find out later. This day, the buyer wanted to meet him on the beach. Alberto didn't like the idea; hotels were his playground.

I was going to sell 4.5 kilos of coke and he wants to do it on the beach. I told him, 'I really don't want to do it on the beach, the beach is wide open.' And he says, 'Nah, I want to do it on the beach; it's the best way. I want to meet you today, I want to show you the spot.'

Alberto drove his hire car to the prearranged meeting spot on the side of a road in Seminyak, spotted the man's car ahead and phoned, 'I'm in the car behind you, a blue Daihatsu Feroza.'

'Okay, follow me.' Alberto trailed him to the beach area, Canggu, by chance near Rafael's house. The buyer turned down a narrow lane, stopped the car and phoned. 'You see this spot right here?'

'Yeah.'

'Okay, this is where we are going to do it tomorrow.'

'Okay, no problem.'

Alberto drove home, parked the car, then walked up to the rental company and hired a second car with tinted windows. He parked it in a random underground supermarket car park. This was a ruse he often used, to lose and confuse police if they were tailing him on the day of the deal. He'd vanish into the car park in one car, switch cars and clothes, then drive out. He'd be long gone as they sat there waiting for him to exit.

At 2 p.m. the next day, three hours before the appointment, Alberto drove his first car, with 4.5 kilos of blow in the door, to a café. He sat at a window table, ordered coffee and watched to see if anyone had followed. Once confident the coast was clear, he was set to commence his mission.

I start putting myself in 007 mode. An hour before the deal, I drove to that supermarket, parked the car, and changed into another shirt, put a cap on, different sunglasses, and then I took out the coke, put in my backpack, went to the new car and drove out. If anybody saw me drive in, they wouldn't notice me drive out in the other car with black windows, cap on, big sunglasses and different shirt. It was just like taking an extra precaution – 007 mode.

Alberto drove to the designated spot in Canggu, parking behind the buyer's car. Both got out, exchanged hellos, then each asked if they had the stuff. It was breaking the rules, exchanging cash for drugs directly, but Alberto felt safe. In unison, they walked to their cars, grabbed their backpacks, and then walked back and switched the bags on the side of the road, with a clear view of the ocean and setting sun. 'So it's all here?' Alberto asked.

'Yeah, it's all there,' the buyer replied, then asked the same.

'Yes, all there.' They each put the bags in their cars, without even a cursory look inside.

I could have put bags of sand, and he could have put bags of paper. It's very hard, you know, just based on trust.

The two men shook hands, looking one another in the eye, intense, loaded looks that said, 'Okay, I'm trusting you', without words but speaking volumes, both aware it was a big $200,000 of trust. Then they got in their cars and drove off.

It was all fully based on trust. That was the quickest deal I've done in my life. And I think that was one of the safest ways I've ever done business. Nobody would ever suspect a drug deal took place; just greet each other, swap backpacks, not open them, shake hands and go.

I went home, counted all the money, perfect, everything beautiful, like not even $100 short. Was like real gentleman business.

So did you meet him again after that?

Many times, we did a lot of business after that.

Alberto was often doing one or two big deals a week, as well as selling to friends or expats by the gram for a high rate. One customer was a big-wave surfer, Gabriel, from LA; another was a famous Australian surf photographer who died, ostensibly from a spider bite, the day after buying some pure Peruvian cocaine from Alberto.

> *I was with him the day before and he wanted to buy coke, and I scored the coke for him. And the next day I found out he was found dead, and I would say he OD'd – that's what I would think.*

Alberto and the other playboys often heard of people overdosing in Bali. Alberto had come perilously close himself when on his birthday his friend put a full gram on a plate in the letter A for Alberto, and he snorted it in one go.

> *I can't believe I didn't OD at that time. I did it all in one go. Bang. That could kill me. It was pure Peruvian flake, the best quality cocaine ... I could have OD'd there and then. I'm so lucky that I had such a high tolerance, but I kept doing lines with them, and then suddenly I started feeling my heartbeat accelerating, I could feel it boom boom boom, it was difficult to breathe, so I started quickly drinking bourbon and coke, vodka and lemonade, just drinking a lot because that stabilises you again. I had to go and sit in the corner. I felt real bad for a while, really paranoid and sick. If you have too much, you feel you are going to die.*

Alberto had many small clients, which were his stable income when the big deals went quiet for a month or two. Selling was just part of his daily routine and his customers knew the code.

'Can we have a cup of coffee later? I think I'm going to bring three friends, is that okay?' He'd know that the customer wanted 3 grams. He sold other drugs too and if he wasn't sure what they wanted, he'd say something cryptic, but translatable. 'Okay, you want black coffee?' for hashish, 'Or would you rather drink some milk?' for coke.

'You use whatever clicks in the minute, talking about white, black, green, okay let's meet for a coffee later.'

He was always wary and often went to a café early to stick the packet of drugs underneath a seat, using tape or a Band-aid, to avoid having it in his pocket when the client arrived. Then he'd change seats, order food or coffee and call the contact, saying, 'Okay, I'm here in Café Moca,' – or Bali Deli, or Zanzibar, or Bali Bakery – always changing spots – 'can you come here now?'

The person would come and sit, 'So, did you mean you wanted 3 grams of Charlie?' Alberto would ask.

'Yeah, yeah.'

'Okay. So you have $300?'

'Yeah, so where is the stuff?'

'Under your seat, just put your hand there.'

Selling drugs gram by gram, the smallest amount he sold, was risky because it exposed him to many people, and entailed always riding his bike with stuff on him. To limit the risk, he usually carried 3 or 4 grams in his helmet, each rolled up tightly in a little plastic ziploc bag and taped – each the size of a 2-centimetre pencil – then tucked into the padded helmet strap.

On his bike, he'd sometimes glimpse a suspicious motorbike tailing him and do a few quick erratic turns to check. If they stuck, he'd ride like hell and outgun them, always losing them, but it would confirm his belief that the cops knew the island's players.

> They had people everywhere doing operations. It was hot. I always kept this in mind, that I could have been followed, so I always kept an eye on the mirror, always.
> – Alberto

When he was busy, he used two phones, often riding his motor-bike with an earpiece in each ear, mikes dangling, so he could talk on the road. Sometimes calls were from overseas – always cryptic, otherwise he'd hang up. 'Good waves in Bali at the moment, good time to bring some surfboards for a surf?'

'Yes, bring as many boards as you can, the surf is great.'

> Those were kind of the most stressful days of my life, cos I was all the time riding the bike with two phones ringing. It was crazy.

As part of his business set-up, he also used the island's myriad four-star hotels to store kilos of blow. He'd book a room, paying $150 to $200 cash a night, using a fake name, promising to bring his passport later on, then stash the backpack in the room for a couple of nights; simultaneously, he booked a second room in another fake name, in a nearby hotel, so he could stay near the blow but not sleep with it.

If days rolled on without finding a buyer, he'd save cash by leaving the bag in hotel storage. 'Oh, I'm going surfing in

Lombok. I'll be back in five days, can I please leave my bag here?' he'd lie, asking just what real tourists asked. In reality, he'd stay in Bali hunting for a buyer. Unwittingly, the hotel would be nursing a big bag of drugs. Most of the dealers were using this trick.

One of Alberto's friends was using it when he got busted. He'd left 1 kilo of hashish and 1.8 kilos of cocaine in storage at the Padma Hotel, telling staff he was going to Lovina in Bali's north for a few days. Actually he had been staying in Legian to find a buyer and was now sitting in a hot, cramped police cell, with all his cash tied up in the drugs in the Padma's storage room. Facing years in Bali's hellhole Kerobokan Prison unless he could get his hands on some cash, he was desperately pleading with his friends to retrieve the backpack. It was a big risk.

He needed money real quick, and asked many mutual friends, 'Please somebody help me, I'll give you 30 or 40 per cent of what's there, please I need help, go and get my stuff and sell it.' But everybody just ran away, as usual if somebody gets busted. Everybody gets so scared, 'Hey, don't call me any more.' They all change their phones, throw the SIM card in the garbage. Nobody answers calls from this guy any more because you never know if he is talking to the cops. Maybe he bargained to be set free if he gives names, sets people up. This happened a lot, people get busted and the police offer them a deal: 'Okay, you work for us and we're going to set you free. You give us someone bigger and we "change heads" and you're free.' And they keep going like that, snowballing to get the bigger guy. So nobody knew if he was trying to set someone up, nobody wanted to touch it. But

I thought, 'You know what, I'm going to do this.' All the guys couldn't believe my courage.

Alberto called the Padma and created a story for why he needed to access his friend's luggage, then called again pretending to be his friend in Lovina, giving permission. It was set. The hotel staff would relinquish the bag to his friend, so Alberto took a taxi to the Padma Hotel, unsure if this was a sting.

Were you nervous?

Fuck yes. I was fucking really nervous. I went in a taxi to the Padma, looking in the rear-view mirror to see if I was being followed, full attention. I arrived there shitting my pants, but looking confident. I went in the reception looking all over, like 360 degrees vision, to see if there was someone watching, while trying not to look suspicious. Everything looked cool, so I went to the desk, 'Hello, my name is Mr Ricardo, I just arrived from Thailand. I am from Buenos Aires and my friend was staying here and left luggage and he told me to come and pick it up.'

They politely handed the drug-stuffed bag to Alberto, who booked a room and organised to meet the buyer he'd already set up. By the end of the day, it was mission accomplished.

I got all the money, and then I called my friend and said, 'It's done.' And all my friends couldn't believe it. That was another situation that I got a lot of respect from everyone. Cos I kept on doing things that nobody else would.

Alberto swung from audacious nerves of steel to giddy paranoia. Most days life was infused with some paranoia, and using excessive cocaine exacerbated it, blurring his instincts. One hot morning, after partying for two days and nights, with friends coming and going, using cocaine in his room, he grew deeply paranoid. Sitting on his bed in the hotel room where he was living, he suddenly started believing the Indonesian people in the next room were cops, getting ready to bust him for the 250 grams of blow he was babysitting. He noticed them darting in and out of their room, peering suspiciously across at his balcony.

'I started getting really paranoid. I had to move it that moment, right then and there.'

In blinding panic, he whispered to his friend, 'There's something wrong, man, they're here for me. I have to move the stuff now.'

'Okay let's do it,' his friend agreed. Alberto took the plastic bag of coke from the room, ran outside, foraged in the bushes for more bags hidden in the garden, and then put it all on top of his head, pulling on a cap to hide and secure it. 'It was like two or three cannellonis of 100 grams each.'

Then, in the midday heat, they jumped in the car and drove from the Kuta hotel to Legian beach. The sand was packed with families on holiday, happily enjoying their days in paradise, oblivious to the frenetic underworld all around them. Alberto found a vaguely secluded spot behind a bit of scrub on a small sand dune. He furtively dug a hole and buried the coke. His friend stood keeping watch, ready to whistle if anyone walked close. Alberto was also careful not to let his friend see exactly where he was planting it. At $100 a gram, it was worth at least $25,000, and he trusted few. Alberto then went back to his hotel and slept the rest of the day and night, catching up after the endless debauched nights of sex, drugs and partying.

The next evening around 9 p.m., his client, who was paying him to babysit the blow, phoned urgently wanting the coke. 'I found somebody who wants to buy the lot,' he said.

'Shit, I can't go and take it right now, it's night time,' Alberto replied. But the client had a hot deal that couldn't wait. He pushed.

'It's got to be now, right now.'

'I'll get it in the morning, it's not safe now.'

'No, it has to be now.'

Alberto capitulated, 'Okay, I'll go and get it,' aware it was a bad idea.

Alberto was no longer high, but his instinctive gut paranoia was kicking in. This time of night that beachfront area was notoriously swarming with Balinese drug dealers, fake drug dealers and Intel police skulking in the shadows with their nets, literally arresting dozens of locals some nights, mostly fake drug dealers who they released the next day. For Alberto, it was a huge risk.

I knew that the place was very, very dodgy to go at night, because a lot of Indo cops hang around there because a lot of drug dealers hang around at night. In the daytime it was full of families, night-time full of cops, so the safest time was like 10 a.m., 11 a.m. I had to go there 9 p.m., 10 p.m. and grab it.

After calling the same friend who'd come the day before, they drove back to the spot, almost directly in front of Double Six, a nightclub renowned for its security guards, Laskar gang members, selling drugs with impunity. Alberto braced himself and walked across to the spot.

My friend was watching to see if there was anyone walking. I had to dig for 20, 30 minutes to find it, and then I grabbed the stuff, put it in the waist of my shorts and walked out to my friend. He says to me, 'Fuck, there's been two guys, real dodgy, look like coppers, Indonesian, they asked me what I was doing here. And I say, I was with a friend who is pissing in the plants. One of those guys there.'

They were walking towards us. I say, 'Fuck, let's go to the beach,' and we walk into the ocean, and then they walk behind us, follow us, and stop. And they pretend they were talking, and I thought, Fuck man, these guys are coppers. I'm not walking out of the ocean, because in here it's safe. If I see the guys come running, 'Hey police,' I can just rip the bags and it's gone in the water. No evidence. So I tell my friend, 'I'm not walking back to the beach. If they grab me, they can grab the evidence.' I was in the water almost to my waist, and he was on the edge of the ocean, and I say, 'Let's walk to Kuta.'

Alberto started wading in the surf, as his friend paddled along in the shallows. The stretch of beach was intermittently lit up by bars and hotels shining lights on the water for effect. But the swaying palm trees cast long dark shadows and between restaurants there were black spots. Alberto could see the two men walking along the sand, fading in and out with the lights. He noticed them suddenly stop, as another two came out of the shadows from the opposite direction. In the surf, clinging to his bags of blow, Alberto was getting more and more pan-icky, propelling his legs faster and faster through the water, and keeping a keen eye on the multiplying dark figures on the beach, certain they were Intel police.

They have the look, little moustache and angry face, they looked dodgy. And I could tell, just the way they walk, you know. Then suddenly I saw another two and another two. I was ... fuck man, now they are talking on the radio, saying 'Hey, two dodgy guys walking from Double Six, in the water, they look suspi-cious?' ... That's what I imagined. I didn't see anybody talking on the radio but I thought like oh for sure they are already on the radio or calling on the phone, telling them come to the beach, 'We've got two dodgy guys walking in the ocean, we're going to have another bust.'

He was sure they were being called to come out from their spy posts, at nearby restaurants or bars. Everywhere he looked, there were more dark figures moving furtively in and out of the shadows. They were closing in.

Every time I walked past another two, and then another two, or another three ... I was like, 'Fuck, now that's it. What can I do?' I even thought about tying a knot and putting the plastic bags in my shorts and just swim, swim, swim, swim far away, where they cannot see me any more.

He'd walked almost 2 kilometres in the water from Legian to Kuta and the shadowy men were still lurking everywhere. He couldn't take it any more. 'Fuck, that's it, I'm gonna throw this shit away,' he said to his friend, still paddling in the shallows. 'I want you to be my witness that I'm throwing it away because these guys are coppers.'

'No, no, you're just paranoid.'

'No, man, I'm not risking my life over 200 grams. They are Intel, so if you want, you go there and look at the guys.' That shut him up.

'No, I'm not going there.'

'Then fuck you, man, I'm throwing this, look look, I'm throwing all the shit in the ocean,' he said as he ripped the bags and tipped the blow into the surf.

Finally free of incriminating evidence, he staggered exhausted out of the water across the sand, past some of the men, now sitting on the beach, noticing a few more sitting at a restaurant behind them. Alberto was sure they'd all been watching his little water show.

I walked past them and they all had like military-look haircuts and one of the guys says to me, 'You want to sell your cell phone?' And they all started laughing. So I think they saw me throwing all the shit, throwing all the evidence away, and they realised I had a big loss, and they saw me talking on the phone and just joked with me. I don't think it was paranoia. Until today I really think they were cops, I fully do.

Soon, everyone would be paranoid.

CHAPTER ELEVEN

TOO HOT

In the days when the boom of the drugs started, there were all these big massive parties, the full moon parties, the theme parties where people would dress up. We were pretty much controlling all the drugs here.

We had that much, and we had the best quality. The best DJs in the world were coming to Bali, so they started throwing these massive parties – the blue party, the white party, the red party, the tiger party – every single person fucked up on drugs. There was a lot of drugs in Bali; a lot of acid, a lot of ecstasy, a lot of cocaine, a lot of heroin. There were a lot of full moon parties. And there were a lot of people overdosing. That was just before they started the massive arrests. So I think it was warming up, warming up, until it gets to the point where it was boiling and they were like, 'Okay, this is too much.' It was a slow process that got to a point that was over the limit. The dark side came.

Did you go to those parties?

Yep, all of them. All of them. You could buy ecstasy in any single nightclub, and cheap new pills all the time – the white dove, the blue McDonald's, the green Batman – they were so good. Bali was flooded with ecstasy. There was massive consumption of real strong drugs, like ecstasy and MDMA powder ... and cocaine, but more for the end of the party. There were lots of parties on the beach, in hotels, lots of drugs.

No one worried about the cops busting them?

People had a bit of worry, but weren't super-paranoid. They weren't selling freely but it was a scene that if you want to score drugs, all you had to do is talk to someone who's been living in Bali or coming to Bali often enough. You would be able to buy drugs at any party back in those days.

   – Alberto

Drug parties were rampant. The paradise isle was rocking to the techno beat of the world's best DJs, with strobe lasers frenetically crisscrossing in the skies, music blasting out of huge speakers on clifftops or the beach, face painters, fire dancers twirling flaming sticks. Many of the crowds of thousands at the full moon parties at Nusa Dua, Gnan Gnan, Canggu or Uluwatu were on psychedelic drugs, as were those at the other wild parties at Ku De Ta, Blue Ocean or Double Six, on the beaches, in the bars and hotels.

Alberto, Rafael, Marco, Ruggiero, Fabio, Andre and Tota were often at the parties, joining in, selling a bit. Rafael would often slip into the girls' toilets and share a cubicle with some babe, to do a few lines together on the closed lid.

One night Rafael rode his Harley to a party on the cliff-tops at Nyang Nyang, near Uluwatu, with pills and coke stashed in his pocket, ready to rock. The sea air was pulsating with techno music, the skies lit up with lasers, and around 3000 people were dancing, but Rafael didn't go to the party that night.

I come a little bit late and then I see the cops coming sneaky. I think, 'Fuck, I have stuff.' So I stay on the bike, make my way back a bit, then stop to see what happens. Bust. The cops go to the DJ, 'Stop, police,' and I go. Then I hear more come, many cars, small trucks with many cops inside.
    – Rafael

Suddenly Bali was red hot. With undercover police now circling like sharks, Rafael was soon feeling his mistake.

I was too famous. I did it the wrong way, too loud, like, 'I'm the man, fuck off.' Was crazy at this time, too many people knew about me; a big quantity of horses were coming here, and talking to their friends; they get drunk sometimes in the club, 'Oh, Rafael's become the big drug dealer in the island, he's rich now, he has a mansion in Canggu, many motorbikes, big car, he's a mafioso.'

His old horse Barbara was still perilously loquacious and loved basking in his glow at parties, pointing to him as he walked in like a celebrity with an entourage, saying, 'You want drugs, he's the guy.'

She fucked me in that time. I was totally blind, I liked to be famous; coming in with my big necklace, black shirt open to waist, my long wavy hair. I was very easy to spot when I arrive at some place, always with group of friends, people calling, 'Rafael, Rafael.' And if anyone says, 'Oh, who's that guy?' Barbara tells them, 'Oh, he's the big drug dealer on the island. I work for him. I picked up the wrong bag once.' Oh fuck, she talked to everybody. Crazy. Everybody was avoiding her because she talks too much.

Other horses were also talking too much, bragging in nightclubs or the surf about carrying drugs for the island's mafiosi. Some of the small-time dealers, who bought from Rafael in hundreds of grams to cut and sell, were also foolishly indiscreet about their source.

People often came up to him in clubs or restaurants, telling him, 'Be careful, man, you're hot', but in the next breath asking to buy some coke. Rafael ignored these remarks; they pissed him off. Until the night at Deja Vu bar when the warning came from Chino's man.

Suddenly someone comes to me in the middle of the rock 'n' roll and says, 'Rafael, be careful, man, some people are looking for you, some Australian police.' 'Really?' 'Yeah, Chino's heard something.' Then I think, 'Oh-oh, serious.'

With police on Chino's payroll, ignoring this tip-off would be foolishly suicidal. He jumped on his bike and sped home, telling his maid to swamp the wooden floors with water. Upstairs in his bedroom, Rafael got down on hands and knees, using a torch to pick out little rocks of coke wedged in the cracks between the floorboards where he sometimes packed. 'Between the wood, I find some small rocks, enough to put me inside for a long time.' He took all plastic and other evidence to the beach and burnt it, took bags of cash to storage, then went all the way to Uluwatu and, standing on a clifftop, hurled his phone into the ocean. 'I go far away on the cliff, it was kind of a good luck ceremony.'

The morning after the frenzied clean-up, he went to see Chino. 'What's happened, Chino?'

'Be careful, man, a cop came here about something else and your name came up. They're looking at you. Be careful, you need to try to be low profile, don't buy so many things, stop going out, lay low.'

Rafael was now ready, waiting for the cops to show. It took just two days. He glimpsed a black Toyota Kijang with tinted windows tailing him, so did a quick test, making two sharp turns down unmade back roads. The Kijang mirrored his moves, but Rafael stayed cool; he expected they'd now search his house, but the evidence was gone. When he drove home, the car stopped 100 metres from his front gate. Rafael raced upstairs, shut the curtains to his aquarium-like bedroom, then looked out with his state-of-the-art binoculars. They couldn't see him, but he could see them spying on his house with their own binoculars.

I have the nice lens, and I was watching to see all their moves. They had this small shit, very small binoculars. I have huge $400 ones from Singapore. Very nice, I can see all the moves they make through them; three guys, most of the time in the car, *sometimes they go out to piss, smoke a cigarette, get inside again. But so obvious, easy to see they're Indonesian cops.*

And then I was, 'Shit, they're gonna come, they're gonna come,' and actually I call my friend Chino. 'Chino, the guys are here, what do I do?' 'Don't do anything. Be quiet. Watch the TV. They're not going to do anything. Relax. But clean your place, don't let there be any evidence.' 'Okay, it's already clean.'

That night the car left around midnight, but another car was back, in a slightly different position, a few hours later. Next day, Rafael was ready to play with them. He went surfing.

I think, 'Okay, my friends, let's rock,' and then I make these guys do a tour of Bali. I check the website, where are good waves today? . . . Nusa Dua. 'Let's go to Nusa Dua, my friends,' and then I drive fast to Nusa Dua. They follow me. I just surf for two hours, they wait for me, they play like not interested, whistling, looking around, but I know they're undercover cops. Not very undercover . . . so stupid – the moustache, Ray-Bans, the kind of haircut you know, with jeans and boots, like a uniform.

Each day Rafael spent hours in the water, and walked past the police as he came out, amused as they feigned lack of interest, then cruised the roads again, laughing as they tailed him on a wild goose chase. But after several days of a relentless tailing, he was feeling agitated. Spying on them through his fancy binoculars he'd see them lighting up and smoking cigarettes in the car. One night, he walked out with an unlit cigarette, and cheekily asked for a light.

Sometimes I was pissed, you know, fuck these guys sitting at my door. I can see the light from the burning cigarettes in the dark. I went out wearing only a sarong, just to show off, naked, with an unlit cigarette, and I come to their car, knock on the window, 'Ah, can I have a light?' They give me a light. 'Thank you.' And then I walk to the beach. Walk back, 'Hi, bye. Good night.' And I walk home again, and they drive off half an hour later.

For the next week they followed him, and he acted like a surfing monk, giving them nothing more than a good look around their island and some beach time.

I stop using, I stop everything, I just surf and they follow me everywhere. I play a lot; sometimes I bring them out to Tanah Lot, or Uluwatu for a tour and then come back home. I laugh in the car . . . so stupid. And then in the end they say this is the wrong guy. He doesn't even go out to dinner. I think I was lucky too, because they are not so professional. They never come to my house . . . not this time.

Rafael knew now he needed to deal more discreetly – not accepting any new small clients, only dealing with the people he knew, and avoiding parties and dinners.

In my glamour time, I show-off, like, 'I am the man.' And then I pay for this because it was hard to hide myself; people always phone to ask, 'Oh I have a new buyer.'

Using less coke himself also gave him a clearer focus and stripped him of his sense of invincibility, casting a more realistic light on his precarious dream life.

I can think more to protect myself. Because when I was high ... 'No, fuck off, I don't care.' But I get more conscious of the situation, and I keep quiet.

He became tactical; strictly keeping drugs out of the house, except a tiny bit in the end of his electric toothbrush for personal use. He used hotels to store kilos of coke, or under the seat of a motorbike that he'd pay in coke to park at friends' houses, and he regularly switched storage rooms. He lay low, using a regular Honda, a black helmet and black jacket, vanishing among the thousands of Balinese motorcyclists. Rainy days became cherished, as he could cover himself entirely with a Balinese plastic poncho and become indistinguishable.

Riding around Bali now, he often glimpsed a tail in his rear-vision mirror. Sometimes he'd see the car or bike turn off and realise it was nothing but paranoia; other times, it was cops – they were still watching him. Everything he did now was with caution, including going to his storage place. He'd try to go only once a week, always circling the block a couple of times before ducking down the lane, incognito in his black jacket and helmet and riding his nondescript Honda.

To continue the façade of a simple surfer and family man, he would hit the water at 6 am every day, whether he'd had a big night or not. He'd started partying again after a few weeks of acute paranoia and monkish life. But it was a different person who emerged, his exhibitionist nature eclipsed by survival instincts.

That's the start of the careful time. Before I was like, I don't give a shit. And then I start feeling my mistake to be too much of a show-off. I start thinking, 'Oh, I'm going to sell the bikes, the bikes make me an easy target. I'm not going to go to some places any more, because the undercover cops, they know fancy restaurants, some dealing happened there.' I still keep partying, but carefully.

He was using tricks, like parking his Honda bike outside one of the clubs in the afternoon, then that night driving there in his recognisable big car and zooming off to a party on the other side of the island on the bike.

Then people see my car; 'Oh, he's here.' Many friends say, 'I saw your car last night in Ku De Ta; I was there; how come we don't see you, man?' ... 'Ah, because I met two girls, I went to their house to smoke some ganja' ... always bullshit. But that shit works, it was very helpful to me.

If friends or regular customers rang asking for drugs, he'd tell them he'd bring them that night, but to be quiet: 'Be careful, don't tell anyone ... I'm hot.' Other nights he'd ride one of his ostentatious bikes, because it could outrun anyone if he had to. 'Nobody can catch me. I am a very good driver too, nobody can follow me, impossible.' If there was no off-street parking where he could stash his bike under a piece of fabric, he didn't go. Or he'd park his car a kilometre from the party and walk from there.

As the months passed, the paranoia subsided, but he often sensed lurking shadows and kept playing strictly by the rules. Fabio one day came to him, shaken. The day before he'd been standing on Legian beach in front of his restaurant, watching the waves, when undercover police snatched him off the beach, piling him into a car – essentially kidnapping him. They drove him past Rafael's house with a gun to his knee, demanding information. He kept repeating, 'Rafael's a family man, a surfer.' After a few hours of interrogation, they let him go, but Fabio was freaked out, now anxiously talking about selling up and ditching paradise.

Rafael wasn't sure whether to believe Fabio's story – he didn't want to believe it.

There was more bad news when a horse carrying for Rafael and Poca was busted after arriving in Bali with 2 kilos of coke. Poca dealt with it, quickly and quietly paying $30,000 to police to have the horse released and sent home after two weeks in the police cells, with the arrest kept low-key and out of the media. But Rafael was still edgy, because he didn't know whether the horse had spilled his name. He reverted to a quiet lifestyle, doing a clean sweep of his house, again soaking the floors in water, and tightening up his habits.

When I get the news, 'Oh shit' . . . I threw my phone, second time, this time from the cliff at Padang, then all the procedure again; quiet, not using. I was so afraid, I just quit everything for a couple of months, I disappear. I hid myself; I stay in my

house, surf and sleep, surf and sleep. Very worried. After that I
stopped doing the small things, like selling 1 gram here, 1 gram
there and focused on selling kilos. Much safer.

Rafael was now using only horses who didn't live in Bali, so as
soon as they cleared customs and made the drop, he could turn
them around and send them back home. Protecting his freedom
was his priority, but it was getting harder.

Out of the blue one day Rafael got a call from Alberto, telling
him about a drug dealer's nightmare, literally.

Alberto called me and says, 'I'm so afraid. I had a dream last
night where I got caught, and then someone was looking for you
too.' I say, 'Alberto, forget it, man, be clear. Now is August, time
to be quiet, so if you feel like that, follow your feeling, go to
Lombok.'

But Alberto was busy dealing for the parties. It was high season
and Andre had just hit the island with a horse bringing 3 kilos
of coke and 2000 ecstasy pills from Amsterdam, and he'd given
some pills to Alberto to sell. It was a dry patch in Alberto's big
business deals, so he was taking risks, not only selling lots of
small amounts, but also dealing with the small-time locals,
which all the westerners knew could be lethal.

Indonesians, when they are small players – everybody gets real
edgy about it, because they are the ones who are really dan-
gerous; everybody knows they talk to police. The big players
nobody is worried about, the small players everyone is worried

about. They won't think twice before giving some names up;
they are not strong.

   – Alberto

Two days after his nightmare, Alberto was delivering pills to an
Indonesian he'd done two deals with previously. They'd set up a
time around lunch, but Alberto was delayed. The Indonesian kept
calling, asking for his new arrival time. When finally close,
Alberto phoned letting him know he'd be there in a few minutes.
Alberto was wary about dealing with a local, but was focused on
what else he had to do that night, because he still had another
three people lined up for deliveries – one at 10 pm in a restaurant, another at 11 pm in a supermarket and another after that
– but only ever taking the drugs for one deal at a time. It had
been a busy day. He parked his bike and walked towards the shop.

When I was walking inside this guy's place, I had a funny feeling
– just my instinct. I look to the side and there was some guys,
like three or four, sitting on the stairs right next door to his shop
and talking, all Indonesians. I had one split second of eye con-
tact with one of those guys; he looked right into my eyes with
an evil look. Right then I had an electric shock all through my
whole body like I'd just been hit by lightning. Right then, I knew,
that's it, something is really wrong. It gave me chicken skin, goose
bumps. I had the feeling.

Were you tempted to run?
No, I was already walking inside, so I couldn't just turn and
run. If I ran out of there they would shoot me, or run after me

and bash me, and if I run I'm accepting guilt; you don't run if you're not guilty. I knew there was nothing I could do. There was no way out. I didn't have time to think. This happened in three seconds. We are talking about a four- or five-second situation.

So I walked in and he was waiting for me. Instead of shaking hands and, 'Okay, let me see the money,' and counting the money first like we did, I put my hand in my underwear and I was like, 'Here, here, here,' and gave him the bag of pills, and he gave me the money. I wanted to get rid of it quick. I didn't want it on me. Without thinking – it was instinctive. I was feeling really weird. I just wanted to check the money, I wasn't even going to count one by one, just to see like if the amount looked correct; it was a US$1500 deal, tiny deal. Then I would go and jump on the bike and count it at home. I was like, 'Okay, that's it,' and I put it in my pocket.

Suddenly, all those guys who were sitting outside came running in. One guy grabbed me by the shirt and put a gun to my head, says, 'Police, don't move.' And I was like, fuck, this was the shit. The whole thing took less than five seconds.

Another guy came and put his hand on my heart, just to see my heart beat and it was chchchch, and he smiles, an evil smile, like, 'Ah, we got you.' Fuck, it was evil as can be. I was like, 'I don't know what you're talking about.' They search me and they couldn't find anything, and they couldn't believe it. They thought I had something in my pocket, but I just had the money.

They were real angry, pissed off, like they are doing arrest, *they are all like fucking angry. I remember seeing two guns on that scene, one at my head, another in another guy's hand.*

They ask, 'What's this money for?' and I say, 'This is my money. What's the problem? It's not against the law.' They were like, 'Okay, search the other guy.' They couldn't believe it was on him, because it was supposed to be on me. I was the one, but because I was that quick, I'd just walked in and given the stuff to him.

So they search the guy and find the stuff in his pocket, and they were like, 'Who did you buy it from?' And I look him in the face, like fuck, don't fucking snitch ... it's not me, it's not mine and then he points his finger at my face and says, 'Him, I just bought it from this guy now.'

I just thought fucking motherfucker, not strong, like little bitch giving me up. I say, 'Bullshit, I've never seen you in my life,' and then the guy holding the gun to my head hit me in the face. 'Shut up' ... boom ... 'Bullshit.'

After that, they put me in the back of a car and, while we were driving, they were like, 'We got you.' I say, 'No, that wasn't my stuff.' The guy slapped me and says, 'We know it's your stuff. You think we're stupid?' They stop the car and park in this quiet place, a car park, and they turn the light on inside the car and the guy in the front seat starts interrogating me. 'Who was this from blah blah blah?'

There were four or five guys in the car and I was still thinking I could buy my way out. I was like, 'Okay, how can I solve this, can I give you some money and get out of this?' They were like, 'How much money you want to give?' 'Okay, I give you $20,000 cash to get out; just let me go, I can arrange the money in one *day.' That's what I heard was the standard price. Then the guy in front just comes out of the blue and – bam – punches me in the forehead.*

That's a weird place to punch you?

It doesn't break your nose; it doesn't bleed or give you marks. He says, 'You think we're stupid? You think you're just going to pay $20,000 and walk away? It's not that easy. We've been watching you for a long time, we know you are doing this business. We need names.' Oh fuck.

And that's where it all started. They say, 'Okay, where do you stay?' And we went to my place, then they start searching in the garden with flashlights, checking, checking everywhere. Then we all went into the house. I think there were five cops. They say, 'Sit down and don't move,' and one guy sat next to me. They were all pissed off and angry. I was just sitting down with my mouth shut. They went through my wardrobes, through every pocket of all my clothes, through my bags, all the cabinets, everything. They kept on asking me, 'Where is it?' and I say, 'Please, be my guest, bring dogs here if you want, I don't have anything.' Every five or ten minutes, they would say, 'So, where is it? Come on, tell us' – screaming, pissed off, angry, never being gentle or nice.

I say, 'You won't find anything; you're wasting your time.' And they were real mad because they wanted me to say, 'Okay, I have a stash.' I was just thinking, 'Okay, how can I get out of this now?' I didn't know what to do. But I was expecting it to be okay, thinking this is going to end soon, like tomorrow I will be free. I was thinking maybe they're going to settle for US$20,000 when they don't find anything.

They searched for one and a half, two hours, and didn't find anything. And then they took my phone and said, 'Okay, call someone now, organise a deal and you walk free.' I was like, 'Fuck, I don't know what you are talking about, I don't do this business.' They say, 'Bullshit, we're not stupid. If you want to do this the hard way, we do it the hard way.'

– Alberto

The cops blindfolded him, cuffed his hands behind his back and made him sit in the back of the black Kijang. As the back door slammed shut, Alberto knew this was very bad. These cops weren't going to take him to the police station like this; his fate was to be far darker. This was it – his years of paranoid thoughts and nightmares exploding in his face. The game was up.

CHAPTER TWELVE

DARK PARADISE

Bali can be heaven one minute and hell in the next. You live the fantasy, you live the dream, but one day you wake up. And that day you wake up, you don't know where you will wake up, what sort of hell.

   – Alberto

People come here and think it's a paradise for sure, but it becomes hell, really, really quickly.

   – Andre

With his eyes covered, Alberto crouched in the car, scared and vulnerable, desperately trying to focus on every zig and zag to keep track of where they were taking him. But it was futile. He quickly lost his bearings and when they stopped about 45 minutes later, he had a vague sense they were near Ubud – renowned as the peaceful, hippy heart of Bali, ironic considering what he was about to experience.

As they yanked him out of the back of the car, below the blindfold he could see lights directly ahead and dirt underfoot.

The night was eerily quiet, but in the far distance he could hear the drone of a busy road. Here, darkness surrounded him and he imagined vast rice paddies, which tied in with stories he'd heard of people being taken by Bali police to isolated windowless houses, and bashed.

They pushed him through a little iron gate into a house. Tipping his head back slightly, he glimpsed unpainted walls, raw brick and a bare concrete floor – an unfinished house. He saw five pairs of feet in leather sandals – each slightly different; soon the trait that he would use to distinguish his captors. The air was full of tension; the cops were angry and for Alberto, standing impotently blindfolded, cuffed and vulnerable, every sound and touch was magnified by fear and blindness.

He flinched as the cops grabbed his arms and shoved him into a room, pushing him to sit down on the edge of a bed. A door slammed shut, then boom, it was on, fists raining brutal blows into his stomach, ribs and back, a hand slapping his face, as someone else used a plank of wood to slam into his head. He was helpless, the handcuffs preventing him from even lifting his arms to shield his face. It was against every human instinct, but he had to just surrender his body to the blows. Even gritting his teeth, he could not stop crying out in pain.

After an hour or so, the cops slammed the door behind them, leaving him slumped on the bed, hurting badly and trembling. He knew that was only round one; that they would be back to hurt him again, until they broke him down into helping them set someone else up. Right now Andre, who owned the pills, and Rafael, whose name the cops had already tossed out, were blissfully unaware of his predicament, oblivious to how close they might be to falling into the same dark hole if their friend broke. As Alberto sat there, trying to slow his ragged breathing and pounding heart, he was praying that he had the grit to take whatever was coming without capitulating.

The worst thing was the hits on the head with a wooden stick. They have this big piece of wood, solid, heavy. They hit like on the side of the ear, on the top of the head, close to my forehead, on the back of my head. One guy hitting and another guy punching on the ribs or slapping the face, together, two guys, at the same time. My hands handcuffed behind my back. They hit me for one hour, two hours, then they go out of the room, and lumps come up on my head, and then they come again two hours later, and hit the lumps. That's fucking painful . . . You want to cry; they make you see stars. That was heavy. That's the real pain, the real pain.

– Alberto

Whenever they left the room, Alberto slumped on the edge of the bed, feeling fainter and sicker, but his mind was trying to figure a way out. So far offering cash hadn't worked. They wanted to create a domino effect because it meant far more cash in the end, as well as a bunch of high-profile arrests.

Sometimes he just sat zombie-like, waiting for the door to burst open, the sandals to stride in and the next onslaught to begin. Listening in the quiet intervals, he sometimes heard faint cowbells in the distance, or a car horn, and always the constant drone of the motorway. The sounds of the normal world outside seemed surreal now that he'd been kidnapped to this place, which felt like a world spinning on a different axis, a parallel universe to the rice paddies and cowbells outside.

He still thought he was somewhere near Ubud – where people very close by were probably finding inner peace, meditating and doing yoga classes, or relaxing by the infinity pool with a cocktail. They might as well have been on another planet. He thought of the irony of the Balinese image as being peaceful, gentle people, when these same people were sadistically bashing him with relish, trying to break him.

During the beatings, every so often they'd pause and snarl, 'Come on, use your tongue, give us names.' They were pushing him to set up a sting so he could 'change heads' and walk free. They held his mobile phone under his nose, taunting, 'You want to make a call? Look, here's your phone,' then dropped it in his lap. They spat names out. 'You know the coke guy? Rafael?' Alberto kept shaking his head. His phone was full of dealers' numbers but he knew there was no chance of the cops deciphering the nicknames.

The cops were randomly texting messages like: 'Can I score some hash?' But no one in the game ever used direct words, only euphemisms, so nobody was stupid enough to reply. Alberto kept singing the same tune, 'I don't do drugs business,' aware his denials were perilous, but now sure – to the core of his being – that he would never snitch.

Fucking rats. I don't even share the same table, the same bar, with people like that. Will you be strong and quiet and eat your own shit or will you give your mother to get away from your problems? That's what it boils down to, and that's what matters the most.

– Alberto

He knew these brutal bashings would eventually end, but if he turned rat he knew his soul would never recover. So he kept stoically denying and absorbing the pain, trying to figure out a way to end the torture as fast as possible.

All the time I was sitting on the bed, handcuffed and blindfolded, just sitting thinking, 'How am I going to get out of this?' I would hear the door opening again, I would go, 'Here we go again.' I could see through the bottom of the blindfold the feet arriving, the leather sandals, so I knew if the same guys came back.

Then they would start all over again, bang, hit me on the head, bam, slap on the face, bam punch in the ribs, saying, 'Come on, use your tongue, say some names, help us to help you, come on,' and just hit hit hit. Sometimes, they put a piece of wood on top of my bare toes, and one guy comes with a real strong kick, bam, and you see stars and always like screaming, 'Ahhh fuck.' 'Come on, talk,' and just keep on going and going like this.

So in the end, after two days, they realised I wasn't going to talk or set anyone up – I was already a fucking zombie – and they finally came in, saying, 'Okay, let's go. You're not going to help us so you're going to go to jail for 10, 15 years, is that what you want?' I was like, 'Okay, if that's it, that's it, but please take me to the police station. I wish I could help you, but I can't.' 'Bullshit.'

So you were polite to them?

Very polite; they have you by the balls, the last thing you want to do is go, 'Hey, go fuck yourself motherfucker pig,' or something like that. I was already getting enough.

In two days they'd never left me for more than two hours; I didn't sleep one single minute, didn't go to the toilet, not once, I didn't eat once. Maybe I had one or two glasses of water when they played good cop, bad cop. One guy hits me, bam bam bam, and the other guy, 'Hey, stop, get out.' And then, 'Hey, I really want to help, you talk to me.' I say, 'Please, can I get a glass of water?' 'Okay.' They bring a glass of water and I still don't talk ... boom, the bad guy comes back in, starts bashing me again. Always two guys bashing me.

– Alberto

Finally, he was piled into the car, his blindfold removed, and was driven to the police station to start the next phase of hell. He was in a bad state, but said nothing as he was processed. As he walked into the crowded cell, all 30 or so pairs of eyes turned to look at him. 'Hi,' he mumbled, then found a spot on the concrete floor among the sea of men. He was hurt and shaky, with no clue what his future held, but was praying he didn't have to stay in here too long. The prisoners were packed in like battery hens, and with no windows and only a small vent, the air was stale and had a blue smoky hue from the endless cigarettes dangling from most lips.

The concrete floor exacerbated his pain, but during the interminable days there was no choice but to sit in the cramped cell, usually playing cards, unable even to properly stretch out his legs. He nicknamed the hellish hot concrete cage 'the freezer' – because here life froze, with nothing to do but wait to learn your fate. He spoke little of his bashing, but if anyone asked they were usually blasé and thought he'd got off lightly. The locals suffered far worse brutality, with no possibility of consular intervention, not that Alberto reported to his consul. Indonesians were routinely shot in the leg, with many walking around in the jails with bullet scars to prove it.

Alberto had long feared being busted and locked up in a tiny cell, but the reality was even worse. He was sharing a single filthy squat toilet with 30 men; they had no bedding, no sheets, not even a pillow – he used a book to rest his head. At night the sweaty men lay like tightly packed sausages, sleeping side-by-side on the bare concrete, uncomfortable any time, but with his bruises, Alberto found it excruciating, and it ensured they didn't fade fast.

There were always tensions and spats, with everybody hyper-stressed about their cases. Most were trying to cut a deal before the cops handed their case paperwork to prosecutors, at which point it became impossible to quietly slip out – avoiding jail time or a court case – and the price for a deal shot up, as more people required payment.

Alberto had many visits, but often from locals sent by his friends to deliver cash and food. None of the dealers could risk going in and drawing attention to themselves. Immediately after arriving, Alberto had borrowed a phone to call Rafael, warning him that the cops had repeatedly brought up his name. Rafael already knew he was on their radar, but this was another red-hot alert, and he returned to strictly surfing and abstinence.

I clean everything again, stop this, stop that, cut phone, change my phone number. I was already hot, because when Alberto got caught, I was wanted for a couple of years. I stop selling. Be quiet. Wake up 5 am, yoga, surf, come back. Bring my kids to school. Swim, surf. Not using coke, oh sometimes I use a little bit because you know I hid a little bit in the electric toothbrush.

– Rafael

Alberto also rang Andre, to warn him and ask for help, given the pills were his. Andre promised to talk to Alberto's lawyer to try to organise a deal with the cops, but no deal was struck before he was moved to Kerobokan Prison.

By that time, Alberto was looking forward to going to jail where, he'd heard, he could walk outside, play tennis and use weights. If someone had told him two months earlier that he'd be upbeat about going to the notorious Bali prison, he would have called them nuts, but with withered muscles and sickly pale skin, he couldn't wait. As he walked inside, he felt sheer relief to see blue skies and green grass. But his surge of optimism deflated like a pricked balloon when the vivid greens and blues faded to the smoky bluish grey of another concrete cell. When the guard slammed the barred door, he was again banged up in a hot, smoky, windowless, over-crowded cell. This time a putrid stench hung in the cloying air.

There were a lot of ugly, disgusting things; the toilet in the first cell I arrived at was broken, so people had to shit in plastic bags,

tie a knot and throw the bags out the window. It was like 12,
15 people in one room.
    – Alberto

Life improved substantially after he slung a bribe of about $150
to a guard and was moved to a less crowded cell in a block
that held most of the 50 or so westerners. It was the party block,
with non-stop music, drugs and booze. The cells had stereos,
TVs, DVD players, and his cellmates threw him a welcome
dinner of feta cheese, olive salad and cold beers – one of the
best meals he'd ever tasted. The inmates were from around the
globe, mostly doing time for drugs, and gave him tips, like
slinging a bribe to the guards so he could have friends bring
in a mattress, pillows, clothes, food, books and magazines.

So then I started organising having a little life inside. We painted
the entire cell. I ordered some speakers to be made by the pris-
oners so I had my music. I felt, 'Okay, I'm still in hell but the hell
is much better than where I was for the last two months.' The
biggest stress was waiting for my sentence, because you never really
know what to expect. I started to get a rash, and it grew and grew
and was real bad, itchy and painful. It was caused by stress and
also, I think, because when they cleaned the water tank, there
were three dead cats in it – one was like half decomposed. It was
the water supply for the whole jail, and we were using it to shower.
    – Alberto

Andre was still battling for him outside and had paid a lawyer
$30,000 to cut a deal with the police and judiciary, who were

promising a light sentence if the price was right. But the guys knew anything could still happen. Andre felt it was his responsibility to help Alberto, because they were his drugs, but he had to ensure he didn't make it obvious he was involved and get ensnared in the case. He used the ruse of being a family friend who was just helping him out.

You pay, you pay, you pay. I paid the lawyer, but I didn't get close because for me it's dangerous. I just paid the lawyer and said, 'The family sent money to me, because I'm a friend of his family.'

Did you visit him?
No, just send money and food sometimes.
   – Andre

Six interminable months passed before Alberto knew his fate.

The defendant, who was involved in the sale of 33 ecstasy tablets, was only sentenced to 1.5 years in prison yesterday at the hearing at Denpasar State Court.
   – *Denpost*, February 2003

The jail was literally around the corner from the luxurious house Alberto had previously shared with the fat Diaz brothers, Mario and Poca, and dealer Jerome. It was a dizzying dichotomy between his old life of decadence and this life of primitive concrete cages and decomposing cats, but they were insanely close, separated only by whitewashed concrete walls. Knowing his beautiful life was so tantalisingly close was hard and depressing, but he placated himself by ruminating on the fact that he'd actually been lucky.

I was playing with fire for years and years and years and I burned the tip of my finger. A lot of people they just played once and they burned their whole body. I got busted with a very small amount, and I just did a bit of time – a fucking lot of time for me – but still, compared to what I was playing . . .

If you hadn't paid the $30,000, how long do you think you would have got?
Probably, eight to ten years.

Is that what the lawyer told you?
Yeah.
– Alberto

The sudden blitz by narcotics police was shaking everything up. No one was safe; everyone was a target, from the big dealers like Rafael to the rich expats enjoying a quiet spliff at home in the evenings, to local dealers, users and tourists on holidays. Narcotics teams were working frenetically to set up stings, working with their captives to do the notorious 'changing heads', paying cash for tip-offs – especially to catch a westerner, their prize target – and then kicking in doors.

It was not just about cleaning up drugs in Bali; far from it. That had been the catalyst, but the crackdown and tougher sentences suddenly created a shiny new business, producing a torrential cash flow making some Balinese richer overnight than in their wildest dreams. Westerners living and partying in Bali had previously understood that, if busted with a user amount, they could buy a 'get out of jail free card' for between $1000 and $2000. Now, if caught with a joint or a few ecstasy pills at home, the fee to avoid the problem leaving your lounge room had jumped to between $30,000 and $50,000. Police, whose average wage was less than $200 a month, were winning the lottery just by kicking in doors.

There was all the police force running around like crazy, just trying to arrest as many people as possible. Everyone was like, okay, the 'arrest race' has started, they are going for everyone, they are just arresting people, every single day you would hear stories, 'Oh, someone else got busted.' So there was a time they started competing; there was a lot of competition between the narcotics teams. The ones that bust the most are the ones that make more money, that is a fact.
  – Alberto

Was like very good business – don't have any cost, police just kick some door and go out with $50,000 easy money. Good business. If you don't pay, you stay. Shit.
  – Rafael

Most foreigners arrested on drugs charges in Bali avoid serving their sentences by bribing authorities in Indonesia's notoriously corrupt legal system.
  – AAP, 25 July 2002

I tell you, everybody was getting paid. The foreigners were making these guys rich. The judge was driving a brand new white Mercedes. They realised that finally they could make money out of this, because they think all foreigners like us, if we're having a beer on the beach, we're millionaires. And they rounded up a bunch of foreigners all at one time and they started this business. The cops I think are the ones that figured it out – that there was a money machine, a cash cow, in their town.

– Gabriel, American surfer

It wasn't just the police cashing in on the new business; everyone from snitches to prosecutors, lawyers and judges, were all suddenly getting windfalls. Even local journalists were benefiting. Lawyers were approaching them to keep their clients' stories out of the papers, or at least restrict it to a small story off page one, to avoid the spotlight so cops and courts could more easily accept a bribe for a light sentence without scrutiny.

If I'm a western expat busted with 4 grams of cocaine at home, how much do I need to pay to keep it out of your newspaper?

It depends how rich you are. More rich you are, the more expensive the price. If I know you have a yacht, you have your own aeroplane, maybe a different price. Sometimes I wouldn't take money, if it's a big story.

How does it work?

Mostly the modus operandi is via lawyer. 'I have client, and my client doesn't want you to expose them, would you help me please? I have a fortune, I want to share my fortune with you, okay, am I clear enough?' Something like that.

What are the big cases lawyers often want to keep quiet?
Drug cases with a foreigner suspect.

And do you tell your journalists, 'Don't cover that court case today'?
Yeah.

And what if the journalist asks why?
That's my own business. 'You have to choose, you obey my order, take it or you leave from this office.'
— Editor, one of Bali's major newspapers

While expats busted at home could usually manage a sling to avoid the problem leaving their house, it didn't always work. Some didn't have ready access to big cash, or their case had already hit the newspapers and gone too far to avoid the spotlight. At that point lawyers, together with police and judiciary, had to devise tactics to be able to deliver a light sentence for cash, without red-flagging the bribe and alerting Indonesian Corruption Watch (ICW), an active non-profit organisation initiated in June 1998 as an anti-graft watchdog.

Tricks used were sometimes as simple as obscuring the quantity of drugs found, or having one sentence read out for public scrutiny in court and then quietly changing it on the court paperwork that was sent and held at the jail. Conveniently, the files were not stored on computer.

Englishman Steve Turner slung a $35,000 bribe to covertly reduce his six-year sentence, announced in court, to three years, avoiding questions being raised over why he was doing three years for thousands of ecstasy pills, while penniless locals routinely served four years for possession of one or two.

> *Money talks for drug criminals. Indonesia is notoriously corrupt, routinely languishing near the bottom of global corruption indexes, and the rot has spread through certain sections of the police and judiciary. One source says some of the wealthier and more savvy foreigners caught with drugs can bribe police officers and avoid court altogether, while others, less lucky, are kept in prison paying bribes until their funds are exhausted, at which point they are promptly deported.*
> – The Australian, 13 November 2004

Lawyers, dubbed negotiators, kept their slippery tactics under tight veils of secrecy for obvious reasons, but in the case of English chef Gordon Ramsay's brother Ronnie, busted in a public toilet in Kuta with heroin, his lawyer used the media to call on Gordon for cash, making it clear that money talks in Indonesian justice.

> *Ronnie's solicitor added his own criticism of the celebrity chef. 'Money can certainly help the lawyers here . . . help the wheels of justice turn a little smoother,' he said. 'I don't know how his brother can be so cruel. He can help but he chooses not to,' the lawyer told the* Daily Express.
> – Daily Express, 18 July 2007

All westerners were seen as potential cash, but when it was revealed they were super-rich or at least had connections to big money, they became possible gold mines. When the press exposed Ronnie as the brother of multi-millionaire chef Gordon, word spread like wildfire in Kerobokan Prison that the new inmate's brother was chef to the Queen of England – not quite accurate, but close enough. Ronnie might not have had a yacht or an aeroplane, but his brother might, and that was good enough.

With his piercing blue eyes, Ronnie was the image of his famous brother, despite his rake-thin, drug-ravaged body and sickly appearance being the antithesis of marathon-fit Gordon. But for all the potential cash his capture could create for the Balinese judiciary, nobody was getting anything, because Gordon had cut ties with his addict brother. Ronnie had no line to his brother's fortune and almost no cash.

Heroin addict Ronnie, 38, faces ten years in a grim Balinese jail after being found slumped in a public toilet on the island, clutching a syringe and a £10 wrap of the killer drug. The walls of the toilet are smeared with faeces and crude graffiti. A blood-stained bandage lies discarded on the floor. Only a truly desperate man would consider even stepping inside, let alone rolling up a trouser leg to inject his feet with street-bought smack.
  – Sunday Mirror, 11 March 2007

Gordon was refusing to send cash, having reportedly already spent £300,000 to help Ronnie try to kick drugs. So Ronnie and his lawyer started a shame campaign, pleading through the media outside Denpasar court for his brother to send him cash.

'I told him, "Gordon, please help me. I have no one else to turn to." It has been made painfully clear to me – with a lawyer I could be out in a few months, but without one I will be left to rot in this hellhole for the full ten years. I could die in here …

'Gordon's kitchen alone cost £500,000 and he drives a Ferrari. For less than a new set of wheels he could get me out of jail. I feel I've been hung out to dry.'

– *Sunday Mirror*, 11 March 2007

'I asked him for help. He knows I need help,' the 39-year-old addict complained of his famous brother, who is said to have a fortune of more than £60 million from an international string of restaurants plus TV shows and books. 'But he made his decision not to help me. I've heard nothing from my family. It's heartbreaking.'

– *Daily Express*, 18 July 2007

Ronnie served just 10 months, with the judge explaining that he was lenient because Ronnie had pleaded guilty and expressed remorse. Without greasing the outstretched palms, it was impossible to get such a short sentence, so somehow he'd secured the cash needed to 'make the wheels of justice turn a little smoother'.

Australian Richard Stephens was in Bali for a holiday when he was busted after buying a few straws filled with heroin from a dealer at the island's notorious heroin mecca, Kampung Flores, in Denpasar. Richard had stood there as the dealer unzipped his adidas bum bag, took out his packet of Peter Jackson Extra Light, tossed out the last cigarettes and inserted six small straws of heroin, weighing a total of 0.3 gram. When the police stopped him on his bike moments later, they went straight to his adidas bag, pulled out the cigarette packet and found the heroin straws.

I wasn't a smuggler or anything, it was personal use, but we were set up by the police and I actually watched the police pay the informant out of my wallet.
  – Richard Stephens

It is not uncommon for dealers to inform police if the buyer is a foreigner, sometimes snaring a lucrative payment for the information.
  – WA *Today,* 7 October 2011

The police took Richard to a café, gave him a cup of tea, and told him to pay $10,000, explaining in broken English, 'It will help you, you go home soon.' To communicate more easily, Richard pulled out an Indonesian phrase book, and the cop pointed to *uang lebih,* 'more money'.

'Oh, do you want more money?' Richard asked.

'Yeah, yeah.' Their eyes lit up.

He realised I had understood what he said, but stupid me goes, 'Nah, get fucked, I don't co-operate with the police.' I said, 'No money, you are not getting no more,' and he laughed. I wondered why he was laughing and didn't really care. And then I realised, when I got to the police station, [and] in the next days, that you can buy your way out – that we had our chance but now it had gone too far, too many people had seen us, and too many people had to be paid. So I had to go to jail. If you keep

your mouth shut and pay money straight away, you can basi-
cally slip out without anyone knowing.
    – Richard

Missing your chance to deal early only guaranteed the cost of
the bribe would skyrocket, as more people required payment
and camouflaging a deal got trickier. Richard hired a female
lawyer, who did the negotiating.

The lawyer came to me and said, 'They've offered us a deal;
they want 275 million rupiah' – we worked it out as A$55,000
– and she goes, 'If you don't pay that by a certain time, a cer-
tain date, if you are one day late, they won't accept the payment.'
    Otherwise we would have had to pay $180,000.

To whom?
The police wanted that; it would've got split up between the
lawyers, judges, everyone. They're parasites, they are real para-
sites; everything is money, money, money. It ended up costing
my family $55,000 for me to get home. If I didn't pay that, I
would have done 15 years ... they were asking 15 years.
    – Richard

Richard ended up doing three months.

Cash wasn't always the reward for snitches; spite also played a
hand, with some expats' villas raided after a tip-off by a vengeful
local. Komang had been working for a Swiss furniture export
company, being paid $250 a month plus commissions, a very
good salary for a Balinese. But when Frenchman Gerard moved

to the island to do marketing for the company, Komang lost his job. Bitter in the belief that Gerard had bad-mouthed him to the boss in Switzerland, he executed a plan of revenge. Using Gerard's Balinese maid to steal a joint from the house, he passed it to a police friend to test. It was marijuana; so two police searched his house, found a small stash and busted him. Without ready access to big cash, Gerard was taken to the concrete police cells, and then moved into Kerobokan Prison. After raising the cash, he cut a deal and got a lenient two years.

Komang didn't get his job back but got great satisfaction seeing the Frenchman fall.

I was a little bit happy he went to jail. I really hated him because
I lost my job, I lost everything, my life, and I was very angry.
— Komang

Alberto regularly saw his Balinese snitch in Kerobokan Prison, but didn't waste time exacting revenge. There were many locals in the jail who had 'changed heads', but then been denied their promised freedom and who casually hung out with their victim. It shocked Alberto because, in South America, a snitch's fate was usually a wooden box. But in Bali snitching was common, which was why the 'changing heads' scheme was so often used.

They're natural-born snitches.
— Alberto

But Alberto and the crew would soon see one of their own turning rat.

CHAPTER THIRTEEN

MISSING ENGLISH GIRL

As Alberto languished in Kerobokan Prison, he heard zilch from his Peruvian drug-dealing friends, fat Diaz brothers Juan (Poca) and Mario and Jose Henrici (Borrador). Rafael had come in laden with bags of food from the Bali Deli, but the Peruvians didn't visit, call or send him cash or food; they stayed clear, because they had their own strife. Not only were they hot on the police radar, but Borrador's English girlfriend was now threatening to snitch on them.

Poca's usual feverish paranoia, exacerbated by Alberto's bust and the police blitz, meant this girl's threats, perilous anytime, were exquisitely bad timing. The Bali dealers might have been smart, educated, multi-lingual guys who often surfed, loved parties, five-star hotels and fine wines, but it could be lethal to forget they were drug dealers – often high and paranoid, precariously teetering on a high wire, with much further to fall than most. At any given moment, their ritzy lives could take a spectacular nosedive into the darkest pits of hell, as they'd just watched Alberto's do.

One evening Rafael was sitting in a Seminyak restaurant,

Made's Warung, when he noticed a 'missing persons' poster on the wall. He recognised the face of Borrador's English girl-friend. After the roadside beating that Jando had given Borrador for undercutting prices, Rafael had seen little of him and only knew this girl in passing, but had heard Poca and Mario talking anxiously about her.

They complained she was trouble, 'This bitch talk too much, blah blah, she talks so much.' She was giving shit to Poca and Mario ... like, 'I'm gonna tell police what you guys are doing.'
  – Rafael

She was cool. She was kind of crazy, but she was cool.
  – Alberto

British girl Kate Osborne had been dating Borrador for a couple of years, living with him and, she confided to her mum, hoping to marry him. She was an attractive, effervescent girl from Carlisle in England's north – seemingly an unlikely person to get mixed up in the drug underworld. She'd grown up second of three sisters in a close upper middle-class family, hanging with a group of smart, urbane, ambitious friends. She loved travelling and backpacked the globe, with many trips to Bali, as like so many, she was captivated by the little island's sun, smiling people and exotic culture.

She'd had an early sense she didn't want to live a boring upper middle-class life. So she didn't. She moved to Bali and fell in love with a drug dealer. She perfectly fitted the cliché of good girls falling for bad boys. Borrador was a volatile, coke-addicted, drug-dealing Latino. She was a feisty, well-bred good girl, who inevitably became ensnared in the Bali underworld – watching their play up close, seeing the intricacies of the game, but not liking it.

But she loved her bad boy. Then one day they both vanished.

Her dog's food had run out and her friends hadn't seen her for weeks. Kate's parents, Patrick and Liz, didn't yet know that when they sounded the alarm. A world away in the UK, they were worried that they hadn't heard from their daughter for more than a month, as she usually rang every 10 days. Their fears that something was rotten on the Island of the Gods turned to reality when Kate failed to call home on her birthday. Her parents were the first to alert authorities.

'The situation builds up gradually and suddenly you think, "Crikey, what is going on?" when there is no contact,' Mr Osborne said.
   – The Times, 4 June 2003

'All sorts of terrible things go through your mind' – Mr Osborne.
   – Daily Mail, 4 June 2003

None of Kate's Bali friends had reported her missing. Those dealing drugs obviously ducked for cover, but other expat friends also stayed quiet. Westerners were cynical of Bali police, with corruption so endemic that you had to sling cash even to get a police report written. The closest most came to the cops, unless busted for drugs, was being pulled over in a roadside blitz, sometimes for riding without a helmet, sometimes for nothing, but always being asked for a 50,000 to 100,000 rupiah (about $5–10) sling before being permitted to ride off. This roadside dance was as accepted as gamelan music for being a part of Bali life.

After Kate's parents called the British Honorary Consul in Bali, British and local police and Interpol, they were suddenly in a waking nightmare. It was not good news, as their worst fears were being confirmed by disturbing facts.

Kate had last been seen weeks earlier on Good Friday night. Her maid had seen her leave home at 10.30 p.m. dressed up to party. She'd gone to the Woodstock Bar in Legian, drunk beers – in good spirits, according to the barman – and then given a Dutch friend a lift home at 2 a.m.

A week later her rented Daihatsu jeep was found abandoned in the car park at Denpasar International Airport with doors locked, keys in the ignition and a flat tyre. But there was no record of her flying out. Her beloved dog Maisie had been abandoned without food or care arrangements; her two bank accounts had been untouched; no activity was recorded on her email accounts and her passport and purse were missing.

Kate's parents set up a website and held a press conference in England. Their story was every parent's worst nightmare and it instantly created global headlines.

The parents of a British graphic designer who went missing in Bali nearly six weeks ago spoke yesterday of their fears that she may have been kidnapped or murdered. Yesterday her mother told a press conference: 'We are staying strong. We have to believe

*that Kate is somehow going to turn up. If someone has kid-
napped her then I would say, "Please, for god's sake, return her
safely to us. Get in touch." I pray every day for her safekeeping.'*

– Daily Telegraph, 4 June 2003

But the story held more intrigue. Borrador was also missing.
In Kate's last phone call to her mum, she'd said that 'Joseph'
had gone to Peru to see his family and was due back soon.
When it came to light that he was now also missing, that he
owed Kate at least £20,000, and that he sometimes brutally
bashed her, he was the obvious prime suspect.

*The mystery of the car, the abandoned dog and the vanishing
friends from Bali's surf set would not normally cause serious
alarm on an island where most people come to escape from
everyday life. The real concern has been raised by Henrici's violent behaviour, all too typical of a small group of Latin American
surfers who have a reputation for aggression and hard living.*

*'She really, really loved him,' said Osborne's live-in maid, Ni
Ketut Dya, 32, 'but they fought all the time.' In a statement to
Indonesian police, the maid said that on one occasion she became
so frightened by their fighting that she called the police station.
The row had subsided by the time officers arrived, she said.*

*One night in mid-March, an eyewitness said, Henrici hit her
in front of customers at the Woodstock Cafe. 'The management
threw him out but he waited for Kate outside, hid behind her
car and attacked her when she left,' said the witness. She was
left with bruising and cuts that required hospital treatment.*

– Sunday Times, 15 June 2003

'I cannot tell you much about him at all,' Mrs Osborne said. 'I have only spoken to him briefly on the phone once.'
  – The Times, 4 June 2003

Sitting on their hands in the north of England, with the Bali police investigation agonisingly slow, and suspecting little effort was being made, Kate's parents decided to fly to Bali – their first trip to Indonesia – with two British detectives.

Mrs Osborne, fighting back tears, said: 'It's difficult, and, quite frankly, slow, increasingly frustrating and exceedingly worrying.'
  – Yorkshire Post, 3 June 2003

Kate's father, Patrick, 64, a former director of Cavaghan & Gray, a Carlisle-based food company, and his wife said that they were 'incredibly frustrated' by the paucity and slowness of information filtering through from Bali. They aim to travel there to talk to officials and local people in an attempt to shed light on her last known movements.
  – The Times, 4 June 2003

For the sake of diplomacy, the UK detectives were quick to point out the investigation was 'Indonesian-led', careful to avoid treading on toes while trying to nudge Bali police in the right direction.

Detective Chief Inspector Bill Whitehead, of Cumbria police, has liaised with the Indonesian police, making it clear that tracing

the boyfriend should be a priority. Later this week he is meeting officers from Interpol.
    – The Times, 4 June 2003

Mr Whitehead said if he was in charge of the investigation he would be keen to find and speak to Kate's boyfriend. He added: 'It would be one of the first things we do in this country, as a matter of course.'
    – BBC, 3 June 2003

The detectives also warned the vulnerable parents about corruption in Bali and people offering false information for cash.

The difficulty with sources from that area of the world is that they tend to report on uncorroborated hearsay with the sole intent of financial gain. Part of our job was to warn the family against such exploitation.
    – Detective Chief Inspector Bill Whitehead

The day the Osbornes flew out, Kate's mum told journalists, 'We will never give up the search for Kate and believe we will find her.' But ten days later they came home, no closer to unravelling the nightmare.

Instead, they had a new question – who was the mystery person their daughter had called at 4.14 am on the day she vanished? Kate's phone records, obtained in Bali, showed she'd not only made that very early morning call but had also sent six text messages to the number throughout the night. It was the last trace of their daughter's existence. As yet, they didn't know whose number it was.

The strongest lead has to be to find the person Kate contacted at 4.14 am, to find out the nature of the conversation and why there were several text messages to that phone earlier in the day.
 – Detective Chief Inspector Bill Whitehead, in *The Journal*, Newcastle, UK, 3 July 2003

Although the trip to the island hadn't turned up any answers, it gave the distressed parents an intangible connection to their missing daughter.

Mrs Osborne said: 'It was very hard going through her home and all her stuff, but it was good to do, because it resonated of Kate and we felt very much with her.'
   Her father said: 'We live in hope that she is alive, but with the passage of time that hope is diminishing.'
 – *The Journal*, 3 July 2003

The Bali drug dealers were super-aware that the disappearance of Borrador's girlfriend had exploded into global headlines, with gossip among them that Australian cops, Scotland Yard and Interpol were now all lurking and spreading tentacles in Bali to investigate, including hot young cops infiltrating private parties by acting as tourists. Some of the dealers actually knew where Borrador was, but everyone vamoosed, staying as far away as possible from the problem.

No one wanted to be snared into the spotlight or see their

name in print. Journalists had already latched on to Borrador's drug connections, even writing stories specifically naming Alberto as Borrador's 'notorious' friend – although ironically the ugly white walls of Kerobokan Prison were protecting him from the fire outside.

One of Mr Henrici's reportedly good friends, Alberto Lopez, was sentenced to 18 months imprisonment in February for possessing ecstasy tablets. Lopez, a notorious figure among Bali's surfing set, was convicted of possessing ecstasy tablets at the High Court in Denpasar, Bali, in February this year and was sentenced to 18 months in jail.
   – Sunday Times, 15 June 2003

Matters are complicated by widespread but as yet unsubstantiated rumours that Ms Osborne's partner, Jose Henrici, was involved in drug running and that he owed her up to £21,000. He is thought to have had at least three other aliases.
   – The Guardian, 17 June 2003

They are keen to track down her estranged boyfriend, who was linked to the South American underworld. Peruvian Jose Henrici, also 35, has a history of arrests for drug offences.
   – Daily Mail, 16 June 2003

Kate's parents had been back in England for several days when news broke explaining exactly why they hadn't found Borrador in Bali. An indisputably clear reason: he'd been busted trying to smuggle 4.2 kilos of coke across the Peruvian border to Brazil and was now locked up in a dungeon-like cell in the middle of the Peruvian jungle. Because he'd travelled on a false Argentinian passport as Carlos Navarro Lanatta, it had taken authorities time to discover his real identity. He'd used the passport to leave Bali three months earlier – three weeks before Kate vanished – ostensibly to see his family, but in reality to do a drug run for Poca. He'd been busted 10 days after Kate vanished, so he had the perfect alibi.

The boyfriend of a British woman missing in Bali for more than ten weeks has been arrested on the other side of the world. Jose Henrici, 35, is in custody in his home country of Peru ... Henrici, a professional surfer thought to have links to the underworld, was arrested on drugs charges in the town of Puerto Maldonado in the Andes.
   – Daily Mail, 1 July 2003

Henrici, 35, described as a professional surfer is being held at the 'hell hole' Puerto Maldonado jail in the heart of the Peruvian jungle.
   – News of the World, 6 July 2003

Henrici is now awaiting trial in Puerto Maldonado, almost 500 miles east of Lima. If found guilty, he could face up to five years in jail.
   – News and Star, UK, 24 July 2003

Borrador talked about Kate to a Peruvian journalist, claiming she had threatened to tell police he was a drug dealer. He was blasé and mocking of her disappearance, not in any way a loving, concerned boyfriend.

> 'She could be in a hotel in a remote island in Indonesia, laughing about everything that is happening,' he says. 'That's what I think is happening. That she is doing this to point the finger of blame at me. I did not kill her and I have absolutely no idea where she is.'
> – *Caretas*, Lima, 24 July 2003

Days after the breaking news of Borrador's arrest, Britain's *News of the World* newspaper ran an exclusive story, with shocking claims by Borrador, that Poca and Mario had ordered Kate's murder to stop her exposing a dark secret they all shared.

> *Missing Briton Kate Osborne may have been murdered by drug barons – after she helped them fake their deaths in the Bali nightclub bombing. The men were facing trial in Indonesia and realised confusion over who died in the horror provided the perfect opportunity to 'disappear' for ever. Kate is said to have added three drug traffickers' names to the list of dead after volunteering to help officials as a translator in the wake of the attack.*
>
> *The sensational allegations in the riddle of missing Kate are revealed today by Kate's lover, Jose Henrici. He admits he is one of the three drug dealers – and is now in prison in Peru facing a massive sentence for smuggling cocaine. He believes the other two men, brothers known as Juan Mendoza Diaz and Mario Alfonso, ordered 35-year-old Kate's killing to ensure their secret could never be revealed ... Henrici's claim is the latest*

intriguing twist in the mystery of what happened to Kate...
the News of the World *has confirmed that Kate – who spoke*
the local language – worked with aid agencies and British Con-
sulate staff helping to compile lists of the dead, missing and
injured ... Police in Peru and Indonesia fear Kate could have
been targeted as the loose link in the conspiracy. The source
added: 'It is feared that the dealers decided that Kate was the
only one not at the heart of the gang who knew what had hap-
pened.'

  – News of the World, 6 July 2003

Poca and Mario weren't facing drug trials in Bali, but they were
hot and hunted. The *News of the World* story was dismissed by
DCI Whitehead, saying that Kate had only been 'linking in
with British victims and their families, so she will not have had
the ability to impact on other nationals'.

Despite telling the *News of the World*'s journalist that the Diaz
brother Juan was a drug dealer, Borrador denied it in his interview with the Peruvian journalist, who knew Juan's nickname
was Poca.

You know Juan Jose Mendoza Diaz, aka Poca?
  Yes, a Peruvian friend who lives in Indonesia.
  He dealt drugs?
  No, he is a photographer, he takes pictures of surfers. He
made videos, edited, that's his job. I don't know if he had con-
tact with drugs.
  – Caretas, 10 July 2003

Adding significant weight to the theory that Kate was murdered by Poca, or a paid assassin – not difficult to find in Bali among the mercenary gangs like Laskar – was the revelation that Poca was the mystery person she'd called at 4 am. But police didn't get the chance to talk to the Diaz brothers, as they'd fled the island.

It was an unsettling time for all the dealers, with Interpol involved and British police sniffing around. Most dealers had their own theories, with whispers circulating that Poca had overdosed Kate, then dumped her body in a rice paddy, though no corpse was found. Everyone was keeping a distance. No one wanted to talk to the cops. Rafael was hitting the waves like a crazy man, taking long surf trips away, selling kilos but no small stuff, and keeping a low profile.

I was a little bit hot anyway ... and when I know all this shit about them, I keep distance, because the Peruvians were in trouble. Also, they didn't come to me, they just disappeared; with the British police coming here, for sure they shit in their pants and run. I think that's why they disappear – Borrador [Jose], Poca, Jerome. I think they never come back, that's the last time I saw them, they just disappeared after this thing with this girl.
    – Rafael

It was six months later, with Borrador in jail, no trace of the Diaz brothers and no more news, that Kate's parents let go of hope. They knew their daughter would never ever put them through this torture if she was alive. They issued a statement to the press.

After an extensive investigation into the disappearance of our daughter Kate, we are now forced to conclude that she has been murdered. It has been an unimaginably stressful six months for the whole family while we have lived in hope of Kate being found alive.

   – The Journal, 11 October 2003

A year after Kate vanished, her family held a memorial service in England. Their nightmare would never end, but they said goodbye. DCI Whitehead, who'd been with them throughout the investigation, confirmed that UK police believed Kate had been murdered.

Speaking for the first time about what he believes happened to Kate, Detective Chief Inspector Bill Whitehead said she was visited by the brothers two days before she vanished. She sent six text messages on the night of her disappearance to Juan Diaz's phone and her final call – at 4.14 am on 18 April – was to him.

   'The brothers were associates of Jose Henrici and I feel that Kate suspected Jose was drug-running for them,' he said. 'Indeed his capture in Peru with 4.2 kilos of cocaine supports that. There is some evidence that she was outspoken about that activity and it may be that posed a significant threat to their venture.

   'There were four things that could have happened to Kate – she could have disappeared of her own volition, had an accident, committed suicide or been murdered. On balance, I think it is highly likely that she was murdered.'

   – The Journal, 21 April 2004

CHAPTER FOURTEEN

CATCH ME IF YOU CAN

While the search for Kate had been going on in Bali, Lemon Juice boss Marco was in Peru, doing what Borrador had been busted doing weeks earlier – buying coke in Lima and taking it out to Brazil, en route to Bali. Like Borrador, Marco wasn't risking the Peruvian airports, dangerously manned by ruthless locals and America's DEA, FBI and sniffer dogs. Instead, he was floating peacefully down the Amazon on a boat.

Marco was sleeping in his hammock, slung up with others, like a blur of colourful ribbons slashed across the deck, as the charter boat cruised down the river. It was cramped and noisy, but Marco was seemingly without a care in the world, having the time of his life. None of the 200 or so tourists camped out on their hammocks would have had a clue that the relaxed Brazilian's hang-glider was loaded with blow.

Marco was back trafficking coke, with several of the Bali dealers – including Dimitrius, Rafael and himself – investing. Having just done a 3-kilo run to Bali, he'd decided to up the ante and show the young horses how it was done. This time he was carrying an audacious 13.7 kilos. He'd just picked it up in Lima, Peru, and taken a boat to the city of Iquitos, where he switched boats and was now spending three days and nights cruising towards the triple border of Colombia, Peru and Brazil.

I went by river from Peru all the way to my grandmother's house in the Amazon. Beautiful trip ... you must do it. Nice boatman, restaurant, air-conditioner, like a house in the river. More than 200 tourists, all had backpacks. At night we sleep on hammocks like you're in a tree. I arrive in Manaus [Brazil], nobody checks anything, and I go to my grandmother's house.

With nearly 14 kilos of coke?

Yeah, in Peru I had more than 100 kilos. In Peru, cocaine is like Coca-Cola.

    – Marco

After saying goodbye to his 92-year-old grandmother, he set off from Brazil to Bali, confident of breezing across the globe like all the other times. En route he flew to Amsterdam, where he casually flouted a basic rule, calling friends in Bali and giving his arrival day on a mobile phone. It was potential suicide. Andre took one of the calls.

He says, 'Hey Andre, it's Marco. I'm the man; tomorrow I arrive in Bali – big goal, big money. Let's go to the club tomorrow when I arrive.' I say, 'Don't talk bullshit in the phone, motherfucker. In 20 years, don't you learn anything? Please, don't talk

*like this. Come safe.' You never talk about the day the shit is
coming.*

– Andre

But Marco wasn't fazed. He flew out of Amsterdam on a KLM
flight to Jakarta, where he planned to clear customs and take
a domestic flight on to Bali. He flew into Jakarta Airport at
5.15 pm on Saturday afternoon.

Things were about to turn.

He walked across to his hang-glider on the floor and slung
it on his back. One of the hustling trolley boys picked up his
other bags and they headed for customs. The bags went
through. But Marco was far from safe. He sensed it, too.
Tonight, something was up. Police were highly visible. His long-
time customs officer friend, who regularly helped him slip
electronics from Singapore through customs, walked across,
warning him there was a bomb threat; anti-terrorist police were
working the airport and the customs chief was insisting they
X-ray the hang-glider.

Marco was ready. It had passed machines before. But this
time, as it went through, four of the six tubes reflected a dark
image. 'What's in here?' the customs chief asked. Marco fid-
geted, incessantly tapping his foot, quickly explaining that some
tubes were made of carbon fibre and blocked X-rays. Unsatisfied, the officer pulled out a Swiss Army knife and started
tapping the tubes; the hollow ones sounding tinnier than those
loaded up with coke. 'What's in here?' he asked more sternly.

Marco was rifling through his bag. 'Wait a moment, boss,'
he rasped.

Now agitated, the officer barked, 'Where's your passport?'

'Cool down, please. Wait a moment.' Marco was still fumbling in his bag, finally pulling out his professional book. It contained more than 300 photos and a CV, something he always carried as proof he flew the glider. Now he was ready to fast-talk.

'Man, I'm a professional,' he said, pointing out the pictures. 'These are special tubes for aerobatics, for making a loop.' The officer was shaking his head. Marco's slick spiel was failing; he was twitchy, nervy. Things were about to get worse. The officer ordered him to 'wait there'; he was going to get equipment to cut open the tubes. It hit Marco – he was going down with the biggest load he'd ever carried. Unless he did something fast.

He knew he had only one chance. It was make or break, right now. There was no time to think. He couldn't fight, so flight was his only hope. The airport was frenetically busy, people everywhere, with two packed Garuda flights arriving simultaneously with Marco's flight. He glanced maniacally from side to side, his heart racing.

The split second the customs officer turned away, he took his chance. In the blink of an eye he was off, the adrenalin shooting through his body, giving him an uncanny agility, despite his limp, to weave, duck and slip out of the crowded airport, untouched by police. In the car park, he leapt on the back of a random motorbike taxi, rasping, 'Let's go.'

'Terminal One?' the guy asked.

'Yes, yes,' Marco yelled, clinging to the driver as they tore off.

I'm David Copperfield, brother, I can disappear in one minute,
that's why you have to lock me up. I can fly with no wings.
   – Marco

The wind whipped Marco's face as the motorcyclist raced along the road. He felt alive. He was on the run, an escapee. For these moments he felt elated – he'd done something no one else would have dared. It flashed through his mind that this was like a movie. When they got to Terminal One, he vaulted off the back of the slowing bike, slung 50,000 rupiah at the motorcyclist and leapt into the back seat of a taxi. 'Find me a cheap hotel,' he said, jerking his head from side, watching out for a police tail.

When the driver pulled in at the front of Hotel Central Jakarta, at least 20 cops were swarming at the front gate – nothing to do with Marco, but he had to stay invisible. 'Oh my god, let's go. Take me to a shopping centre.' He could hide among the crowds. Cops were outside the shopping centre too, but he got out anyway.

He had about $120 and bought some cheap clothes to change into. Then for the next few hours he wandered aimlessly, round and round in circles inside the shopping centre, not sure what to do, his panic rising. By 11 pm, the long corridors were ghost-like, with only a few straggling shoppers. Lights were sporadically going out and the roller doors being pulled shut. It was no longer a sanctuary of camouflage, quite the opposite. It was time to go. He walked up the steps into the night, quickly finding a cab to take him to a cheap hotel.

Without wanting to expose the passport still tucked in his

pocket, he created a story, telling the receptionist his girlfriend would arrive later with ID. Once inside his room, he pulled a beer from the fridge, sat on the bed and lit a Lemon Juice joint that he'd smuggled from Amsterdam – an insane thing to carry when he was trafficking kilos of blow, but it was this insouciant confidence that had kept him untouched, until now.

He'd bought a phone card and late that night went down to reception to use it. He called Carlino, the prime investor in this run, who'd paid for the flights, hotels and equipment, and was waiting in Bali for his 5-kilo slice of the 13.7 kilos. He answered, but refused to believe Marco's implausible story.

Carlino says to me, 'Don't fuck with me, man. If you don't bring my glider now, I will kill you. Where is the fucking dope?' I said, 'Believe me, brother, I had a problem.' He says, 'You talk fucking bullshit. I'm going to kill you, motherfucker. You steal the cocaine.' 'No, believe me it's true, brother, the police caught the wing.' Dimitrius, Carlino, were all suspicion because they think, 'Why is the guy here and not the glider?' They think I hide the glider somewhere.

– Marco

Marco went back upstairs to lie down, exhausted but unable to sleep, with acute paranoia keeping him on high alert. This was now a deadly game of cat and mouse.

At 6 am, wearing the new pants, shirt and Nike cap, he went outside. The sun was just rising but the streets were already busy. After eating breakfast at a nearby five-star hotel, he took a taxi to the bus depot, on the advice of the receptionist. It was full of police. Marco stood out as the only westerner, but hid his face beneath his cap, bought a ticket and climbed aboard, relieved he'd soon be in Bali with his friends, who had to help him. This was their problem too.

On the bus, Marco didn't sleep, as much from paranoia as a sense of panic as the bus driver hurtled like a maniac along the roads. Headlights flashed and horns blared constantly as they wove in and out of traffic. Marco tried to stay calm. He had to keep his wits. A wrong step now would be fatal. The bus crossed on the ferry from Java to Bali, where there was the routine police document check. Marco had already bribed the driver with 100,000 rupiah to let him stay in the bus, ostensibly for a sore foot. He pretended to sleep, evading the police again.

Three hours later, the bus was close to its destination, Denpasar Bus Terminal. Exhausted but in survival mode, Marco approached the driver. 'Listen, my friend, I have to go to Kuta, can you open the door now?' He slung him another 100,000 rupiah. With cash the magic password, the doors swung open and Marco jumped as the bus slowed.

His instincts saved him again. The depot was already under surveillance, with police passing around photos of the fugitive. They'd suspected he'd flee to Bali, as many of the 300 photos in his professional book left behind at Jakarta airport were taken on the island.

Now on familiar turf, Marco's ego and cockiness resurged with gusto. He was acting bizarrely, almost tempting police into a game of catch me if you can. Instead of going straight into hiding, he took a taxi to his favourite restaurant, the bustling La Lucciola, an expensive beachfront place patronised mostly by westerners. There he phoned Rafael, who'd unwittingly invested in the run but planned to stay well clear. Dimitrius, another investor, turned up, as well as Ron – a wealthy friend who'd flown at the same time as Marco as a back-up horse to help him on arrival. Andre, his rental partner in Amsterdam, came too, although he wasn't an investor in this run.

Marco was sitting at an exposed table at the front, wearing his pink and white Nike cap and sunglasses, waiting for his friends. He was typically restless, indiscreetly leaping up and down from his chair, pacing back and forth, with a glass of wine in his hand, to a little footbridge that led to the car park to see if they had turned up. As soon as he spotted them, he dashed across the footbridge to meet them.

He was happy like a kid. 'Hey guys, nobody can take me. I'm Mad Max, David Copperfield, nobody can take me. I'm the man.' Dimitrius the Greek, fuck he's angry. 'What the fuck, shut up. Are you crazy, man? You left the cocaine there. Ron tells me you sniff coke on the flight. What you fucking doing with my money? You lose all the money for the operation, now the police are running behind you. You are fucking stupid.' He's really angry. And everybody is really angry, you know – me, Rafael, Greek, everybody is really angry, because it's not a happy situation, but Marco was happy. 'Oh, Mad Max, blah blah blah.' Max was happy.

– Andre

They took Marco to their car to show him that day's *Jakarta Post*. 'This is real, brother, this is the *Jakarta Post*,' Dimitrius said, pointing. 'Look, look ... Marco Archer Moreira, the fucking Brazilian drug smuggler, page one. Look!'

A Brazilian paraglider reportedly failed to smuggle in 13.7 kilos of cocaine through Soekarno–Hatta International Airport in Tangerang on Saturday afternoon, but did manage to escape arrest. His whereabouts is unknown, but customs and excise officers at the airport suspect that Marco Archer Moreira fled to Bali. It is the biggest smuggling attempt of cocaine in the country this year. If convicted, he could face the death penalty.

– Jakarta Post, 4 August 2003

When he looked at the newspaper, he realised he was in trouble. In this moment he realised he had a big problem – 'Oh, I cannot stay in La Lucciola', but after a couple of seconds he was back to being the same stupid guy again. 'Ah, I go to Lombok. Carlino is going to help me.' Carlino is the Italian guy who was supposed to receive most of the cocaine here. Carlino was also really angry, because everyone knows Marco was using drugs while bringing it.

On the plane?

Fucking stupid. Every time, sniffing, sniffing inside the aeroplane, not normal. Call attention. Marco was really, really high on cocaine when he fell. I know all this cos I listen, 10 times, to Samuel. They arrived together. If Marco was a normal guy, no problem, but he was really nervous and this call attention to the cops. If he is professional, he come in easy easy easy. Stupid. Totally. Because you are playing with money, millions of dollars,

and you are using. It doesn't make any sense. Can you imagine
he escaped ... this is so crazy, just one guy, leg with a limp
like that, how can he escape the airport?
   – Andre

Despite their fury, it was the rules of the game to try to help
a busted horse, especially their friend. Dimitrius drove Marco
to Carlino's house. Carlino was fuming, quickly arguing hotly
with Marco over why he got busted. The run costs were about
$40,000, but the real issue was the huge loss of potential profits.
Andre deserted ship, this wasn't his gig in the first place – he
wasn't an investor. Carlino, though, had to ensure Marco didn't
spill his name if he got caught. He drove him to a simple hotel
in tourist hotspot Sanur, telling him to stay put. For the next
couple of days Carlino came and went with supplies and news.
Typically restless and hyper-active, Marco got bored fast. Several times, after dying his hair red and painting his face with
fluoro-coloured zinc cream, he went to the lobby to stretch his
legs and watch the communal TV. He realised he was undeni-
ably hot news when he saw his own face up on the TV screen.

It wasn't surprising. He'd vanished right from under the noses
of dozens of clearly inept, red-faced police and customs officers during a bomb alert. Security was meant to be watertight,
but they had failed to stop a 42-year-old man with a limp. It
was an international story and excruciatingly embarrassing; the
Indonesians had lost face. This could cost jobs and now it was
personal. They wanted Marco nailed, especially after they'd cut
open the hang-glider tubes and found 13.7 kilos of blow. They
were hunting with unprecedented force for a drug trafficker.

The customs and excise officers have closed down access to all airports and seaports in the country in an effort to find Moreira, who is still at large. Head of customs and excise at Soekarno–Hatta airport, Jusuf Indarto, said that Moreira was not only a courier, but that he was part of an international drug syndicate. 'He's a Brazilian athlete,' he said, showing Moreira's picture in a Brazilian newspaper.
  – *Jakarta Post*, 6 August 2003

Eluding police would have been a lot easier if Marco hadn't left his professional book behind. It gave them hundreds of pictures of himself and his friends, and the cops were hotly pursuing the photographic trail, raiding all his haunts – the club, Bali Village, his friends' villas – and interrogating people, making the Kate Osborne search two months earlier look like a picnic.

After three days in the hotel, Carlino told Marco it was time to move. 'Marco, it's very hot here, you have to go. Police have photos everywhere.' They decided to stock Carlino's luxury catamaran with food so Marco could sail to Brazil.

But Carlino, motherfucker, he doesn't want to give up the boat. I'm ready to sail from Indonesia to Brazil and he changes his mind. I say, 'Brother, don't forget me – I have a death sentence, man.' But he didn't want the boat going back to Brazil; he wanted it in Bali for the girls and everything. The boat is a killer boat, worth US$250,000. Big one. Fantastic boat.
  – Marco

Marco continued to behave bizarrely. He was scared but had a fatalistic confidence that all would be okay; after all, he'd defied the odds for years, twice even cheating death. But this time his sense of invincibility was deluded. He was being sloppy, casual, behaving as if this was a game he could afford to lose.

Marco was really, really calm. He didn't realise his life was in danger at this time. For him – just another adventure.

How could he not realise?

Marco after the accident, he was a little bit crazy. He think, 'I will never die. If I don't die in my paraglider accident, nothing is going to kill me.' This he repeated 10,000 times, 'I saw death up close, but death cannot take me.' But he's stupid, you know, he doesn't have any plan. Just go to Lombok. He didn't realise really how dangerous the situation was. If he realises for a couple of seconds how hot the situation was, he wouldn't stay on the beach doing barbecues.

    – Andre

He had no strategic plan, making it up on the run; it was a series of erratic moves – paying locals to take him island-hopping in their boats and finding random places to sleep – that kept him in front of police by a nose, but left a blatant trail.

I escape by motorbike, car, motorbike, boat, and Samuel came with me. He went one time to Bali to get money, get ganja, get food and everything. The second time it was all dangerous; he went to get my passport but it was gone. My friend set fire to

my passport. He was afraid. I'm very stupid, man, you know, I escaped from the airport – nobody does that – but I made a mistake to trust my Brazilian friend Dimitrius with my passport and he burnt it.
– Marco

All the dealers were feeling the white-hot heat around Marco. Those close to him were terrified of getting entangled, especially the investors. Dimitrius had agreed to hold Marco's passport for him, but with police crawling everywhere, he was petrified of being busted with it, so first tried to palm it off to Rafael, then burnt it.

He showed me. I say, 'Man, go far away from me, this passport is too hot.' He says, 'Marco told me to burn it.' I say, 'Don't burn it, man, keep it, maybe he will need it to escape, but I don't want to know. Ciao!'
– Rafael

Marco had slipped into a fake identity, calling himself Mr John Miller, a half-Mexican, half-Californian tourist. Together, he and his loyal friend and back-up horse Samuel were renting bungalows on Nusa Lembongan, an island close to Bali, and spending their days surfing, barbecuing fresh fish and lobsters, drinking white wine and beers and using cocaine and hookers, courtesy of $3000 and a bag of blow Carlino had given him.

After a few days, Marco sensed it was time to move on. They hired a small boat through a Balinese kid, Roni, who'd become their friend, and cruised to the nearby island, Gili

Trawangan. Trying to create a break in their trail, they immediately took another boat to a famous surf spot, Scar Reef, on the island of Sumbawa. Roni didn't go, but knew their plan – somewhat undoing their strategy. There they spent more time surfing, drinking and using cocaine. They also both chose a whore from a local brothel to take back to their bungalows and use for a few days.

Marco kept up on news of the police hunt in regular calls from Carlino. Despite his bravado and swagger, he was feeling insanely paranoid. No amount of cockiness or blow could immunise him from the bone-chilling reality that hundreds of armed military and intelligence police were hunting him down like a dog. He hadn't slept for days.

But far from trying to be invisible by blending in with the tourists, gregarious Marco soon had the locals waving and singing out 'Hola John, como estas, comrade,' whenever he walked past in his big Mexican hat. After eight days the surf went flat and Marco decided it was as good a time as any for Samuel to take a boat back to Bali to get supplies. He also felt it was time to split up for a while, given that in his professional book there were dozens of photos of the two of them together in Bali and Peru.

A day after Samuel had left, Carlino phoned with a red alert – 'Get off the island now. Police are in a boat and on their way.' Marco hung up, then moved quickly, paying a local kid to take him to the marina on his motorbike. He escaped again; he was blessed, charmed, invincible, and was soon sitting pretty in a small motorboat, drinking cold beers in the hot sun, shaded by his Mexican hat, while a toothless old man steered him towards Moyo Island, on Carlino's advice.

Hours later, as the sun started to set, there was no sign of the island. The old man seemed to be going around in circles. Marco had been told it was only 15 kilometres from Sumbawa and he was starting to worry. Then finally, they saw lights.

As the old man dragged the boat onto the beach, several security guards and an Australian resort manager walked briskly across the sand towards them. Still wearing his Mexican hat, Marco asked if he could rent a cheap room. No, he couldn't. On this small nature reserve island, there was only one place to stay – the luxury five-star Amanwana Resort, comprising 20 stylish air-conditioned tents. This place was for A-list tourists who blew thousands of dollars a day on their ultra-posh holiday, flying in and out in private Cessna C-208 seaplanes.

The Australian manager told him the cheapest room was $800 a night. Marco knew exactly what he'd stumbled into. He'd stayed at one of Aman's three Bali resorts, paying about $1000 a night for a room.

Tonight he definitely couldn't afford it, but the manager offered him a bed for one night in an employees' bungalow beside the resort. Marco gave him his name – Mr John Miller – instantly cursing his mistake.

An hour later, he lay in a clean, comfortable bed, but couldn't sleep. He knew he shouldn't have used the name John Miller – police would know it by now. All night he fretted and by sunrise he was up, packed and standing on the beach with his bag at his feet, waiting for a fishing boat to pick him up. He'd booked it the night before with a local boy. Relief swept over him when he saw the boat in the distance and he waved. It was too late to run when he realised his mistake. The boat was full of police, all with guns pointed at him, twitching to shoot him if he made a move.

'So, Marco ... we caught you,' one of the police officers mocked, as he stood on the beach pointing a gun at his legs. 'I'm going to put a bullet in each of your legs. The boss at the airport told me to do it.' It was something Indonesian police casually did to locals, usually defending their action by claiming the suspect had tried to run.

Marco instinctively started his fast-talking. '*Tunggu sebentar*, boss [Wait a minute, boss], I'm already hurt.' He pulled up his shirt and revealed terrible scars from his gliding accident. He begged them not to shoot him. He'd tell them everything.

It was most likely not their compassion, but the gathering crowd of 100 or so local witnesses that stopped the bullets that morning. Instead, police circled Marco, handcuffed him and tied his legs and arms, ensuring David Copperfield didn't have the slightest chance of performing his vanishing trick this time.

As the elite shores of Moyo Island faded into the distance, the police started opening hatches on the boat, with heads popping up of people they'd collected and arrested along the trail to find him. Balinese boy Roni had been badly beaten and given up all he knew, which took police as far as Sumbawa. There, locals all talked freely about the charismatic Mr Miller and the police soon found the boy who'd taken Marco to the marina the night before. At the marina, they had arrested the toothless old man as he'd docked his motorboat late the previous night. Not one of the suspects had had the faintest clue that they'd been aiding and abetting Indonesia's most hotly hunted fugitive.

Everywhere police went, they find these guys and beat them, and lock them in the boat until they find Marco on the beach.
– Rafael

On the trip back to Sumbawa, Marco was told that he'd caused acute embarrassment and rage, and the sacking of many officials. His story was breaking news, with people keenly following the hunt; even inmates were watching. After seeing his photo in a newspaper, one woman at Bali's Kerobokan Prison, nicknamed Black Monster, claimed Marco had fathered her baby – although the baby had actually been conceived through the bars of her cell door with a Scottish prisoner.

Now, as they pulled into the marina, police and spectators were swarming around the boat laden with the notorious fugitive and his suspected cohorts. Armed police took Marco from the boat, through the throng and across to a black Kijang with dark, tinted windows – and four armed police sitting inside.

The boy Roni sat beside Marco, and asked him en route why he had lied to him; if he'd known the truth he could have hidden Marco so well that police would never have found him.

They took the ferry to another island, Lombok. Again swarms of locals and police were at the harbour. It wasn't every day they caught such a big fish. The police blindfolded Marco, then pulled a black hood over his head. He was petrified, making no wisecracks now, not knowing what torture lay ahead. Roni, still sitting beside him, tried calming his anxious friend. At their destination, Marco was taken into a five-star hotel and handcuffed to a bed. When they took off the black hood and undid the blindfold, he saw a dozen police around the room, holding submachine-guns, with a continuous stream of others coming in and out, taking a look at the notorious fugitive.

The relentless interrogation went for three days. They were accusing Roni of helping the fugitive to elude capture. Marco kept telling them the kid had no idea, asking them to let him go. Police were also trying to locate the other man locals had told them about, Mr Miller's friend Samuel. But after the bust, Samuel had fled, flying from Bali to Batam Island, on to Singapore and home free. Marco was glad his friend was safe, but he now felt truly alone.

During the interrogation, Marco was treated surprisingly well, surrounded by guns, but watered and fed endless room service; mostly his choice of shrimp, *nasi goreng* and beers. Unlike Alberto, he was ostensibly co-operating, using his gift of the gab to answer their inexhaustible questions pleasantly and politely, telling stories of his boat ride up the Amazon, and confessing the name of his boss – the Californian man John Miller, who unfortunately had vanished.

I make a professional story. I say the boss is John Miller, the big drug dealer from America. I can never really tell the boss's name, because the only person to help me is my boss. If I report him,

who will help me? No way, man. You have to shoot me to say
my boss's name.

   – Marco

John Miller is a fake name. John Miller doesn't exist. John Miller
is Samuel and Carlino and Marco, because they were the bosses.
They use John Miller because Miller in Brazil is a beer, an Amer-
ican beer.

   – Andre

Three days later, Marco was again moved in a police convoy
back to Bali and handcuffed to another hotel room bed – this
time in downtown Kuta. He was finally charged with drug trafficking under Law No. 22/1997 on narcotics – which carries
death by firing squad if convicted – and was sent to Tangerang
Prison near Jakarta, to await trial.

Three days after Marco's escape, while he was hiding in Bali,
a bomb had exploded in Jakarta. A 28-year-old Indonesian man
had driven a Toyota Kijang through the taxi rank at JW Mar-
riott Hotel and detonated his car bomb in front of the lobby.
It killed 12 people, including himself, and injured 150 others.
Six days later, the terrorist organisation al-Qaeda claimed
responsibility, stating that the bombing was 'a fatal slap on the
face of America and its allies in Muslim Jakarta, where faith
has been denigrated by the dirty American presence and the
discriminatory Australian presence'. Police had received a tip
from a captured militant two weeks before the blast, which had
been the reason for the heightened airport security. Marco was
another of its casualties.

His Bali partners all still blamed him for the bust, claiming his use of cocaine on the flight had made him nervous, fidgety and highly suspicious.

His fate was now in the hands of the courts, and that decision would be a year away.

CHAPTER FIFTEEN

FATES

As the dark cloud of death hung over Marco, he managed to stay upbeat and jocular in jail, regaling inmates with stories of his magician-like escape, but hoping Carlino could create some magic too, by finding a good lawyer and a loophole to get out. For the moment, Carlino was lying low; things were too hot and dangerous, though he would soon put in place a plan to try to save his friend's life.

In Bali, the charismatic Lemon Juice boss's bust had caused a freeze – momentarily. It shook the dealers, as they all knew him well and many of them had also invested in the run.

Unwittingly, Rafael had gambled on Marco's fatal run too, cast blindly into it by his broker. Rafael had started using a corrupt Brazilian cop, a childhood friend of Andre's, to put his cash into projects. The cop often flew to Bali with blow confiscated in busts in Brazil. This time he'd met up with Marco in Rio, learnt of his run, and backed the horse. Aware that Rafael refused to work with Marco after the Japan ecstasy con, he'd kept it quiet.

My guy didn't tell me it was Marco because I'd be like, 'No, I don't want to work with this motherfucker.' And after the shit got busted in Jakarta, he says, 'Sorry, we lose the money.' I say, 'What ... why?' He says, 'I give it to Curumim [Marco]; we were in the project together with him.' I say, 'What, are you fucking crazy, man? Why did you give money to this bastard? He doesn't know what he's doing, he's always high. That's why he got caught, cos he was high on the flight.'

This was a bad project. Too many people were involved. There were 20 people who put some money in, and many people knew the shit was coming because Curumim talked too much on the phone to everybody, totally unprofessional bullshit; no planning, use coke and make everything crazy. He fucked up. I believe he was high. Badly behaved. They suspect and then he runs.

– Rafael

Rafael had also just had 2 kilos arrive, but put it on ice; it was too hot for snow in Bali.

It was like this; hot and cold, hot and cold, but actually when Marco got caught I had 2 kilos just arrive. We celebrated the goal, then suddenly Marco's on TV. 'Oh shit, oh my god, fuck, the police are going to be all over us.' My friend says let's sell quickly. I say, 'No, I'm going to keep this shit, hide it, wait for a couple of weeks and then we will move it. Now we're not moving anything, forget it.' But we were so careful to sell the shit because nobody wanted to do anything. Everybody was saying, 'Oh it's hot now, so hot.'

– Rafael

Rafael was trafficking increasingly more from Brazil to Barcelona and Amsterdam, where he had buyers, and Sweden, his wife's homeland. In Bali, it was now a game of stealthy tactics. He was surviving on his instincts, moving carefully, freezing when it felt too hot, waiting, then starting again when the coast was clear, but always discreetly. Sometimes he'd spot shadowy tails behind his bike, or undercover cops lurking outside his house, and would go to ground.

I go quiet, I don't go out; wake up at 6 am, surf, go home, eat, surf again, sleep early, wake up early, for a couple of months.
   – Rafael

Around the time of Marco's arrest, Rafael had seen more of his friends also busted in Bali. One guy, Ruggiero, a Brazilian surfer, was selling for him and Andre, when Rafael got an urgent call from Chino: 'Tell your friend Rock he's going to get busted.'

'What? Why?'

'Just tell him – fast.'

Nicknamed Rock 'n' Roll, Ruggiero was selling small packets of coke, retailing Rafael's wholesale stuff at top prices to rich expats and keeping a boutique stash in a cheap hotel room. He was small-time, a middleman, but his drug sales subsidised his endless surfing and playboy lifestyle. With few people now risking selling small stuff, the dark-haired fast-talking Latino had picked up the ball. He had many customers, including some of Alberto's, and was busy selling, surfing, snorting, as well as trying to get into a legitimate business of renting and selling luxury villas.

It was a well known fact these guys were falling like dominoes,
so when the other guy [Alberto] got busted, that's when Rug-
giero picked up the ball. There is only one fool at the time brave
enough to do this, so it was lucrative, but it was hotter than
hell. He was making money hand over fist, but he was lining
himself up to go down.

  – Gabriel, American surfer

Despite being hot, Rock 'n' Roll was blasé, flapping huge wads
of cash about. Out one night, he showed Rafael $10,000 cash.
'I say, man, you crazy. Stop, Ruggiero, calm down. Keep your
money in the safety deposit; why you show it to everybody,
you crazy?' He rode around drunk, loud, with blow or hash in
his pockets, often snorting coke off counter-tops at places like
Ku De Ta, so blatant that his friends were all telling him to be
careful.

One of Ruggiero's customers, American big-wave surfer
Gabriel, had seen his previous dealers, including Alberto,
busted. He'd been coming to Bali every surf season for years,
buying coke from Rafael, then Alberto, and now Ruggiero. He
was no good boy himself, using drugs and notoriously riding
his big motorbike around the island topless, in his pink
hibiscus-flowered Quiksilver board shorts, slurping on a Bintang beer. He also usually flew from LAX to Bali with a tiny
bag of dope in his underpants, always slinging $200 to an offi-
cial at Denpasar customs to avoid a search.

We would just tuck it into our underwear and cross our fingers.
But we had a guy there ... I'd go to the office and pay the guy

a couple of hundred bucks and we'd walk out without them searching any of our shit. Money is the trick.
   – Gabriel

Although he took his own risks, Gabriel felt his friend and dealer Ruggiero was way over the top, perilously acting as if he were Bali's Scarface.

I was a bit scared to be around him, because I knew he had a big fat bag in his pocket, and I could be in trouble just being around him. I went to his place one time and he was there weighing up shit; he had like a kilo of coke, and was weighing it all up in grams, hundreds of packets, and I was like, 'God!' I just turned around and left. Just seemed crazy, he was just doing it right there – you know, not even hiding or anything – he just threw a towel over it . . . fucking crazy hot.

So I kept him at arm's length. He was so loose, driving around in the middle of the night with 50 packets of blow.

Fifty packets?
He had packets galore. He was the guy at the time supplying everybody; he was the only one who had it, and he wanted to have it all ready, so he could be out on the streets, selling if someone needed one – here you go, like a 7-Eleven.

And you saw him pulling it out of his pocket?
Yeah. I'd tell him, 'You're out of your mind,' shaking him by the arm. 'You're going to get busted.' But he was just bringing

attention to himself, all drunk and loud, doing snorts right at the fucking dinner table.

Did you see that?

Yeah, he didn't hide it, he'd do it every time I went out for dinner with him. He had a Scarface kind of attitude. I'd seen everybody go down; I'd seen three guys before him who were supplying in town and they got busted and people were telling him he would get busted, but he didn't seem to listen or care.

– Gabriel

After Chino's phone call, Rafael raced around to Ruggiero's house to pass on the warning.

'Ruggiero, be careful, man. Chino says they're looking for you.' But he spurned the tip.

'Fuck off, I'm a street boy, you're a family guy. I know what I'm doing, man; you're just paranoid.' Rafael left with a sense of foreboding. Chino didn't issue gratuitous warnings. Chino had also alerted Andre, who zipped around to warn him.

I take my bike and go to Ruggiero's house with my girlfriend. When I arrive, he's sitting Ruggiero-style, legs spread, scratching his balls, and I say, 'I come here just to tell you Chino says you must be careful.' And Ruggiero says, 'I don't care if police come to me – I'll kick their ass if they step in my house.'

– Andre

The next day, after watching a blazing sunset at a Seminyak beach bar, Ruggiero rode off on his motorbike. It would be the last ocean sunset he'd see for a long time. Two bikes with four men suddenly blocked his way and within seconds cops were leaping from the bikes and out of a car, surrounding him, screaming, 'Police, police'. They pushed him up against the car, pinned his hands behind his back, then searched him and found a plastic container of hash in his pocket. Ruggiero was in shock watching the police laughing and hugging each other. They held the hashish, taunting, 'You see? What is this? You're going to jail.'

I fell down from heaven to hell in a blink of an eye.

The police already knew where he kept his stash, and drove him to the hotel, where they allegedly found 146 grams of hashish, 43 grams of cocaine, and one green ecstasy pill, though in court Ruggiero disputed this, claiming the amounts were a lot smaller.

The next morning at 9.30, Argentinian hashish dealer Frederico was sitting in Yopa café in Legian with his Israeli girlfriend Hanna, doing a delivery. As Hanna ordered a tea and a coffee, Frederico walked towards the bathroom. He sensed something wasn't right. Suddenly, four men sprang up, surrounding him. It was a sting, a bust, an unbelievable nightmare. Frederico went ballistic, shoving a cop to the ground and hurling the dope over the wall. In the next second, he was flat on the ground.

Hanna watched in shock. Outside on Double Six Road there was a sudden traffic jam as motorbikes abruptly stopped, gridlocking; a crowd quickly gathered to watch the morning action – a big guy was being held on the ground by three men, as another was scaling the wall to retrieve the package, which contained 301 grams of hashish. Like spiders, these cops had created a web and caught their prey. And the dealers suspected who'd helped them to spin it.

Word spread fast when guys got busted. Andre got a call asking him to help his salesman Ruggiero, but he was dismissive. He'd already tried to help, but his efforts had been blithely fobbed off at the crucial point in time as puerile babble. Now it was too late and his altruism had expired too.

> *I got a call, 'Oh Ruggiero, Ruggiero, Ruggiero's been arrested, you need to help him.' I say, 'I knew this two days ago. I advised him and now I don't want to see this bullshit guy. I don't want to send money, I don't want to help. He had his chance. This case is too stupid for me, sorry, please don't call again.' If somebody says, 'Run away because tomorrow you're going to get busted,' you need to listen; we don't play. The guy was just really, really arrogant.*
> – Andre

Rafael also refused to help when it became apparent to him that Ruggiero had set Frederico up to try to save himself. He denied it, but the dealers were all sure and the police divulged it to the press.

> *Ruggiero revealed his network, which also involved Frederico Vieyra Garcia, 24, from Argentina.*
> – *Jakarta Post*, 16 July 2003

This is why I have a little bit of a problem with Ruggiero. When they catch him, he gives up the Argentinian guy. Ruggiero was supposed to be released, but in the end he got fucked up too, both go to jail. Lucky for him Frederico was a pussy. In Brazil, he would be dead.

I should have helped him much more, but I didn't because he did this. I don't think it's fair. For our group this was a little bit sad, we don't give too much support to him after that. I was good friends with Ruggiero, but when he did this, my feelings changed totally ... I was pissed off with him, but was sad too.

– Rafael

Now Ruggiero, Alberto and Frederico were all in Kerobokan Prison together and, like most prisoners, they were quickly trying to cut a deal. Frederico did so, paying for a five-year sentence to be quietly cut to two, the figure simply changed in court paperwork sent to the jail.

Ruggiero wasn't so lucky. News of his snitching had spread, with the crew sure that, not only did he set up Frederico, but had tried with others, including a rich expat girl who was a regular customer. Out of the blue, he'd gone to her house with some coke and although she didn't have cash handy he, unusually, gave it to her on credit. After he left, the girl sensed a sting and flushed it. Thirty minutes later, police were banging on her door.

The girl he tried to set up, she's from an aristocratic family somewhere in Europe, really important, and well connected with a lot of rich and powerful people in Bali too, and everyone got pissed off. And they all went okay, fuck this guy, he is going to have to pay for what he just tried to do. He did exactly what we grew up understanding was the worst thing you can ever do ...

Everybody was pissed off that he tried to set people up, nobody wanted to help him, everybody was like, 'Fuck him, he can burn in hell.' And a lot of people did what they could to fuck his case.

Does he know that?

Yeah, he does know that. That's why he got such a long sentence for such a small amount. If he got busted, held himself like I did, he'd get three, four years, guaranteed. But there were a lot of people telling prosecutors and judges, don't help this guy.

The prosecutors would listen?

Yeah, if you have people coming and say, 'If you help this guy we're going to Corruption Watch,' it's a very delicate situation. So his case just went down.

— Alberto

Ruggiero's lawyer had been promising to get him six months, for 300 million rupiah ($43,000), but on the eve of his court case, after he'd already paid, the lawyer delivered bad news.

He came to see me right before I got my sentence and he says, 'Listen, there's a problem.' I said, 'You promised me six months.' He says, 'They don't want the money any more and they're even

considering asking for a life sentence.' I said, 'What? Sorry, can you repeat that?' He said, 'Life.' I felt the earth shake.
   – Ruggiero

Ruggiero got 11 years – drastic compared to others like Englishman Steve Turner serving three years for 8000 ecstasy tablets, and Alberto's and Frederico's two-year sentences.

Soon after, Ruggiero's customer, American big-wave surfer Gabriel, joined them in Kerobokan Prison. As part of the party set, he'd watched his friends get busted. 'That's why I was so blown away, I'd been witnessing this shit first-hand.' He'd followed the waves from Hawaii to Tahiti, Bali and Australia, where he once had a fiancée. But for the last year and a half he'd settled in Bali, planning to start a surfboard storage business with his brother. He'd been hanging out with Marco in the days before his last fatal trip and saw Ruggiero, Alberto and Frederico all fall, like this was some kind of bad movie.

Marco was another one of these Scarface guys – he got some kind of notoriety and glamour out of it. It was an image I didn't agree with. Marco is a really good, great guy, but he still had that same stupid mentality – they can't touch me – and these guys were running around like Tony Montana.
   – Gabriel

One afternoon, leaving his luxury rented villa, close to Kerobokan jail, and about to climb on his bike, three men approached saying they had a warrant to search his house. Initially, Gabriel didn't believe they were cops.

One guy pointed to his T-shirt that had 'Police' written on it, and said, 'Me police,' and I said, 'I can buy that in Kuta. I don't care what that T-shirt says.' The next guy goes, 'Look, I have this, a badge.' I say, 'You can buy one of those too.' And then the third guy shows me a gun and I thought, okay, maybe you are police. I didn't want to believe it. I wasn't dealing; I wasn't selling drugs like Ruggiero. I didn't want to let them in just because of some police T-shirt, but the old Balinese man whose daughter's husband owned the villa talked me into it. He said, 'They're real police and that's a real warrant and they're going to search your place.'

I kept them outside for about half an hour. I was worried about being set up. I've always had that thought in my mind; you don't want to mess with the cops, they can just put something on you, do anything they want. And I was thinking I don't want these guys in my room, maybe a joint or something will fall out of my golf bag, something stupid. I just didn't want them in my house. There was seven, one boss and six plain clothes, they all came in at the same time. And they all did the search at the same time.

– Gabriel

As police searched his villa, rifling through his clothes, bags, drawers, cupboards and under his bed, he was watching, pissed off, but staying calm. But every time they touched his impressive stack of 22 surfboards he imperceptibly winced, tensed,

Drug dealing in paradise; the view from the foyer at the Nikko Bali Resort where Rafael and Alberto did many of their drug deals. Rafael often used it for his trysts too.

The Canggu Club, Bali's nod to the Hamptons. An exclusive members-only club with a pool bar, tennis courts, a gym and restaurants – and where Rafael did deals with customers over lunch.

Jose Henrici (Borrador) holds a photo of Kate Osborne, his English girlfriend missing in Bali, while in jail in Peru. 'If I knew where Kate was, I'd tell you in a second,' he told a Peruvian journalist. He admitted to a British newspaper that he believes the Diaz brothers, Poca and Mario, ordered her murder to shut her up after she threatened to reveal a dark secret.

British woman Kate Osborne, missing and presumed dead in Bali. She was a good girl attracted to a bad boy. British police concluded she was murdered.

Desperate parents – Liz and Patrick Osborne – hold a press conference to alert the world to their missing daughter. A world away in the north of England, they were the first to sound the alarm; Kate was missing in Bali. Their story turned out to be every parent's worst nightmare.

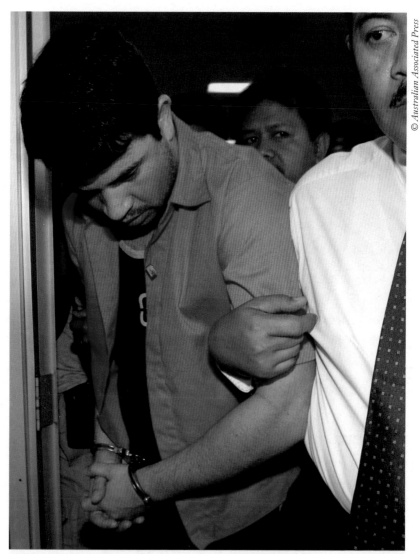

Rodrigo Gularte being led to his press conference after being busted with 6 kilos of cocaine. Despite his rich family, and loving mother who'd tried to set him up in various careers, he chose to traffic drugs.

Customs exhibit Rodrigo Gularte's surfboards – they were opened at Jakarta Airport and 6 kilos of cocaine was found embedded inside them. He was en route to Bali.

The rich boy from Brazil, Rodrigo Gularte, hides his face as he's made to sit at a press conference with the 6 kilos of cocaine he trafficked on the table in front of him.

© Picture Media/Reuters Pictures

In court, Marco turns to the camera the moment after he's been given the death sentence. He'd told his photographer friend, Danilo, to be ready for a photo opportunity. 'He said, "Pay attention, when they give the death sentence, I'm going to turn around"' – Danilo. This picture was actually taken by a Reuters photographer as Danilo was too far back.

© Australian Associated Press

The two Brazilians, Rodrigo and Marco, now live together on death row in the Super Maximum Security (SMS) Prison on Nusakambangan Island, dubbed Indonesia's Alcatraz, off the west coast of Java.

Italian Juri Angione, 24, is made to sit for a press conference with the 5.26 kilos of cocaine that he trafficked to Bali. Juri had done at least 20 runs previously, but always for himself. This run was for Carlino who needed cash to help Marco's case. Ironically, Juri and Marco now live together in the SMS Prison.

Rafael invented the method of using windsurfer booms to traffic cocaine. This is now widely used. The coke is crushed baby-powder fine, then pounded hard into the aluminium tubes to avoid any air bubbles or small rocks, making it X-ray-proof.

M3 Car Wash Café in Bali's Sunset Road was used for pimping and washing sports cars, but most importantly it was a giant laundry to wash drug money. For years its owner, Chino, was Bali's biggest drug boss, operating with impunity, until the Jakarta Police arrived. Chino fled the country to evade arrest.

held his breath, aware they were close. They'd shuffle through the boards, getting hot, hotter, scorching, then ... they'd walk away – until the next time. They were so, so close. In a tiny Velcro pocket on one of the leg ropes, Gabriel kept his personal stash of coke and maybe one or two stray ecstasy pills.

While they were searching, they picked the boards up in their hands 10 times, and every time I was like, 'Whooo, oh god.' I was thinking they might find it, even though I knew they probably wouldn't, but I was worried.
  – Gabriel

The boss kept intermittently taking him outside, playing good cop, repeatedly crooning, 'We want to help you; tell us where your drugs are.' After six long hours, and no drugs, a different cop took him outside to do the same little tap dance. This time, when he came back inside, the boss smirked at him.

I came back into my bedroom and the guy had his arm buried in my pillow. As soon as I walk in he goes, 'Ahhhh' and pulls out of the pillow a little blue plastic ziploc bag and says, 'Gentlemen, drugs, heroin.' I'm like, 'No way, that ain't mine.' First, I don't fucking keep drugs in my pillow and second, how does he know it's heroin if he's just discovered it?

They changed as soon as that guy pulled the drugs out; they got mean. They were laughing with a smirk on their faces, 'Aha, we got you,' and I was like, 'Noooo.' Running around the room, stamping my feet, pounding on the bed, screaming, 'Noooo.

Nooo, man, no, no, no, don't do this. It's not mine. Don't do this to me, guys.'

He was just smiling at me, going, 'We got you,' and I was just fucking pissed, man. I was thinking, 'This isn't real, this isn't real, this can't be happening.' Cos I knew that the worst thing is to get busted in a place like Bali, so when it started to hit that this guy was serious about busting me with his fucking shit, I got scared and worried then. They handcuffed me right then, they started tearing my place apart, even worse you know, they grabbed all my money.

They stole half of everything I had. The guys were packing bags for themselves when they were leaving; they were stealing stuff from me. I was walking out, so humiliated, and the guy's wearing my best Quiksilver duds – they didn't even fit him. He got my jeans vest. They took as much as they could carry when they walked out of there. I was so humiliated looking at these little short guys wearing my clothes. Like, I'm a big guy – they were walking out of the villa with me like a trophy, in my clothes. They looked stupid because they were like midgets wearing my sized clothes – they didn't look good, they thought they looked good.

I can't believe these guys loaded me up, man. I thought this only happened in the movies. And they took me to the police station and shut the bars on me and it was as real as it gets.

– Gabriel

In the police cells, he met Juri Angione. Juri was a 24-year-old Italian jeweller, who it turned out, was Carlino's failed plan to help Marco. Carlino had asked compatriot Juri, living in Bali with his Timorese girlfriend, to do an emergency run to get cash to save Marco from a firing squad. Juri had already done between 20 to 30 international drug runs, carrying both in his stomach and in bags.

This time Juri took Carlino's job and flew to Brazil to pick up the surfboard bag of coke. Juri instantly knew it was badly packed, but decided to risk it anyway, flying from Brazil to Amsterdam, and then via Bangkok to Bali, avoiding Marco's failed, tainted route. But instead of helping Marco, he joined him. Customs in Bali busted Juri with 5.26 kilos in his surfboard bag.

Airport authorities on the resort island of Bali arrested a 24-year-old Italian national on Wednesday afternoon for attempting to smuggle some 5.26 kilos of cocaine with a street value of about Rp 4.5 billion ($600,000) into Indonesia.

A thorough search of the bag produced three surfboards, two swim suits, two pairs of surfing shoes, a snorkel and 29 plastic packages hidden in the inner lining of the bag. Wrapped in black carbon paper, the packages contained suspicious white powder, which a simple test confirmed as high-quality cocaine. [Juri] Angione admitted that the bag, clothes, shoes and surfboards were his, but denied any knowledge of the cocaine.

– Jakarta Post, 4 December 2003

How were you feeling?

Juri: Fucked up. Yeah, fucked up. Way bad ... It was the first time I bring something for somebody else. I always bring my own stuff. I always pack my own bags. I'm a user. But I do it this time because there was an emergency for Marco. They had to find someone to bring more stuff to make money to help Marco. I didn't know Marco that time. But to help my boss, I say, 'Yeah, okay, I go.'

Was it going to be sold in Bali?
Juri: No, in New Zealand and Australia.

Were you going to take it there?
Juri: No, not me. Somebody else take it by boat.
Fellow inmate: By catamaran.

Carlino's plan had been to send the coke to Australia in his catamaran, as he'd planned to do with his slice of Marco's load.

Instead, he now had two guys potentially facing the firing squad.

I remember the community of drug dealers, was a little bit . . . even me . . . say, 'Fuck man, who does this guy think he is?' He just has a problem with Marco and tries to send another guy to help and fucks up another one – actually he was my good friend.
   – Rafael

CHAPTER SIXTEEN

WHITE CHRISTMAS

Marco after the accident repeats a thousand times, 'If I don't die in my accident, nothing is going to kill me.' It's like he challenged death; he chased death. This is so crazy, like karma, you attract the things you think about too much. Fucking crazy, one guy repeats every day, 'I can't die, I can't die.' Now he is on death row waiting to die. Looks like his energy attracted death. Like the book The Secret, *it's exactly like that.*

    – Andre

Everybody in Brazil who was a friend of his, we all tried to get money from everybody and send it to him, try to pay the police. But the thing was so big, they could not make a deal, you know. He's not a bad guy, he's a good guy.

    – Sparrow

American Gabriel often spoke by phone from his Bali cell to Marco in jail in Java awaiting his court verdict day. 'I was on the phone to him all the time. And he would be all upbeat, amazing how he can do that.'

Another friend, Danilo, a Brazilian photographer living in Bali, was often visiting him in jail to take photos, and Marco would use his culinary talents to cook up the food he brought in, then serve Danilo lunch in his private cell, always the same lively, laughing company.

Only once did Danilo see any trace of worry. They were together in the holding cell at court, a week before the verdict, and Marco looked at him, asking, 'Do you think they are really going to kill me?' It was a poignant moment, and Danilo took a photo. In court, Marco testified that he'd needed cash from the run to pay a several years overdue $80,000 hospital bill in Singapore.

On the day of his verdict a week later, Marco's demeanour was as upbeat as always, as he stood at the barred holding cell door, chatting and laughing with journalists.

He wasn't taking it seriously, he thought he would get out somehow, he didn't show any emotion – he wasn't scared.
– Danilo

Before going into court, Marco told Danilo that he'd give him a good photo opportunity. 'He said, "Pay attention, when they give the death sentence, I'm going to turn around."'

The verdict of death was widely expected as Carlino hadn't been able to cut a deal for him – the case was too high-profile, and raising big bucks had failed at Juri's bust. So, the little boy with the big personality from the Amazon jungle sat in court with his head bowed as he listened to his fate.

'He is guilty of importing a type one narcotic, cocaine, and the court punishes the defendant with the death penalty,' said presiding judge Suprapto. 'The defendant was one link in an international narcotics network that has threatened the country.'

Moreira, 42, gave a courteous hand gesture to the court after the verdict and his lawyer said he would appeal. The judge chided Moreira for escaping at the airport in August when customs officers quizzed him about the hang-glider. Asked by reporters how he managed to slip away from airport authorities, Moreira said: 'I'm David Copperfield' – a reference to the US magician.

– Reuters News, 8 June 2004

Marco's story was headline news in Brazil, with reports that he could be put to death by an elephant crushing his head.

The Brazilian sentenced to death can be executed with an elephant kick crushing his skull. Or, if their executors employ what they call a 'more humane method', then he may be shot.

– Istoé Independente, 16 June 2004

The Brazilian Marco Archer, known among the communities of surfing and hang-gliding by 'Curumim', was sentenced to death yesterday by the Indonesian court ... The executions are carried out by a firing squad or by crushing the head by the leg of an elephant.

– Waves, 8 June 2004

The head-crushing stories continued despite being refuted by the Indonesian embassy in Brasília.

> *The Indonesian Embassy in Brasília denied, as was reported by the press, that if convicted and sentenced to death, Moreira will have his head crushed by an elephant. The convict is executed with rifle shots.*
>   – *Folha de São Paulo*, 26 May 2004

Straight after his verdict, Marco was loaded back into the police van, and through the window asked Danilo to bring him two beers to the jail.

> *I actually got three beers for him. I went straight after to the jail to see him, he was kind of shook up, you could tell he was a little bit emotional, he didn't say anything, but he needed a beer to digest everything. I didn't stay long, I didn't really want to because it was kind of hard for me too, what are you going to say to the guy?*
>   – Danilo

Seeing Marco get a death sentence, with his future now a dark tunnel towards a firing squad, was sobering for all the dealers. Execution had always been a vague unthinkable chance, but now it was a reality, and smart horses were suddenly thin on the ground. But it served as no deterrent for Dimitrius, who set up another run to Bali only weeks later, using a 32-year-old rich upper middle-class guy from South Brazil to do a run.

Rodrigo Gularte was the black sheep in a rich family. He'd

started sniffing solvents as a teenager and, despite his mother trying to set him up in various careers, he chose to traffic drugs. He was softly spoken, handsome and nicknamed Fraldinha (nappy) by the Bali crew 'because he complained like a baby'. He flew out with eight surfboards, six loaded, and two friends to help camouflage the trip as a boys' surfing holiday. At 3 pm they flew into Jakarta, transiting to Bali.

Customs officers noticed the men acting 'nervous and agitated' and when the X-ray showed foreign objects inside six of the boards the three friends were taken to a security room. As they watched, one of the boards was cut open and it revealed two embedded plastic bags, each with 500 grams of white powder. The rest of the boards were then cut and another ten bags uncovered.

Surfboards are very suspicious, obvious, doesn't work. Frank [De Castro Dias] already fucked up that equipment. It was a bad job too. You don't need to even put in an X-ray, you just hold it up to the light and you can see.

– Rafael

Incredibly, Rodrigo had agreed to do this run for Dimitrius just weeks after Marco was sent to death row.

The death penalty handed down to Brazilian Marco Archer Cardosa Moreira on 8 June for attempting to smuggle 13.7 kilos of cocaine from Peru apparently failed to deter three of his countrymen from attempting the same thing last week ... On Saturday, officers of the Interdiction Task Force at Soekarno–Hatta

International Airport arrested the three Brazilians for trying to
smuggle 6 kilos of cocaine from São Paulo in six out of eight surf-
boards they were carrying ... 'The agency strongly suspects that
the three have a link with a John Miller, the person who gave
Moreira the order to bring in the cocaine,' Makbul [National Nar-
cotics Agency Director] said, adding that Miller was still at large.
– Jakarta Post, 6 August 2004

Rodrigo admitted guilt straight away, absolving his two friends, and now faced the probable death penalty alone.

Meanwhile, in Bali, Italian jeweller Juri and American surfer Gabriel were trying to cut a deal.

The two westerners had shared the concrete floors of the police cell, sleeping on towels, until Gabriel splashed out cash. 'I always had $1000 in my pocket.' He was the first to be allowed a thin mattress and was soon getting margaritas delivered to the police cell. When he moved to Kerobokan Prison, he slung the boss $1000 to transfer instantly out of the vile initiation cell into the foreigners' block, sharing with Argentinian hashish dealer Frederico. Quickly renowned among the guards for his cash-splashing, they nicknamed Gabriel 'America'.

Like most, he was anxiously trying to do a deal and get out. One morning the police drove him and his lawyer, William, to a meeting with the prosecutors. Afterwards, William met with the judge and the deal was set. For $50,000, Gabriel would be sentenced to three years, six months. William just had to slip them the cash an hour before the courts opened at 7 am on the day of his verdict.

Handcuffed in the bus, en route to his last day in court, Gabriel was stressed, desperately hoping the deal would work.

William had the money in time for the deal, it was all set, and I was just ready to get this behind me, because your head is just so foggy when you don't know what you're going to get. I was all worked up. I went to the court, I'm sitting there in the cell waiting, and they called my name. But I hadn't seen William yet; he was always there when I went to court – he would meet me at the bars.

Then the prosecutor came to take me into court. He had an angry look. I was asking, 'What's wrong, what's wrong? Where's William?' I was freaking out and he wouldn't even look at me. He just grabbed me by the arm and dragged me into the courtroom and rammed me down. I was sitting in court and William never showed up. So all the judges who were supposed to get paid that morning, they didn't. They were pissed off, man. They were all stinking mad at me and I got eight years. Then the prosecutor dragged me back to the cell and didn't say a word.

I was speechless. I'd given the shirt off my back to help my cause and it had been working. Then I found out when I got back to jail that William died the night before. We'd just sent like $50,000 and he died before he handed them the money. All that time I had built up hope, all the money spent, all the planning for this one big court date and the guy croaks the night before. I couldn't believe it, but it was true. Everyone was completely blown away. I thought, 'Oh my god, my problems aren't ending, they're just beginning. I can't be here for eight years. The guy who set up the Marriott bombing in Jakarta and killed 12

*people got ten years.' I'm thinking I got eight for this pillow dope,
and this mass murderer got ten. I couldn't live with that. That's
when I turned into a ghost. I was like a walking dead man.*

Did you get your money back?

*No, not a dime. His wife was a rotten bitch, she took all my
money.*

– Gabriel

Italian Juri had also been working on a deal to try to avoid literally being a walking dead man. Busted with 5 kilos of coke
at the airport, he was facing Marco's fate. His devoted family
in Italy was trying to scrape together cash to help, but airport
busts were intrinsically more high-profile, more scrutinised
and trickier to deal. Anything less than life would create suspicion. Using the priciest lawyer in town saved him. Juri was
sentenced to life in prison, with a very expensive wink that it
would drop to 15 years later.

Gabriel was devastated by his double whammy of bad luck.
He was trying to figure it out; make sense of it ... maybe it
was karma for the drugs he had tucked away. Moping around
the jail, he was miserable, zombie-like, drinking beers to blur
reality, dazed at the idea of waking up in hell every day for the
next eight years. Then he got a tip from the prison boss advising
him to call Juri's lawyer.

*I call the guy and he comes in all cavalier and swagger, 'Yeah
Gabriel, tell me how much time you want.' 'How much time do
I want to do?' 'Yeah, tell me how much time and I'll tell you*

the price.' I open my mouth and say, 'I can't do more than two years.' I should have said one. Stupid. But anyway, he says, 'All right, two years, I give you two years for $30,000.'

I call my parents and they're like, 'What, more money? Another scam?' They didn't want any part of it. And the worst thing I could say to my brother was, 'More money?' But I talked him into it. So I ended up paying some crooked lawyer to get my sentence brought down. He got some lady at court to change it from eight years to two, so that when the paperwork came from the court to jail it said two years. The warden knew about it, but it was a secret at the courts. This one lawyer, he was doing a lot of the foreigners' cases, he was the guy.

– Gabriel

Like most westerners, Gabriel was also flinging money around just to survive, paying for all the basics in Kerobokan Prison like toilet paper, soap, water and food. For his sanity he was also bribing the guards to bring in beers, dishes from his favourite restaurants and for days out. The westerners were injecting a fortune into the coffers of guards, police and the judiciary.

Hotel Kerobokan was just a cash cow for the Indonesians who were involved in it, from the cops, to courts to the jailers. They don't see $30,000 in their life, and then all of a sudden there's this blitz by the cops and they're all getting the money – the judge, the warden and the staff at the jail. These people had made this Kerobokan a machine to make money.

They set out in a way to extort money from westerners with their little bit of drugs, that's the way I saw it. It wasn't so much they were trying to stop crime or drugs, they were trying to get these people, like me . . . to try to get all the money out of them, scare them into having their families send money.

The cops were busting everybody doing anything. People were coming in once a week, from all different countries – Greece, France, Brazil, Peru, Australia, you name it, Africa – and every one of them like me, thinking the same thing: we need to raise money to bribe these people to let us go home. Everybody had a plan or a deal to make. I didn't know any foreigner in there who didn't have a deal worked out about how they were going to get out of this mess.

It's incredible just how much money they make. I had to pay the warden $1000 just to go to [a better part of] the jail; the chief of police took my $2000 set of golf clubs; I paid them to type up my paperwork; it's just pay, pay, pay. They are just bloodsuckers. It cost me $200,000, that whole thing.

– Gabriel

Rafael went only once to visit the guys in Kerobokan, arriving with armfuls of bags of food from the Bali Deli. The guys swarmed, happy to see him, passing on letters to send, asking him to buy phone credit. Ruggiero offered to sell Rafael cheap drugs, explaining the jail was a frenetic drugs market with the best and cheapest prices on the island. Ruggiero was already selling to customers, often girls who he'd instruct to come into visits wearing skirts so they could insert the package like a tampon to avoid any risk of being busted as they walked out.

I always say, 'The only condition I make is you put it in your
pussy, not in your pocket. If you get searched and arrested, I get
a problem.'

– Ruggiero

Rafael also saw Chino's twin brother Toto inside. 'All his teeth
were black. He was addicted to heroin, I think, and looks like
a junkie.' After his first visit, Rafael didn't go again. It was
depressing and too chillingly close to the bone.

I had to go home and lie down, it sucked all my energy. That's
why I refused to go there again. I sent people to take food, money,
phone credit, but I didn't want any connection any more, I didn't
need to go there.

– Rafael

While Gabriel and the guys were dealing with corrupt guards
and cops in Bali, Rafael was about to fly to Brazil to buy 10 kilos
of confiscated blow from his cop broker Claudio, who worked
for the São Paulo *Polícia*. When Rafael arrived, Claudio told him
the bust had been delayed; he'd have to wait a week. Rafael wasn't
keen. So, Claudio suggested they go to talk to his boss, who was
already sitting on 100 kilos that he could sell right away.

Rafael was incredulous. Dealing with cops was dicing with
the devil and the idea of walking into their lair was insane.

'Are you crazy, man?' Rafael retorted. 'The guy's gonna give
me the cocaine, take all my money, then give me a bracelet.'

But Claudio assured him it was safe. 'No, the guy's cool, he's
a surfer too. I've talked about you, about your surf camp.'

'No man, no way,' Rafael snapped.

'Okay, man, but unless you make a deal with him you'll have to sit and wait for a week.'

Denying his screaming instincts, Rafael acquiesced. 'Okay, let's go ... let's go to meet this motherfucker. But is he going to give it to me today?' Rafael asked.

'Yes, he has storage of 100 kilos.'

Then I see myself go inside the police building in São Paulo, six floors, lots of rooms. I take the elevator, walk, look, everybody looks at me too, all the police, you know. They're full of gold, they're so bad taste to dress. Ah fuck, like farm people, like they are not good dressers, they have boots, hats. Then he brings me to the office of the boss to negotiate. The big boss is the fucking drug dealer. I was thinking this must be a dream when I sit at the table of one of the biggest delegados [police chiefs] in São Paulo to buy coke.

– Rafael

After a quick introduction, they got down to business. 'How much?' Rafael asked.

'€7000 each kilo.' He'd been promised €5000 by Claudio.

'Come on, man, you say €5000, why now €7000?' he hustled.

'Because this is good stuff,' the police chief argued.

'Well, I brought €50,000 to buy 10 kilos. That's my offer,' Rafael countered.

The cop played hardball. 'Whoa, cannot. It's €7000,' he said.

Rafael quickly created a convincing white lie. 'You're gonna fuck my packing because my cargo fits 10 kilos and I don't have money to buy 10 at €7000,' he argued. 'So please, man, €5000 a kilo is a lot of money, you don't have any costs, man. You just go out and kick some door to get this shit. Come on, you guys, don't be greedy.'

And then it works, my words work. The guy says, 'Okay, €5000.' And then he says, 'Where are you gonna pack this shit?' I say, 'Man, I talk about the miracle but I don't tell the address of the angel.' 'Okay, well the coke is here in the police car, and I can deliver it for you, otherwise you might get busted on the way.'

So we go in the fucking black and white camburão *[police car]. My friend and another cop, not the boss, they sit in the front, I sit in the back seat with the window open, the big bag of 10 kilos by my side, and then they say, 'Let's smoke a joint.' I say, 'Yes, let's smoke a joint.' There was a little bit of traffic, so I say, 'Let's light the joint and put on the siren, let's go fast.' 'Okay.' ... Everybody pulled their cars to the side of the road, and we just pass through. So funny, you know. I was like ... the world is crazy.*

– Rafael

Rafael's crew of packers was waiting to put it into windsurfer booms. He was sending the coke to Amsterdam in two lots. Often now he was using FedEx and DHL. The success rate was slightly less than horses, but with fewer hassles. He could easily send one board with two sets of booms – a smaller one for strong wind, bigger for lighter – which was normal for windsurfers to carry, and meant he was able to traffic more coke without it looking odd.

This time he put 1.5 kilos in each of the four tubes and sent the 6 kilos via FedEx to his friend Fabio, aka Psychopath – a top horse, who'd already done about five runs to Bali. But there was a hiccup. Despite computer tracking showing its arrival in Amsterdam, the courier didn't deliver to Psychopath on the due day. He phoned Rafael, who was still in Brazil waiting for news of the safe delivery before flying in to pick up the cash; 'Fuck, man, the stuff hasn't come.'

Instantly, Rafael's radar went off. It was a red alert. Too suspicious. 'Abort, abort, run run,' he warned.

'Okay, yeah,' Psychopath agreed. But then he disappeared. For 10 days, Rafael couldn't reach him, until he got the bad news. Psychopath had ignored his warning, gone into FedEx, given his name, confirmed the package was his, then snap – he was wearing a bracelet. He got two years. Rafael lost a chunk of cash.

My friend got busted with this. Fabio Psychopath; he's a young guy, cool, crazy psycho. He loved drugs. He didn't give a shit. That's why he got caught.
   – Rafael

The other 4 kilos were carried by a horse and successfully reached the buyer in Amsterdam, covering the loss.

Although Rafael was now selling a lot of coke in Europe and Sweden, Marco's death sentence hadn't stopped him dealing in Bali. When he arrived back, he had a new project with Fox – the young French guy who'd first worked for Andre – 5 kilos arriving from Peru, transiting in Malaysia, then going on to Bali and Sydney.

But the project was hexed. Rafael and Fox flew from Bali to Malaysia to meet the horse at the airport, with their flights booked to coincide. But the flight from Bali had been delayed by two hours, and when they finally arrived their horse was missing. This guy was not bright, more a mule, who spoke no English. Strangely, he hadn't called Rafael's batphone – a cheap phone he bought for every job, using it exclusively for that job, then tossing it. The horse had simply vanished. Rafael didn't know if it was a bust, a theft, or stupidity.

Fuck, I think, where is the guy? Where did the guy go? We don't have a clue. First I think he got caught, because when I came into the airport he didn't call, and I say, 'Fuck, we lose 5 kilo of coke, ah we lose everything.'
  – Rafael

By uncanny luck, they found their lost horse. Jumping into a taxi, exasperated and mystified, Rafael heard the driver uttering magic words. 'I picked up a guy with the same bag as you a few hours ago.'

'What, the same bag as this?' Rafael asked, pointing to his windsurf board bag.

'Yeah.'

'Where did you take him?'

'To a hotel,' the driver said.

'Oh, take us there quick.'

Then I come to the hotel, knock on his door, he says, 'Who's this?' I say, 'It's me,' and the horse opens the door. He was in a

G-string . . . I look at the guy's underwear, you know the string one, normal men don't wear this. I say, 'Man, put something on, why you wearing this shit?' He goes down on his knee, crying, 'Whoa, thank you god, thank you god.' South American people are very religious. I say, 'What you doing?' He was afraid; he cannot speak, cannot call, lost my number, already hours in the hotel, he doesn't know what to do. He was so stupid this guy, he tries to call his family, but he can't dial, because he can't work out the code.

    – Rafael

Relieved, Rafael went to another room to organise the booms, putting one set containing 2.5 kilos in the spare bag to courier to his surfer buyer in Sydney. In the other bag, he put 2.5 kilos for the G-stringed horse to finish his run to Bali. Transiting in Malaysia was a tactic to deflect suspicion and more easily slip the booms past Australian and Bali customs. The horse breezed into Bali, but the Sydney deal bombed.

Rafael's longtime Australian buyer went off the grid, unresponsive to all calls and messages. It was an expensive mystery. So Rafael sent Sparrow, who was back in Bali, to unravel it. Sparrow was an unlikely detective, with things always going awry around him.

He's always got black eyes, broken arms, because he's always involved in shit. He likes to argue, to fight, but he doesn't know how to fight and always gets punched. People beat him because he's skinny.

    – Rafael

But Sparrow was available after flying in for a surfing holiday, staying in the small room under Rafael's water tower, sharing with Fox. Rafael offered him $1000 to fly to Sydney to chase up the buyer and spindly legged Sparrow, who'd never been to Australia, gladly took the job. Before leaving, Sparrow and Fox sat huddled together on the internet tracking the Fed-Exed windsurfer booms to see if they'd arrived in Newcastle. They had.

Sparrow flew out of Bali and straight into trouble. A routine bag swab at Sydney Airport detected traces of cocaine on his suitcase. With his UK passport showing a travel route – Rio–Bali–Sydney – combined with his swarthy looks and edgy, nervy demeanour, Sparrow fitted the trafficker profile. Suddenly, officers were surrounding him, creating a spectacle. People were staring. Sparrow wasn't happy. He knew he had nothing on him.

Rafael had rolled up a poster of Ganesh (the elephant-headed Hindu God revered for 'removing obstacles'), unzipped Sparrow's suitcase and put it inside, saying, 'This is for good luck.' Then he'd zipped it back up. Sparrow felt sure some coke must have leached out of Rafael's pores and left a faint trace on the zipper. Now, old Ganesh was creating obstacles; customs officers were pulling out his socks, underwear, stuffing their hands in his jeans pockets, rifling through everything. Sparrow was piqued but stayed calm. He was already thinking about how he was going to sue for damage to his 'image'.

I look like a criminal, cos police were making like a party with me; two or three policemen were playing with me. It was not good for my image. They check all the stitches in my bag, they check my shoes, all my pants, all my coats, all my shirts, and the bag they put a lot of times in the X-ray. They're not satisfied, they put it through again, not satisfied, they put it through again. Finally, not satisfied, they took me to hospital for a stomach X-ray.

– Sparrow

Sparrow was furious, but it was either a stomach X-ray or being held for 48 hours waiting to defecate. Customs officers were sure they'd nabbed a drug trafficker. They had, but it was his day off.

Sparrow was released after four hours, indignant and pissed off, but free to fulfil his mission. He took a train to Newcastle, checked into a cheap hotel and phoned Rafael, updating him. Instantly suspicious, Rafael advised him to check his bags for a tracking chip. Paranoid at the best of times, Sparrow chaotically rifled through his clothes, before flinging them onto the floor, then held the suitcase up to the light, twisting and turning it in every direction. Finally he gave up, still unconvinced his suitcase was free of spy devices.

The next day he confronted the surfer, who explained that trusting his sharply honed instincts, he'd been sure the blow was hot, and rejected the package when FedEx tried to deliver it. Using Rafael's system, the surfer's name was written incorrectly, so he could deny ownership if he felt it necessary. Forty-five minutes later he'd seen a suspicious car lurking around the corner. Something was off. He felt convinced the cops were ready to snap on a bracelet the split-second after he accepted the package. So he hadn't. For extra caution, he'd also cut all contact with Rafael in case calls were being traced. Sparrow understood, but his mission was incomplete until the surfer phoned Rafael. He did that night. Rafael was disappointed. It was a big loss, but better than a bust.

Now, Sparrow couldn't wait to leave Sydney. It was cold and unfriendly, not like he'd imagined. But his quick turnaround sparked suspicion again at the airport. He was questioned and his bags taken off for a search. In his conspiratorial mind, he was sure they were removing the tracking chip. He lost it, yelling that he didn't like the country, and was leaving fast because he was treated like a criminal, humiliated, and it was cold.

I say a lot of things ... I don't know why they don't put me in prison, because I didn't respect him. I began to shout loud at him, 'Friend, I wanna go, I don't have any drugs, you're crazy people in Australia. I want to go to Bali. I don't want to stay here any more, where is my bag? Why do you do this with me? Three days ago they did the same thing, took me to hospital, they did something to my bag.' They try to make me calm; he says, 'No, we did nothing to it, here's your bag, go.' I think maybe they took out the chip from the bag when they took it for searching and give back.

– Sparrow

When he returned to Bali, he told everyone he planned to demand the British consulate sue Australian customs for hurting his image. It was typical Sparrow. Making it more farcical was the fact that just a couple of months later he was actually doing a drug run. Incredibly, it was only a few months after the triple whammy of Rodrigo's bust, Juri's life sentence and Marco's death penalty. And Sparrow knew Marco well. He'd even helped him to exercise his legs after his glider crash by walking all day with him on crutches around the beaches in Nusa Dua.

Everybody said this to me, 'How can you do this with Marco sentenced to death now?' But in my head, I think I'm just going on the same plane as Narco, but I'm not carrying it. I was afraid for my friend. He was a little bit afraid, because he was friends with Marco too. We were crazy.
– Sparrow

This was another project with Fox and Rafael as partners. Their horses Sparrow and his friend Narco, whose father was a Brazilian police chief, flew out of Rio to São Paulo to meet Fox, who collected them from the airport. Fox took them to his mother's ten million dollar mansion, where he gave them two loaded booms; the bigger one packed with 1.7 kilos, the smaller with 1.3 kilos. To boost their confidence, he dunked the booms in his mother's swimming pool. If the water didn't seep in, no smell would seep out.

Narco was the carrier, Sparrow the back-up. Deciding to try a different route, they flew to Buenos Aires first, then to Bali, where they breezed through. Despite the increasing numbers of high-profile busts – including Australian beauty school student Schapelle Corby, arrested with 4.2 kilos of dope in her boogie board bag, a month prior to their run – most horses were still getting through easily. Chino, who made it his business to know, estimated only 2 per cent of traffickers to Bali were getting caught.

After taking a taxi to their hotel, Sparrow and Narco picked up a hire car, tied the windsurfer board and booms onto the roof, and phoned Rafael as they drove to his house. Rafael was sitting at the beach café, drinking Coca-Cola and watching the waves. He didn't want to say anything on the phone, but the place to keep the booms wasn't ready. 'Bro, can you stay with the booms until tomorrow? The boy in the bungalows where I want to keep them is busy,' he asked Sparrow.

'Okay, yeah.'

That night Sparrow parked his car, with the loaded booms strapped to the roof, in the hotel car park in Legian. The next day he delivered them to Rafael and moved into his small room under the water tower, ready to start his surfing holiday. It was a couple of weeks later that Rafael asked Sparrow to move into the bungalows behind his house, where he still had one boom. Rafael needed Sparrow to babysit it for a while. He agreed. But typically, things went awry.

Sparrow was leaving on Christmas Day, and a couple of days earlier had asked Rafael for a little present of four or five grams. He wanted to sell it to his friend Beans, in Uluwatu, to make cash to buy sarongs to take back to Rio.

On Christmas Eve, Rafael and Anna threw their lavish annual Christmas party. It was a sumptuous spread of food from Brazil, Sweden and Bali, with fresh fish, turkey, beer, champagne, soft drinks and cocaine. Twenty-five people turned up. Kids ran around, music blared, people swam in the pool, dived from the balcony – and discreetly did lines of coke upstairs.

Towards the end of the night, Sparrow asked Rafael for his little Christmas present. Rafael told him, 'No, you can sniff a bit upstairs, but that's it.' Rafael didn't want to risk Sparrow running around high with a little bag of coke. Things were too hot.

Sparrow was furious and a bit drunk. 'You make me sleep one week with this coke, if police get me I'm fucked,' he shouted, slashing his hand across his throat.

Rafael was adamant. 'Sorry, my friend. No. If I give you this, you're going to get crazy. You're gonna talk bullshit.'

'Okay, no problem,' Sparrow snarled sarcastically.

As the party wound down, his pique rose. Sparrow felt he deserved some blow after sitting on a bomb for a week. Another mutual friend at the party, Julio, an addict – the guy Andre had once got Laskar thugs to threaten by putting a gun in his mouth – was inciting Sparrow. Sparrow had already proved Rafael's point that he was a risk by mouthing off about the boom to Julio. No one was supposed to know.

'Come on, we can cut it open. Look what he has done to you,' Julio goaded. 'You slept one week with this thing. Come on, let's get some coke from Rafael. You need money, you're bankrupt, you can't go to Brazil without money. You ask him, he says no, so let's go get it,' Julio urged, dead keen for a white Christmas.

Julio was putting a lot of pressure on me, and all day he was in Rafael's house, a friend of Rafael's – what a friend. If I was alone, I would not do it.
  – Sparrow

About midnight, Julio raced to his nearby house, grabbed a sharp knife and silver tape, then met Sparrow at the bungalows.

Sparrow hacked into the boom. It wasn't easy. Rafael had perfected a technique using a pipe-cutting tool to clamp around each tube and slice it cleanly. It prevented aluminium shavings from mixing in with the coke. Unsurprisingly, Sparrow's method was slapdash. He sawed like a maniac, cutting his hand, while Julio sat like a panting puppy, holding a curled up restaurant menu, ready to catch the coke. But it didn't just spill out. It was compacted like concrete. Sparrow scraped out about 10 grams – $1000 worth – into the cardboard menu. Julio took four grams, Sparrow six, tipping it into the plastic wrapper from his cigarette packet. Before leaving, Sparrow used the silver tape Julio had brought to try patching up the boom. Then he fled to his friend's house in Uluwatu, aware Rafael wouldn't be happy to discover it had snowed on Christmas night.

Rafael learnt of the theft early the next morning. After trying to call Sparrow, he walked across to the bungalows, unlocked the room with his spare key, checked the bag and saw the traces of snow and the destroyed boom. His temper blew.

I get crazy . . . I want to catch him and punch him very hard. But he escapes.
  – Rafael

What made this worse was that the boom was set to fly to Singapore. Now it would be a huge job to get the coke out and repack it in a new boom, minus the stolen grams and the stuff mixed with aluminium shavings. Rafael picked Narco up from his hotel and spent Christmas Day tearing around Bali, hunting for Sparrow. He didn't find him. Sparrow had gone to the airport hours before his flight to hide out.

Rafael was chasing me like a cat catching a mouse, 'Where's Sparrow, fuck him,' fed up with me. All that day he was looking for me; he ran looking for me in a lot of places, couldn't find me, then took Narco to the airport. Narco told me on the aeroplane, 'Rafael's very fed up with you.' I was fed up with Rafael, too. If I saw him, maybe I want to fight him – want to punch him. He was angry but he had a lot of money in his pocket. I was angry and no money. I was bankrupt. I knew it was going to make trouble for Rafael, but fuck him.

When I arrive in Brazil he says all the time on the internet, 'You better watch out, I'm going to kill you, I'm going to kill you,' all the time, 'I'm going to kill you.' I say, 'Ah, you're going to kill me ... Remember you have family here, your father, your mother ... I like them, but don't talk too much because even if I can't get you, I'm going to get your family.' Nobody's good all the time. I'm not perfect. If I have to kill someone, then I would do it. I was fucking crazy.

There is not too strong friends in this business, in drugs. We think we are, but any trouble we have, all the friendship's gone. We become enemies.

– Sparrow

CHAPTER SEVENTEEN

OPERATION PLAYBOY

It hadn't been a very good Christmas for Andre either. It was the high season in South Brazil, which he usually spent at one of his glamorous restaurants. Not this year.

The Brazilian cops had been watching the zigzagging jet-set lifestyles of the Bali crew.

Andre had known he was hot ever since Rabbit had phoned from jail in Paris, telling him about the DEA asking questions. He was paying more attention now, noticing the zips on his bags always in a different spot after a flight. He was sure cops were waiting for him to do something stupid, catch him red-handed. But he was too smart; they needed a snitch. With his girlfriend Gisele, he'd spent most of the year in Bali and Hawaii. He was now wary of returning to Brazil, but he was the best man at his best friend's wedding in his beautiful restaurant in Santa Catarina.

He and Gisele flew in and went straight to the restaurant. They stayed at the wedding for two hours, then drove to Andre's house. Nobody but those at the restaurant knew he was back, but his home phone rang. He looked at it, debating, then snatched it up. 'Hello.'

It was the mother of a horse who'd been busted weeks earlier, but not on a run for Andre. 'Hey, you need to send money to my son, he needs your help.' Andre's pulse was racing. This was not a conversation for a landline.

'Sorry, you have the wrong number. I don't know you. I don't know what you're talking about,' he replied.

She hit back. 'I know who you are, Andre.' He hung up. It was a trap: she'd used his name to link him in. The cops were closing in and he had to get out fast. Within moments he vanished. After telling Gisele to go to her mum's house, he grabbed his bag, switched on the lights as a decoy, then raced out through the garden, and across 3 kilometres of mountain and jungle to a friend's house. His friend drove him to the airport and he flew straight back to Hawaii.

For 25 days he stayed in a friend's luxury ocean-front condominium set on a golf course. But even such a glamorous abode lost its lustre when he wasn't there by choice. The high season was kicking off in South Brazil and his restaurants would be buzzing. Gisele kept calling asking him to return for Christmas.

He acquiesced. The cops didn't have anything on him; he was a reputable businessman. He flew into São Paulo, where his bags were delayed. When they turned up, the zips had moved. Unpacking at home, he saw his neatly folded clothes were disarrayed. It was indisputable – he was in their sights. He had to be supremely careful.

That night he slept in his beach house, waking early for a

sunrise surf. It was a stunning spring morning as he stood in his driveway, putting his kiteboard in the back of his car. Then he glimpsed two men lurking outside his front gates. His pulse raced. They were cops, for sure. He turned and walked briskly around the side of his house towards the beach.

As he strode around the pool, the sun was rising across the ocean – the blue hour, creating exquisite morning light. He barely noticed, focused on escape. It was too late. The garden exploded into action. Men sprang out of bushes, jumped over fences, coming at him screaming, 'Stop, stop, don't move.' They surrounded him, pointing AR-15 semiautomatic rifles, screaming, 'On the ground, don't move or we'll shoot.'

Andre's heart was pounding hard. This was the moment he'd long feared. He fell to his knees and stuck his hands in the air. From all directions men were pointing guns at him, screaming, 'On the ground, get down on the ground.' Andre fell down flat on his stomach, turning his head to the side. Rifle muzzles came in close. They were still shouting, 'Hands behind your head.' Andre clasped his hands at the nape of his neck. A boot smashed down on them, thrusting the side of his face deeper into the grass. 'Don't move or I'll blow your head off,' a cop shouted.

As he lay with his face scrunched into the grass, frantic thoughts rushed through his brain: call a lawyer ... no drugs in house ... bribe the cops. Before he even realised it, he was shouting out, 'I've got money. My money is in my safety box. You don't need to use violence.' If he were an innocent businessman, not expecting cops, he'd think these guys were thieves. So he acted the part. 'My money in the safety box – I'll just open the safety box, and then you can go.'

He then first heard the voice of a man who would become his nemesis. 'We're not thieves, Andre, we're Federal Police.' The cop bent down and flashed his badge in front of Andre's flattened face. 'I'm the Narcotics Police Chief and I've been watching you for three years. *Sua casa cai*, Andre, your house falls.' The chief ordered the cop to remove his boot from Andre's neck. Another took his hands and cuffed them at his lower back. 'Get up,' the police chief ordered, grabbing his shirt and yanking him up.

When he stood, Andre saw at least 15 cops surrounding him.

They are fucking scared. They don't know what's going to happen. For them, it's more stressful than me because this is a fucking big operation. They see I'm a drug dealer, they don't know if I'm going to shoot them, or maybe I have a security guard who shoots them. These guys prepared this for weeks, and 5 am that day they get a call and are given the mission. Before that nobody knows where they're going, so the information doesn't leak. They call everybody 4 am, 5 am ... 'Now we go to this house, you go to this house.' So the guys come full of adrenalin and do this Hollywood scene.

   – Andre

Andre had prepared for this day too. He'd played in his mind how to react to a bust since his last escape dash to Hawaii. He wasn't going to cower, he'd play hardball – he was a reputable businessman. Their guns didn't scare him. Brazil was full of guns; he had one in his restaurant and even traffic cops carried them. He knew cowering and acquiescing to their every demand would just make it worse. He had to play tough, act like the respectable entrepreneur he pretended to be.

The cops took Andre into his house, and he realised the Chief and his partner were the two men he had glimpsed at the gate. Chief Fernando Caieron was head of Operation Playboy, an investigation – one year so far – into the rich playboys trafficking drugs between Indonesia, Holland and Brazil. Andre was his first big catch.

Inside the house, more than a dozen cops were searching and Chief Caieron was asking Andre where he kept his money. Andre hoped this was a sign the cop was interested in cutting a deal, unaware at this point of the scale of the investigation.

'Okay, let's go to my bedroom.' Andre led them through into his opulent stone and marble en-suite. They uncuffed him so he could reveal his hiding spot. He tweaked invisible locks on a marble bench and, like magic, it floated down the stone wall, revealing a safe behind it.

Andre put in the code, opened it and was brusquely told to stand back. Chief Caieron rifled though the safe, finding documents and his passport, but no cash or drugs.

Heading back to the living room, Andre had a quiet word to Chief Caieron, offering him €150,000 to leave now and take his men. The Narcotics boss had worked hard on this, he'd personally instigated Operation Playboy, and even if he'd wanted to take the cash, his hands were tied. 'No, I cannot. A lot of people are involved in this operation and I need to put somebody in the media.'

Back in the living room, the men told Andre to sit down on his wooden Balinese daybed, covered in cushions, as they kept searching his house. Chief Caieron started using the Federal Police's well-known tactic of mind games.

This cop, Fernando Caieron, is a specialist in this kind of mental pressure. He doesn't give one slap to anyone, doesn't punch anyone, just uses pressure on the mind.

   – Andre

'I'll give you 30 years in jail, Andre. It's a long, long time,' he started. 'But if you help us, you will maybe only get ten years. If you don't help us, I'll give you 20, 30 years in jail.'

Andre threw it straight back. 'Hey, don't talk bullshit – you don't give me anything. You're a policeman. If you want to be judge, you need to go and study at least another ten years. Don't treat me like a kid, please.'

'Tell us where your money is and we can help you,' Chief Caieron pushed.

'Ho, right! You want my money to help me? You come inside with guns and want to put me in jail, and you want my money to help me? Please don't play me for a fool. If you want to help me, then tell me how much you want – maybe I can help you or not. But if you just want my money to use against me, don't talk to me; lock me up, call my lawyer.'

'Ah, you think you're smart, Andre, but we got you. Now I can come to your house with girls, use your swimming pool, use your car.'

Andre looked at him with incredulity: he felt the tactic was so blatant, not worthy of the master manipulator. 'You can try,' he said.

'I will try.'

Andre wasn't going to break. 'Okay, do your best, man, you can use my swimming pool, you can bring girls. This is just one of my houses around the world; you think I care about this house?'

'We know you, Andre, we've been spying on you for three years.'

'Well, then you know I don't have drugs in my house; so why do you come here with this big operation?'

'Not just your house, Andre. Right now police are in your restaurant, at your girlfriend's house, at your storage.'

Police came to my four houses in my city, my two houses in the other city, many places, eight or nine places at one time in Brazil
– 6 am.
   – Andre

Andre continued trying to play the cop at his own mind games, as he thought himself a master of mind power, having used it for years on his horses. The more personal Chief Caieron got, the more ironic Andre became, sensing he was starting to rile the cop.

'Now I'm going to Gisele's house and will put your girlfriend in jail,' Chief Caieron said.

'Why do you talk to me like that? One thing ... do your job, but don't make it personal, because you have a family too and I can also make it personal.'

'Oh, so now I can charge you with threatening me.'

'No, I'm just advising you.'

The cops were still searching his house. In truth, this was Andre's dream home, with a huge wow factor. It had graced the pages of Brazil's glossy magazines. It was a large four-bedroom Balinese-style house with a high thatched ceiling, built on a slope in front of the beach. All the decorations, from silk cushions and chairs to the larger furniture had been tailor-made in Bali. Andre's sideline business was importing Balinese furniture – which had also helped him with money-laundering – and this house was the ideal showroom. The business also gave him a good cover story for why he spent so much time in Bali.

This Balinese furniture was a good cover for my family, for the society in my city. Everybody look – the guy's doing well, the guy's working. Sometimes people say, 'Wow, you work a lot; every month you need to travel.'

– Andre

In his back garden was his oceanfront swimming pool, which provided a spectacular view from the living room, with Balinese god statues trickling water into the pool. Beyond that was the beach, then the endless blue of the sea; the house was surrounded by mountains and jungle, huge bamboo plants and scrub. It was the sort of glamour home he'd pictured back when, as a teenager, he collected the pineapple tins on the beach.

Andre was growing angry as he watched the cops still rifling through everything, coming up with what he quickly disparaged as idiotic evidence. They pulled a pile of nearly 80 green striped plastic ziploc bags out of a cupboard and turned to each other, excitedly shouting, 'Look, look this is proof, bags to pack the cocaine.'

Andre interjected. 'Whoa yeah, can you please open my freezer for me?'

'Why?'

'Open my freezer, can you?'

'Okay, you want to show us drugs inside the freezer?'

'No, my fish, my beef, my food, all inside those bags. What, you think I keep bags I use to pack cocaine in my house?'

After about 30 minutes, he lost patience. If he couldn't buy his way out, there was no point being civil to these cops, and the longer they stayed in his house, the more chance they had to plant something. He wanted to get out fast; there'd be no more chitchat. He started using a new tactic – screaming like a maniac, 'Please, please, somebody help me, please help me.'

I get like crazy, freak out. Screaming, screaming for my neigh-bours.

– Andre

Turning to Chief Caieron and his men, he yelled, 'What are you fucking doing in my house? Get out of my house. Where's your warrant? I want to see the court paper. I haven't seen any court papers yet. I want my lawyer. You busted me, now you take me to the police station. I need to see my lawyer.'

Unaware of the Federal Police raid, state military police turned up. They were responding to a call made 40 minutes earlier by a neighbour who'd heard the shouting and seen the dark figures jumping Andre's fence. Two Federal agents walked out to talk to them. Chief Caieron now agreed, 'Okay, Andre, let's go.'

As Andre sat in an office at the police station, a door to the adjacent office swung open. Sitting there on a chair was one of his horses: a childhood friend, Luiz Renato Pinheiro. Andre instantly knew the guy had snitched. He raised his handcuffed hands and slashed his thumbs across his throat. Luiz looked scared, quickly clasping his hands together in a 'please forgive me' gesture. He was deluded. Andre was never the forgiving type.

This guy Luiz, he got arrested with 6000 ecstasy pills. I loaned him the money to buy them because two days before I went on a trip to Hawaii with Gisele, he came to my house and says, 'Hey, Andre, I'm totally broke, please can you help?' I say, 'Man, I'm not working, I'm going with Gisele to Hawaii for a vacation. I don't want to move drugs now, I'm being quiet.' He says, 'Oh brother, please can you loan me some money, call your contacts in Amsterdam?' I say, 'Okay, I will loan you €10,000, you go to Holland buy 10,000 pills, bring them yourself, sell them and just give me my money and 100 grams of weed so I'll have something to smoke during the summer.' 'Oh Andre, that's great, thank you, you are my brother.'

– Andre

Despite being careful with cash, Andre didn't mind floating his childhood friend a relatively small sum, given he was flush with more than half a million euros in his bank and various other places. Luiz and Andre had grown up in the same neighbour-hood, played football in the streets, surfed and gone to parties together. One day, years later, Luiz had approached Andre asking for a gig to pay his family's bills, and ended up doing five runs. So, Andre was confident Luiz knew the ropes and could organise this himself. But it backfired spectacularly. Luiz smuggled the pills inside a paraglider sail safely through the airport. But after a tip-off that he was working for Andre, Chief Caieron was watching him. Luiz and his partner, Cristiane, were arrested with 6000 ecstasy pills in green-striped ziploc bags on the same morning as Andre. Luiz 'spontaneously co-operated', telling the cops the pills were Andre's.

This horse snitched on me. He tells police everything: 'I've known Andre for more than 20 years. He's a big drug dealer in South Brazil. He's the biggest one.'
  – Andre

Later on, Andre would hear his childhood friend was shot 25 times in a typical snitch kill.

In Brazil, they kill snitches like that. Sometimes they cut the throat and pull the tongue through; this is called the 'Italian tie'. They do that to teach everybody, 'You want to snitch on some-body, take a look at this picture, now you sure you want to snitch?' My cop friend told me that somebody shot this guy 25 times. I was in the jail but everybody thinks someone did that for me. I think so too.
  – Andre

Andre twice had people phoning him in jail, offering to kill Luiz. But talking on an unsecured jail phone line, his reply had always been the same: 'Do whatever you think is best.' Andre didn't have proof Luiz was dead, but if he was, felt he'd got his just deserts.

I say, 'Fuck him. Dead? Oh, great.' I lose my life; I lose my house because I had to sell to pay lawyers; I lose my love Gisele; I lose my family. The guy really, really destroyed my life. For what? Because he did bullshit. He did his own thing. Not me. And for this I don't put my head on the pillow and say, 'Oh, the poor guy is dead.' Good luck to him in the sky, heaven, hell . . . I don't know where God send this poor soul, because he is a poor soul. If you don't have enough foundation, enough soul . . . If you're not strong enough to go to the jail, to play with the cops, then don't play with smuggling drugs, because probably you need to do that one day. Like this guy, 'Oh, I go to Amsterdam to buy and sell,' but not enough power, not strong enough when the cops say, 'You . . . ' 'Okay, it's me, it's me.' The guy talk talk talk. And what made it worse is he was like family.

    – Andre

But Andre's poolside ambush wasn't precipitated only by Luiz's ecstasy tablets.

There was another loose-lipped horse who'd given Chief Caieron evidence against him weeks earlier. Again, Andre's unravelling was as a result of a favour. His corrupt cop friend Claudio had called asking if he had a spare horse to run with 8 kilos of confiscated coke to Amsterdam. Andre told him that Diego Amaral was available. As Diego flew out of São Paulo, he was busted. Diego cut a deal with Chief Caieron – whose fervent aim was to catch those who 'lead the operation'.

It's not easy to get those guys, but when you get them, the sensation is matching, is parallel to the difficulty.
– Chief Caieron

It was a great day for him when Diego turned rat on Andre, spilling names as well as explicit details of his runs for Andre. He told police of his previous run a few months earlier; he'd carried 3 kilos in windsurfer booms, delivered to his house by Andre, to Amsterdam – there Andre sold it, and together they counted the €66,000 in the hotel room. Using some of the cash, Andre bought 10,000 ecstasy pills and 2.2 kilos of skunk, which he wrapped together with €25,000 cash, in a kitesurfing kite, and then sent Diego back home with it. A week later he'd introduced Diego to another horse doing another run, offering him a chance to invest his trafficking fee.

But before Chief Caieron was able to use the information, he had to wait for Andre to return. The ambush was six weeks later. Chief Caieron charged Andre for Diego's 8 kilos of coke, Luiz's 6000 ecstasy pills and for money-laundering.

Andre was sent to jail to await trial – a shocking and meteoric plunge from his glamour life. The loss of his status and his liberty hurt him badly, especially since it was his lust for sunsets and flying whimsically across the globe that first enticed him into drug trafficking.

When you get in the jail, it's like a bad dream, a nightmare. It takes weeks or months to go, 'It's true, I'm here.' Because you get so paralysed, so shocked.

   – Andre

With his sharp mind, Andre was never going to quietly submit to his fate. Late one Friday night, exactly 120 days after first being slammed into a cell, he quietly slipped out, thanks to a well-placed payment of $50,000 as security for bail, bypassing the lower courts to avoid any chance of it being overturned.

This day, when I got out, everybody was fucking mad, the cops were pissed off and upset. My lawyer went to the jail about 10 pm, because he didn't want anybody around to see me – no media, because he's smart. If you go to the newspaper, you will draw the attention of other ministers. Just slip out.

But the director of the jail comes to me and says, 'You are going free again because this country is a bullshit country. The Federal Police spent three years looking for you, three years to lock you up, now you pay this motherfucking lawyer, and you can go out – a big dealer like you back to the streets. I'm disgusted in my profession.' The guy is angry. Not angry personally with me, he was polite to me.

   – Andre

Chief Caieron had also got the news, and hurriedly went to the jail to check the paperwork, to see if he could find a loophole or mistake to prevent Andre's release. Being late Friday night, it was too late to get the courts to do anything. Caieron was furious that his big fish had slipped away again and told him, 'I'll catch you again, because I know you're a drug dealer, Andre.'

Andre felt they were arch-rivals, that Chief Caieron was jealous of his life. He taunted back, 'Eh, calm down, man, I buy my freedom. You take your small gun and run after small thieves, people wearing sandals on the beach, *pe de chinelo*. I'm going back to my nice house, back with my girlfriend, and you still carry the small gun, running after pickpockets.'

I still feel really powerful because I went to the jail, stay four months, smoke some marijuana, make calls inside.

Still dealing?

Still dealing inside, and then pay to go out. When I go out, my life is back that same day. I have big money in my pocket; I have everything I want in my life. For sure I felt the impact when I got busted, but I still felt strong, powerful. They catch me, they put me there, but I'm smarter and can go out again, so I can deal drugs again outside, they can't catch me.

— Andre

Andre flew up north to Fortaleza, to avoid the risk of cops planting anything on him.

CHAPTER EIGHTEEN

OPERATION PLAYBOY 2

Chief Caieron was angry – he'd worked hard to get evidence to put Andre away – but he'd had another win four weeks earlier, busting another playboy, dubbed 'the baron of ecstasy', whom he could trumpet to the media as another big drug boss brought down by Operation Playboy.

And the baron of ecstasy was Dimitrius the Greek, who'd just flown in from Bali.

Several months earlier, not long after Rodrigo Gularte's bust, the Greek had moved into a rented house with Fox on the beach, directly in front of Rafael's mansion in Canggu. After a few big losses, the Greek was going to live in Bali for a year and invest in some runs with Rafael and Fox. He'd ameliorated the situation with Rafael by apologising for working behind his back, blaming someone else, and they were again good friends.

The Greek was also starting to live a healthy life, trying to get super-fit by cooking lots of vegetables and taking long bike rides, often 20 to 40 kilometres, through rice fields, up volcanoes, out to the sea by Tanah Lot temple, often with Rafael pedalling alongside. Rafael's eldest daughter also spent time exercising with the Greek.

But after a few months Dimitrius decided to return to Brazil. A week earlier, he'd watched his horse, Rodrigo, get sentenced to death. It was expected, and wasn't stopping him wanting to set up another run. Rafael advised him against going back. 'It's too hot, man, stay here. You have a nice house, good lifestyle. What are you going to do there?' On the beach, other surfer friends were also encouraging him to stay. But he'd decided to leave – unaware somebody had already tipped off Chief Caieron.

With only a vague time frame of the Greek's arrival, some-time after Carnival, Chief Caieron doggedly staked out São Paulo airport. 'We used to go to the airport every single day to check any kind of purchase, booking, boarding or check-in made for him – until the day we got that information ... he's coming from Bali with a connection flight in Paris.'

Dimitrius was carrying €3000 from Rafael to give to Fox for a new project he was doing in Brazil, but nothing incriminating. Using his Greek and not his Brazilian passport, he departed Bali assuring Rafael he'd be okay.

But as he flew into São Paulo airport on the busy Air France flight, Chief Caieron and four other officers were waiting. They'd only seen the Greek in a photo, so it was possible he'd look different, and as the passengers disembarked and streamed past, they didn't see him. As the minutes ticked by, Chief Caieron started to fear they'd missed him. 'It's the most long five minutes we've lived, 'cos lots of people came out from the aeroplane but not a sign of him. It's just a stress situation.'

Then, he saw him. Dimitrius was unwittingly walking towards him. He called out his name and Dimitrius looked up.

And that's the moment he heard, 'You're under arrest.' When I was handcuffing him, he turned his neck, looked at me and asked, 'Why are you doing this? What did I do?' I put my hand on his shoulder and said, 'Think it over, my friend!'
   – Chief Caieron

Rafael found out his friend had been busted when his daughter saw it on the internet.

'Papa, look, your friend got caught.' 'What? Show me!' My daughter had been doing some exercise with Dimitrius, working out with him, and spotted it in the news.
   – Rafael

. . . Dimitrius Christopoulos, 36, arrested during Operation Playboy by Federal Police. Christopoulos is accused of partici- pating in a gang involved in international trafficking of narcotics, specifically to the Netherlands and Indonesia.
   – Federal Court for the Rio Grande do Sul, Santa Catarina
      and Paraná, 27 May 2005

Dimitrius, who also has Greek nationality, is accused of running a gang that in recent years has solicited young upper middle- class people often in extreme sports like surfing to transport cocaine to countries with high tourism flows in Europe and Asia.

The Federal Police said that the gang moved a lot of money, but did not know the exact amount. 'We have arrested one of the largest organisations of drug trafficking in synthetic drugs in the country – a gang which operated using cocaine as a bargaining chip in Europe and Asia,' the delegate Ronald Magalhães said.
— *O Estado do Paraná*, 20 February 2005

Chief Caieron had been watching Dimitrius for 16 months since his horse, Luis Cafiero, had been busted and snitched. Luis was the horse whose 'fair complexion' – incongruous with his surfer cover story – had created suspicion, and instigated a customs search, which uncovered 7.3 kilos of cocaine between his surfboards. The small detail of no suntan had brought the horse crashing down and subsequently his boss too, proving that Rafael's usual pedantic scrutiny of a horse's look – ruffling hair, buying outfits – was worth the effort.

The defendant, Dimitrius Christopoulos was arrested in February this year, after being denounced by co-defendant Luis Alberto Faria Cafiero, caught with 7.3 kilos of cocaine trying to board a flight to Indonesia, with a stopover in South Africa.
— *Federal Court for the Rio Grande do Sul, Santa Catarina and Paraná*, 1 April 2005

Luis Alberto Faria Cafiero, 27, was arrested in São Paulo. 'He did not have a surfer's typical tan,' a police official said.
— *Orlando Sentinel*, 12 October 2003

Chief Caieron had also watched the bust of Rodrigo Gularte, revealing it had sped up their investigations. The Operation Playboy team had proof Dimitrius had bought tickets for Rodrigo and the two surfers he'd travelled with, and had paid for the operation.

In Dimitrius' confiscated electronic organiser, Chief Caieron hit the jackpot, finding more playboy names, including Rodrigo Gularte. .

According to the Federal Police, it was the gang of Dimitrius Christopoulos who sent to Indonesia the Brazilian Rodrigo Gularte, 32, recently sentenced to death by a court in that country for drug trafficking. Gularte was arrested in July last year, at the Jakarta International Airport, as he tried to enter the country with 6 kilos of cocaine hidden inside a surfboard ...

The electronic organiser confirmed the connection between Christopoulos and Rodrigo Gularte, arrested for trafficking and sentenced to death in Indonesia. Names of young people who live in Santa Catarina are also included on the organiser, some accompanied by the word 'horse'.

– Diary of Santa Catarina, 5 May 2005

Four days after the bust at São Paulo airport, police moved the Greek by private jet further south to Florianópolis – the Operation Playboy base. Regarded as a dangerous drug boss with mafia connections, his transfer, supervised by Chief Caieron, was turned into a major operation. All police, and their prisoner Dimitrius, were made to wear flak jackets.

They put him on the TV saying he was a big cartel guy. When they fly they put bulletproof vests with snipers like he was some-body dangerous. They made him out to be the biggest mafia. Bullshit, he was just a playboy, a young guy doing something. He cannot kill one cockroach. If you see his face, you never believe he do this type of job because he look like a mamma's boy, very polite, too polite sometimes, beautiful.

But it was funny because those fools, they make all this shit with snipers and private jet and then they come with the bill for the jet plane and make Dimitrius pay. He had money in the bank at that time ... but anyway, all his money, everything in the bank, everything in his name, they were supposed to con-fiscate because it was money from drugs.

– Rafael

Meanwhile Chief Caieron wanted his other big fish back behind bars. Soon he'd have his chance. Andre was bored up north and flew back to Santa Catarina. He was still trafficking, without pause even in jail – 'Money was running like water' – but he was being extra careful. When he got a call from one of his horses, asking for a job, he agreed, but insisted he wouldn't be going anywhere near the cocaine.

I don't feel the real, real danger around me, I still feel smart. Stupid!
– Andre

After a tip-off that Andre was doing another project, Chief Caieron put a surveillance team on Andre after he'd come back from Fortaleza.

We had information that Andre had gone back from Fortaleza
and was planning to send a new shipment of narcotics to other
countries. Because of that, the Police Chief told us to intensify
the surveillance on him.

    – Federal Police Agent, Macos Cezar Pitangui Pereira, court
    statement

With Andre's 3 kilos of cocaine hidden in one of his kitesurfing
kites, 26-year-old horse Marco Froes went to board a 7.30 am
flight from Florianópolis to Fortaleza, north Brazil. But police
busted him. Within 90 minutes, they were at Andre's house.
Andre knew it was too fast for a random bust.

He was right; the Operation Playboy team had been
watching every move. But Andre suspected it was more sinister, and that his horse, who'd come to him keenly asking to
do this run, had been working a sting with the cops from the
start – probably after being busted for something earlier.

In hindsight, there were many clues. The horse had called
Andre's mobile twice the morning before his flight, despite
Andre explicitly telling him not to. Andre was sure this was to
prove the connection. 'I didn't answer. I think, why is this
motherfucker calling me?' During the organisation of the run,
he'd persistently phoned, asking Andre to come to help him
pack. 'All the time the guy tried to push me to get together
with him, but I was always, stay away, stay away. I say, "I don't
put my hand in this shit, man, I don't go to your place, somebody will deliver it to you."'

Andre had also given the horse a cheque to buy his airline
ticket, insisting he must change it at the petrol station first. But

he didn't; he used it at a travel agent to pay for his flight. This was evidence later used against Andre. He could see that Chief Caieron had left nothing to chance; he'd pushed the horse to gather as much hard evidence as possible.

He hadn't wanted to lose Andre again. He didn't. Andre went straight back to jail on a Friday, 19 weeks after he'd walked free by buying bail.

We never had any kind of doubt that Andre would come back to this kind of activity. So, we restart our investigation and waited for his next move. We're right.
    – Chief Caieron

It's like a personal game between me and this guy Fernando Caieron. This is a real playboy; the chief. This is personal between him and me.
    – Andre

With the prisons massively overcrowded, Andre was sent to live in a shipping container with three other prisoners – another sharp, painful plunge from his jet-set lifestyle. Unsurprisingly, he quickly masterminded an escape plan. Four of the shipping containers shared an outdoor area with a barred roof. For hours every day, the doors to the containers were opened to the outdoor area. Guards sat up top peering down through the bars, but at shift change, there was an unsupervised 20 to 30 minutes. Andre soon had the prisoners sawing the bars, then gluing them back using soap, toothpaste and cigarette ash, before the next shift turned up.

Finally, after cutting four bars, they were ready to run. The plan was to wait for a rainy day, when the guards rarely went up top. On the first wet morning, three months after Andre had been banged up for the second time, he escaped with 11 others. They climbed up and out, then jumped and ran for their lives. An unlucky guard turned up as they were fleeing over the top and a big inmate punched his face, toppling him off the roof of the container.

> *Reginaldo is a fucking big guy, just pow, punch the guard in the face and he falls down from the top.*
> – Andre

The twelve escapees ran out and through the jungle, with guards shooting with machineguns, and chasing after them with dogs and on horses.

> *When I jump the guard starts to shoot with a machinegun. We are running, running, running to the favelas, 2 kilometres. And after 30 minutes we get to this house, 12 people escape . . . woohoo, great, have a big party – drugs, girls, dinner. For me the party was not that great, because I don't like to stay in the favelas, it's a different class of people, but for the other guys, wow, party, girls. And the police can't come into the favelas.*

Why?

> *Because these people would shoot them. There are many thousands of small houses and most of the people who live there are*

*robbers, drug dealers, all criminals, all kinds. And if the police
try to come, these people will shoot with big guns, bang, bang,
bang.*

   – Andre

Andre stayed in Brazil, still dealing, hiding out and living well,
but the image he'd created for himself and relished, as a
respectable and high-flying entrepreneur, was now a shattered
relic. Chief Caieron had made sure his story blitzed the news.

*According to the Federal Police, Andre Mendes is associated with
much of the cocaine trafficked from Brazil to Europe, where it
is traded for synthetic drugs like ecstasy and LSD, which are
brought to Brazil by mules.*

   – *The News*, 19 November 2004

*In Brazil, they call me the biggest exporter of cocaine from South
Brazil to Europe. This is fucking stupid, because the people who
put it in containers are ten times bigger. They catch me, and try
to make me like an example for the society. The guy did university, the guy has money, the big restaurant, but now he's in
jail because he's a drug dealer. It's fucking bullshit.*

   – Andre

Andre was on the run for five months before his lawyer convinced him to turn himself in for sentencing. He'd advised
Andre that, in absentia, the judge was required to give the maximum sentence but would probably give a small penalty if he
surrendered.

My lawyer tells me, 'If you show your face, you have a chance to get a really, really small sentence.' So, I go to my lawyer's office and say, 'I'm here.' They give me 15 years for one crime, 15 years for another crime, and 7 for another crime – 37 years.

Were you shocked?
For sure.

   – Andre

He was also ordered to pay $300 for repairs to the cut bars of the containers.

Andre was slammed into the maximum-security prison in Santa Catarina, a jail from which no one had ever escaped. Most inmates in Section 4, where Andre was now living, were serving multiple life sentences. 'For sure they put me in the worst place.'

The Greek was also there. Before long, both the playboys used their wheeler-dealer instincts to cut deals to make life a bit easier. The Greek paid for a job in the kitchen, and Andre paid $3000 to work in the library. So, instead of being locked up in his cell for the standard 22 hours a day, Andre was free to walk around the jail from 6 am to 8 pm, wheeling a super-market trolley full of books.

The jail is really, really huge, 2000 people inside. It's like a city. At 6 am they open my door, and I take my supermarket cart, full of books, and go everywhere. I go walking the whole day, smoke marijuana, talking to the people, sometimes partying ... because there are six different sections ... 'Today there's

a party in this section, someone's birthday.' 'Okay.' I go there
with my cart. At 8 pm I'm tired, walking around all day, I want
to go back to my cell for sleeping.

– Andre

Despite making the best of a bad situation, Andre had no intentions of pushing a shopping cart around for one second longer than necessary. He had a cunning plan up his sleeve.

He hoped soon to be back in Bali.

CHAPTER NINETEEN

AGAINST THE ODDS

*All my friends start getting caught in Bali, in Brazil, in Aus-
tralia and then I was, 'Shit, man, they're gonna come to me –
I have to be more careful.'*
    – Rafael

In Bali, Rafael had watched his friends falling across the globe.
He knew his tactic of abruptly freezing and going quiet – and
a lucky star – had so far kept him free.

He was still sporadically tailed, still hot, with cops twice
kicking toilet doors in while he was using the bathroom at
clubs. But most of the time he was playing the devoted family
man, despite being a busy drug boss. Early one morning, he
got an alert call from his Balinese neighbour, telling him cops
had a lens pointed at his house. He raced upstairs with his
binoculars, shut the curtains and peeped out. Up the road was
a scrum of men, clearly cops, with their clichéd moustaches,
long hair, tattoos, sitting on motorbikes, smoking, talking,
waiting, and watching through old binoculars.

'I see straight away the fools there.'

There was a bang on the door downstairs. It was a surf photographer friend: 'Hey, Rafael, let's go for a surf.'

Rafael called him upstairs and passed him the binoculars. 'Man, you've come at a bad time, I'm gonna be busted soon. Look in the bushes, the cops are out there; they're so stupid, they're easy to see.'

The photographer turned to Rafael: 'Why don't you run?'

'Run where? Anyway, I don't need to run ... I don't have anything here, so fuck them, let them come ... let's go, the fools can wait.'

With their surfboards tucked under their arms, the two walked down the palm-lined driveway into the street, past the conspicuous undercover cops. Within a couple of minutes they were paddling out, where Rafael planned to stay for a while to spite the cops and delay the inevitable.

I know as soon as I come out, they are going to come. I didn't have any drugs in the house but I was a little bit worried because in my position I don't want any contact with police.

Almost two hours later, Rafael came out of the water and sensed the cops snapping to attention. He walked across the sand with his friend to the little beachfront café, sat down and ordered breakfast. They could wait a bit longer.

Two Balinese police came and sat next to them, blatantly listening, but with no hope of comprehending. 'Look, this motherfucker thinks I don't know he's a cop,' Rafael said in Portuguese. 'He's gonna try to fuck me soon.'

His friend was feeling the heat. 'Rafael, you sure you don't have anything at home?'

'Yeah, I'm sure.'

About twenty minutes later it was time to go. Rafael strode the 93 metres from the beach to his wooden gate, feeling eyes all over him. They were on their marks, set, poised for a signal to ambush. The second he put his hand on the gate, the sleepy street erupted. 'Police, police,' they screamed as they sprang out of bushes and charged. Three motorbikes roared in fast from one direction, three did a short sprint from another. It was hardly shock and awe.

'I know, I already know,' Rafael snapped. 'What do you want?'

They wanted to come inside. 'Nobody's coming inside my house without a witness and you need a warrant.' One of the cops handed him a piece of paper with writing in Indonesian. 'Fuck, I don't understand this, hang on,' Rafael said and called his Balinese neighbour. 'Wayan, please come quick.'

Wayan tore over and read the warrant, looking grim. 'Ah Rafael, Marco Archer has given you up.'

'What?'

'He says you're the man who takes care of all the coke coming from South America to Asia.' It was almost two years since Marco's bust. Rafael grabbed the warrant, staring at the foreign words.

And then, I see the name 'Marco Archer Moreira'. I don't know why he did that to me. He gave me up. He was jealous of my success. Sad.

Rafael had no choice but to let them into his sanctuary, despite his fears of them planting something. A dozen cops poured in through the gate, quickly spreading out across the garden, foraging among the plants, hunting. Finding nothing, they all moved inside the house.

Anna was out, but the kids were home and quickly grew angry with the intruders rifling through their things. 'My kids give shit to the cops.'

'You're so rude, you can't just come into people's houses and open their freezer,' Rafael's eldest daughter objected. One of the toddlers squealed, 'Don't touch my things. Papa, stop them, stop them.'

Despite their protests, Rafael was trying to keep the cops in the children's rooms rather than his own, but they were soon making their way up the spiral staircase to his bedroom, where things turned nasty.

'Where's your cocaine? We know you're a drug dealer.'

'Hey, be careful, you can't just say shit like that, you have to prove it,' Rafael shot back. 'What are you talking about? I'm a family man.'

The cop lifted his shirt, flashing an old .38 revolver. 'I have a gun, so show us your drugs or I'll put a hole in your knee.'

Rafael knew they wouldn't pop a westerner. It was a scare tactic and it didn't work. 'Sure, try your luck, shoot me. It will be the biggest mistake of your life, cos I'll sue you. And I'm not afraid of your guns. My father's a cop,' he lied. 'I grew up with guns everywhere, and I know that old shit doesn't work.'

'Oh, it works and I'll use it if you don't talk,' the cop spat.

'You guys are so stupid,' Rafael retorted. 'I'm a family man. You're in the wrong place. The big mafia guy who really has the coke is laughing at you. You guys are a joke.'

'Come on, Rafael, don't say that,' his neighbour interjected, worried his goading might backfire.

Rafael ignored him. 'I don't have anything to be afraid of. I'm clean, I don't use drugs. Take my blood,' he said, sticking his arm out. 'I have kids to take care of. You can't bring guns into someone's house with kids. That's wrong.'

The cops were now fuming, and searching with more vigour. Two of them went into his en-suite. Rafael tensed. Inside his electric toothbrush was a gram of coke. The faintest trace would take him down. But the two quickly focused on Anna's vast array of expensive perfumes, creams and potions, enveloping the room in fragrant mist as they stood twisting off lids, spraying, sniffing and fingering the products. Rafael's boring toothbrush went untouched.

Other cops were searching Rafael and Anna's designer wardrobes, feeling inside the Prada shoes, the pockets of his Quiksilver board shorts and his Armani shirts.

The boss told Rafael to open the safe, but Rafael asked him to first clear the room. 'Only you, me and my Balinese friend open the safety deposit. I don't want everybody to see what I have inside. This is my private stuff.' The boss agreed, then stared wide-eyed at glistening riches – Rafael's €25,000 Rolex, his 1-kilo gold necklace, more gold jewellery, and about €3000 cash – as well as photos, passports and documents, but nothing incriminating.

'Sorry, my friend, you've come to the wrong guy,' Rafael said, closing his safe. 'I told you, I'm a family guy. No offence, but you are so stupid . . . Marco sent you to the wrong guy. He named me to clear the real drug dealer. Now you try to fuck the good guy and the bad guy is laughing. Why do you even believe this guy?'

'We know exactly what you do,' the cop retorted. 'We've been watching you for the last two years.'

'Right, so you see me wake up every day 5 am, surf, take the kids to school. You don't see me in the clubs every night, do you? Drug dealers, they are in the nightclubs,' he said, now on a roll with his spiel.

'If you really follow me for the last two years, you see I sleep every day at 9 pm. I wake up 5 am, do yoga, do surfing, teach my kids how to surf. Fuck, you don't think about how you stayed here for one month and didn't see anything? I see you guys out there all the time, like you did this morning. You have to be more discreet. Look at my lens ... they're much bigger than yours. I see you; I can see the hole in your tooth from here. You cannot work like that. If I'm a real drug dealer I can shoot you from here.'

The guy feel so embarrassed when I give this kind of comment to him.

They'd been searching for three hours and found nothing. In a desperate attempt to extract something from the morning's raid, the boss asked Rafael, 'Can you give some money?'

'What! Why?'

'Because I have to do a course in Jakarta, I need money.'

'No, I can't give you money. First I have kids to take care of, school fees, visas. Why would I give you money for nothing?'

'Please, *Pak* [Mr] Rafael, just two million rupiah [$200] to help me with the ticket to Jakarta?'

I say, 'No, sorry. Please can you go, take your friends from my house. I want to rest.' Pak Wayan [alias] – you know he's boss of the cops, Intel, long hair, looks like a gangster – I refused to give him money.

The cop changed tack, asking him to set someone up. 'Can you help us by going to a club and trying to buy ecstasy to show us who is selling?'

'Are you nuts?' Rafael retorted. Before leaving, the boss took phone numbers from Rafael's mobile. None were drug dealers, as this was his 'clean' phone, but he took Rafael's number, and soon started using it.

He kept calling me every day. I was, 'Fuck, don't call me any more. Okay, let's make a deal: you can come here now, I'm going to give you 500,000 rupiah [$50] – not to help me, but for you to forget me, never call me again.' He comes like 'Hah-hah-hah' [panting]. He sees my lifestyle, and I think he thinks, 'I have to take some money from this motherfucker.' He tried everything he could.

Rafael was safe, for now, bailed out of the hot spot by his tactic of keeping a squeaky clean house, his quick inscrutable lies and glib tap-dancing. But he was furious at Marco.

I never believed police were going to come like this. I was very pissed off with Marco. I call and say, 'Man, if you put me in jail you are going to die, because I'm going to kill you, motherfucker. Why did you talk about me?' 'Oh I don't say anything, I don't say anything.' But his name was on the note.

So did he try to cut a deal?

I believe so. The cops show me the paper; they have the statement from Marco. I was thinking to fuck him. I was angry. I was boxing training and I taped his photo on the bag and punch so hard. Pow pow pow. I remember it gave me motivation.

Rafael soon got more bad news. Chino was red hot and running for his life. Bali police had never bothered him, but Jakarta police were hunting him down due to a domino effect of snitches from the bottom right to the top.

The unravelling of Chino's Bali-based drug empire started when Jakarta police busted a small-time dealer with 10 ecstasy pills. He snitched on his dealer, who was busted with 713 pills, who snitched on his dealer, a Taiwanese man named David, who was busted with 27,000 pills, who turned things international when he snitched on his dealer, Collin, in Singapore. Police followed Collin's cash trail to a bank account in the name of Henry.

Henry, who was Chino's trusted assistant, confessed everything and told the police about the secrets of their ecstasy business in Jakarta, Bali, Holland, and Singapore.
  – Bali Post, 31 March 2005

Police traced $2 million to one of Chino's accounts. As the *Bali Post* reported: 'Chino supplied ecstasy pills which were worth 19 billion rupiah within the period of ten months.' The story was headline news, splashed across the front pages of the island's newspapers: 'Unbelievable and shocking!' 'M3

Boss; Wealthy, cool, never had clear explanation about his business: The beggar who turned out to be a millionaire and a fugitive.'

Chino's years of immunity were shattered, as Jakarta cops crawled all over his assets. Twenty police with dogs raided his M3 sunset car wash café and pit stop for four hours. They found nothing incriminating, but confiscated documents, made a record of assets, then sealed off the building. The front doors were padlocked, a security guard stationed out the front, and 130 employees blocked from entering. The usual frenetic building with its designer holes in the façade was eerily quiet. Five days later, police searched again, from 10 am to 4 pm, but again found no drugs.

Jakarta police also searched Chino's house on the river in Legian, suspended use of his 20 jet-skis in Nusa Dua and sealed off the water sport business with yellow tape 'since it is suspected as a part of money laundering system', the *Bali Post* reported. They also confiscated 26 cars, 7 motorbikes, 12 personal computers, 6 video games, 7 televisions, 4 go-karts, and some sound system equipment.

They had a warrant to do so, but – in a weird 'only in Bali' twist – the Jakarta police were blindsided. Lawyers for Chino's wife stated that the Jakarta police had suspended the assets based on a search warrant from Denpasar District Court, but that it was 'never issued by Denpasar District Court'.

Police suspended the assets based on a letter from Denpasar District Court number No. W.16.DDP.UM.01.10–665 dated 1 April 2005 regarding the search warrant. However, it was found that the letter was never issued by Denpasar District Court.

– Denpost, 18 April 2005

They were forced to release Chino's assets. Not so curiously, things in Bali were still working in the drug boss's favour. At the same time, his friendships with influential people in Bali were making unwelcome and embarrassing headlines. Despite corruption in Bali being as intrinsic as rice paddies, people lost face when it was exposed and didn't like it. As one source told the *Bali Post*, 'This apparently is a nightmare for the M3 boss, who is a close friend of some high-ranking government officials.'

Another source added, 'He was friends with some well-known government officials, high-ranked police officers, even doctors, but I cannot give their names.' The source was perplexed when he was told that Chino is now a fugitive and a target of the Indonesian Police Headquarters and Greater Jakarta Area Metropolitan Police. 'Why is it the Jakarta police that run after Chino? What is wrong with the Bali police? Do they pretend that they don't know?' the source joked.

– Denpost, 20 March 2005

Even the Governor of Bali, Made Pastika – Bali's former Police Chief – got press when Chino's operations manager, Bejo, said in a statement that he'd seen his car taken out of M3 after the Jakarta police confiscation request appeared.

Meanwhile, Chino's wife had hired an expensive team of lawyers in Bali who argued that she, not Chino, owned the assets, although they were unable to prove it with documentation.

As Rafael confirms, 'Chino had so many connections everywhere in the police.' Unsurprisingly, he had got wind of the police operation in time to flee and evade arrest. His real name was now useless to him, with Interpol issuing a Red Notice – its version of an international arrest warrant – so he established his headquarters in a nearby country, continuing to make millions from ecstasy production under a new false name.

When Rafael heard about Chino's crash, he instantly worried about becoming entangled. 'I say, "Shit, now I'm fucked, they are going to come to me too." Maybe they put cameras there [at M3] and see me there all the time.'

Rafael didn't get arrested, but was still perilously walking the high wire in Bali. Months after the first raid, two cops were back on his doorstep, trying to push their way into his house. 'Police, police,' they jostled trying to get in.

'Hey,' Rafael shouted, 'I don't care if you're police, this is a private house. You cannot come in like this. What's wrong?'

'I have information you are a drug dealer, we follow you for three years.'

Rafael laughed, 'Man, you cannot come inside my house, please get out of my property, you don't have any warrant.'

'They straight away go out, and then I know they're pussies. If they're tough cops, they say, "Shut up, motherfucker" and throw something in my garden to fuck me.' Rafael agreed to talk to them outside his gate, after his neighbour Wayan arrived as a witness. They wanted names, but they didn't have a hope: 'I say forget me, you talk with the wrong guy.'

Around the same time, Rafael chanced an encounter with the chief narcotics cop, *Pak* Wayan, at Carrefour supermarket, still pushing to 'help'. '*Pak* Rafael, remember me?' the cop asked.

'*Pak* Wayan, you still working for the police?'

'Yes, if you need anything, you call', he said, then handed Rafael a business card.

'Shut up, man', Rafael snapped, sure he would never be calling him. Paying off one cop didn't stop another from busting you, as Chino's situation proved.

With the cops sniffing around and the island so hot, combined with the risk of his horses getting the death penalty, Rafael started doing all his business in Europe and his wife's native Sweden.

> *I was not selling in Bali any more because I was afraid of some-body getting the death penalty. I was saying, 'I don't want to have this on my bill. Somebody dead.'*

With his years of expertise in the game, people were often investing in his runs, which he organised by making calls from public phones in Bali. Hells Angel Tota was using Rafael to organise and sell his coke.

> *Tota calls me golden boy because everything I touch becomes gold. He was very keen, 'Let's do it in Stockholm, you have a wife there, easy.'*

Did you do many deals in Stockholm?
Many.

Did you usually fly there?

> Fly. First I send the horse from Brazil. They arrive, call me in Bali, say, 'I'm ready.' I say, 'Okay, tomorrow I come,' because Bali to Stockholm has flights every day. And I meet the horse there in the hotel in Stockholm with the windsurf board. I take the booms to my apartment, open, wait, sell, get the money, pay the horse, kick him back, fly to Bali full of cashhhh.

Rafael's wife also regularly flew in to help him carry the cash home.

Your wife was working with you?

> All the time. She was more like a brain – calculations, numbers – and I was in the action, in the field. But I start to involve her a little bit too much. I'm not born to be a drug dealer, because I was too nice and she was always in my face, pushing me: 'No, this price is too low. Are you crazy?' and pushing me to make bigger bigger bigger. She push me a lot too . . . to take the money and do something else. She says, 'Let's bring 100 kilo, let's bring 200 kilo, and retire in good style.'

Did you ever do that?

> We try, but the biggest amount was 20 kilos in one go.

And did she go on trips to take drugs or money?

> She loved to pick up money.

By doing business remotely, Rafael was getting ripped off by some of his merry-go-round of partners and combined with horses busting, his finances started fluctuating wildly – soaring then crashing to zero. His lucky star seemed to be waning. The day Hells Angel Tota phoned with a project, wanting him to fly to Stockholm in two days time to pick up 2 kilos of coke, he was broke. But this was a dead cert.

'Come on, Tota, how?' Rafael asked, uncertain. Tota told him that a Brazilian Federal cop, his friend, was escorting a Hells Angel on an extradition flight from Rio to Stockholm: 'Nobody checks him.'

'No, no way, man, I don't want to see any cop, are you crazy?'

Tota persisted, 'You're fucking stupid, man; this guy is my brother, he's a cop but he's a *bandito* too. Fuck, don't be a puss, man. Take the plane.'

Tota wanted Rafael to meet the cop at Stockholm's Arlanda Airport in the frenetic international arrivals hall. 'No way, man, there are cameras. I don't want to meet any cop in the airport.'

'Shut up, man, it's fine. He already knows you.'

'What? How?'

Tota told him the cop had once come to Bali and met Rafael when Tota dropped off a bag of coke. Rafael was incredulous. 'Fuck, man, you bring a federal police officer to Bali to meet me?'

Tota sweetened the deal by offering Rafael half the cash. Against his screaming instincts, Rafael agreed.

I was totally bankrupt in that time, crazy for money.

Tota even had to send him €800 via Western Union to buy the plane ticket.

Two days later, Rafael flew Thai Airways to Stockholm, stayed overnight with a friend, then took a taxi back to Arlanda Airport. He'd agreed to wear his sun-bleached blond curly hair out, without his usual masking Gucci sunglasses and cap, so the cop could quickly recognise him. Undisguised and exposed to the airport's CCTV cameras, his life and freedom were on the line on the word of a Hells Angel. Rafael had no idea what this cop even looked like.

It was coming in my mind, 'What am I doing? What am I fucking doing? If my friends know this, they're going to think I'm a rat. How do I get involved with this shit? Hard to get out now. I'm already here; I have to get this done.' Same feeling I had when I go to the police building in Brazil to buy the cocaine. I say to myself, 'Let's get this done.'

Standing at the designated spot in the huge, cavernous and sleekly modern Scandinavian airport terminal, he felt acutely vulnerable. This could be it. He was a sitting duck. His heart was pounding. It was far from his usual covert way of operating. A man came up, passed him a plastic bag, said, 'Sorry, I have to go,' and vanished as quickly as he'd appeared.

He gives me the bag, a lot of magazines, Playboy, surf magazines and 2 kilos of coke very well packed inside a woman's leather make-up case. I take a taxi to my friend's apartment, open the shit, try it, 'Oh, good.' Call my contact, sell and then I send part of the money by Western Union to Tota. And I bring cash to Bali. Like Tota said, 'It's the best deal you get in your *life; we are going to share half and half.' I was stupid – I could say, 'Oh, they pay only $30,000 [a kilo]', but I say the truth – 'They pay $40,000.' And then he say, 'Okay, $40,000 for you, $40,000 for me.' I say, 'Fuck, thank you, brother!'*

With the help of his wife's friend, he sent $20,000 to Bali by bank transfer, but carried the rest on the flight.

They pay me ($80,000) in Swedish crowns. I go to the money changer and change it for €500 bills, so it was easy to bring.

In your pocket?

Yeah, in my pocket, a little bit in my wallet, in my shoes, a little bit in my underwear. I never put all the cash together. When I have €70,000–€80,000, I put €10,000 in one foot, €10,000 in other foot, €5000 in my front pocket, €5000 in back, €5000 in my wallet, €5000 in bag, hand luggage, I put everywhere. You know the military pants, full of pockets, I love to travel with these pants. I put it here, here.

How many times have you travelled with thousands of dollars like that?

Many, many times. I hide it very well.

So it's all carefully done?

Yeah, I do it good. I was very well dressed, too. They never check me in the airports. Some people are afraid to travel with money; I'm afraid to travel without money.

Rafael was travelling more often to Brazil carrying cash to organise runs, to buy the coke and take it to the packers, to try to improve his success rate by being on the ground. His cash was low when he decided to do a high-stakes gamble with Fox, betting all his remaining chips on sending 20 kilos to Amsterdam.

I go to Brazil, I'm going to do, because these pussies there, they don't know how to do. Then, big shit, big shit, fall fall, fall, lose money, lose money. Fox wanted to be partner too, we want to make big shit.

Fox and Rafael had become good friends during the three years they'd been working together, sending coke to Sweden, Europe, Bali, Malaysia and Australia. They hung out in Rio and São Paulo visiting high-class brothels, packing cocaine, organising runs, partying and sniffing blow.

Rafael spent time at Fox's Bali-style house on a lagoon in Florianópolis, as well as Fox's mother's $10 million mansion in São Paulo's ultra-exclusive *Jardins* district. Fox had his own wing, where he played his games of guns, girls and cocaine, often storing his loaded booms there.

At the mansion one day, Fox showed Rafael a new gun and silencer. 'This shit work?' Rafael asked, screwing on the silencer.

'Never tried,' Fox replied. Rafael walked across to the window, opened it, pointed the gun to the sky and fired. The bang exploded in their ears. 'Fuck, man, this silencer shit doesn't work,' Rafael laughed. 'The police are gonna come.'

Fox's well-to-do family had no idea what he did. His

Brazilian mother and grandmother were very wealthy and his father, divorced from his mother, was a consul from France.

His family was very rich. Amazing. His Brazilian grandmother was fucking rich. I met his mamma, his brother, his driver who did everything for us.

Fox and Rafael were unlikely friends. Fox was plain-faced, tall with a stooped posture, a pear-shaped physique, long arms and dark, razor-cut hair.

He looks like kind of pussy guy, not tough guy, skinny, little bit big bum, shoulders smaller than bum. A shy guy; not a charismatic person. Nobody liked him. From the beginning people say, 'Why you go with this guy, man?' I say, 'I wanna help him.'

The charismatic, gregarious Rafael was also opposite to his friend in his sartorial style. Rafael was often aghast at what he deemed Fox's bad taste. Despite splashing a fortune on his wardrobe, Fox dressed in clothes that Rafael wouldn't wear in a casket, like pairing a €5000 Dior leather jacket, which Rafael abhorred, with jeans and white Nike shoes. Fox was obsessed with his collection of Nike's most expensive sports shoes with the Shox feature – foam springs. He kept a dozen pairs on display on special shelves in his living room.

Totally ugly, these shoes. I don't use training shoes with jeans, but Fox loves white Nikes. If he got one drop of something on his shoes, he got so mad, he went home to change. He uses them

one time, brings them home, and cleans them using a tooth-
brush. This guy is sick with the shoes. Sick.

Rafael often had hookers asking him if his friend was gay.

Sometimes we go to the best prostitute house in Brazil, São
Paulo. I don't like this shit much, but Fox says, 'Let's go, I pay
for you.' 'Okay, let's go.' High-level girls. Sometimes people who
work in TV go there. Normally girls cost $100, but if you get
one they call the artists, it costs $1000, $2000, the expensive
programme.

Did you try an artist?
Sometimes we take, cos they do a show with the poles, and we
ask 'How much for this one?' '$2000.' 'Okay, bring.' But we always
play with the girls, pay one time and get the phone number, and
then we meet outside, so they don't pay for the place.

But when we sit in the prostitute house and all the girls come
out and take you to a room, they always think Fox is gay. 'Oh,
your friend's gay?' I say, 'No, why? Fox, they say you're gay.' 'No,
I'm not gay.' But the way he dress, he spent €5000 on the Dior
jacket, totally ugly. I would never buy something like that for
myself. With the pocket down the front, like a suit, so ugly this
shit. I say, 'Fox, how can you buy this shit?'

So he had a lot of cash?
Yeah, but that time he started taking money from the business.
He says, 'Oh, I get money from my grandmother for my birthday.'
It was bullshit, he already started taking from me.

On their latest high-stakes gamble, Rafael desperately needed a win. He packed himself with €75,000, flew to São Paulo and delivered it to Fox, then flew out to Amsterdam to wait for the horses. Often runs expected to take days stretched out for weeks, but as time passed and the horses didn't arrive, Rafael was hearing more and more excuses from Fox.

He say, 'Tomorrow', 'Next week', 'Tomorrow', but they never come, they never show. Then he disappeared, don't answer the phone. The guy bullshit me. He was going behind my back, selling to another friend in Amsterdam while I wait. He robbed me. I didn't know he's gonna fuck me and I stayed in €300-a-night hotel, eat in the best restaurants every night, and then suddenly, he disappears, and I'm poof, totally bankrupt.

I came back to Bali with no money, just thinking, 'I want to kill this fool,' but I didn't have the money to follow him. I have a friend who met him in the surf in Brazil. He says, 'Be careful, Rafael's going to kill you, man. You fuck his family, you fuck him.' He says, 'No, he can't come here, he doesn't have money to follow me.' It was true.

But Fox was served drug dealer justice. As he stood talking on a public phone in Florianópolis, a car load of men stopped, one man jumped out and pointed a gun in Fox's face, saying, 'Hello, playboy.' Fox dropped the phone in panic, unclasped his Rolex and held it out, begging, 'Please don't kill me, please, take my watch.' The armed bandit snatched it, then ordered Fox to get in his new Toyota and take him to his house.

Once there, the men ransacked the place, taking everything

from his PlayStation and plasma TV to his precious Nike shoe collection. Then they beat him up badly, stripped him down to his underpants, and dumped him on the highway 100 kilometres from his house in the freezing cold, driving off in his new $100,000 Toyota.

Two months later, Fox was attacked again at his house on the lagoon in Florianópolis. Fox saw in his security cameras two big black Chevrolet cars, with blacked-out windows, pulling up and five bandits wearing black balaclavas, brandishing submachine guns and pistols, get out.

He was already paranoid; he put in a special security system, full of cameras, and when they come, he saw in the cameras and was pissing his pants. They came calling, 'Fox, Fox' and then they shoot, ba-a-a-a-a-a, the door. He ran upstairs, hid in the wardrobe. They go inside, ba-a-a-a-a-a, come to the second floor, shoot everywhere. The bullets go through the wardrobe but don't touch him. Lucky motherfuck. They didn't know he was in the wardrobe – if they know, they shoot him.
– Rafael

As a parting gesture, the bandits spray-painted 'Rafael $$$' on the front of the house. Then they fled.

Who were these people?
I don't have a clue. Until today I try to find out. I believe somebody I know, who was pissed off with the situation. I was thinking Claudio, the police friend, but I met him and he thinks it's me. Everyone thinks it's me and then Fox calls, 'Why you do that?'

I say, 'Man, you think it was me? You really think it was me? You've known me a long time ... If I come to see you, I'm not gonna write my name. You wouldn't be talking any more. You know what I'm gonna do with you?' 'You threaten me?' 'No, I just tell you.'

Rafael's tactic was to be vaguely civil to Fox on the phone, hoping he might return to Bali so he could avenge himself. But Fox fled, suffering from panic syndrome – fearing someone was trying to kill him – to Teahupoo, Tahiti, on his French passport.

Many people want to kill this guy, he's not gonna live long, he fuck everybody to get rich.
  – Rafael

The next time Rafael was in Brazil, he met with Fox's lawyer, who by chance was dating one of his friends. She told him the cops had been asking, 'Who's this guy Rafael?' She asked Rafael, 'Was it you?'

'I wish,' he replied. Rafael went to Florianópolis to look at Fox's house, which was up for sale.

I was planning to burn the house, make some Molotov bottles and throw in the house to burn it. But I give up. I say it's too hot now. I'm ready to make some money. Fucking Fox, he's lucky.

Although Rafael had lost many of his friends to jail or betrayal, one of his more trusted partners returned. Irrepressible, with a toothy smile on his face and as excited as a kid, Andre flew back to Bali. He'd fast grown tired of wheeling his shopping trolley of books around maximum security and, after 14 months, paid to be transferred to the less secure Complex Penitentiary, the jail where he'd escaped from the containers previously.

The boss from this prison is really funny. He's a fat guy, his name is Shucka. When he sees me, he says, 'Why are you coming here again? You try escaping, you want to fuck my job, yeah?'
 – Andre

Andre's escape was thanks to guards who agreed to leave two doors unlocked for $10,000. The night before, they told Andre he had exactly ten minutes between 6 am and 6.10 am to slip out. Andre didn't sleep that night and in the morning, it went perfectly to plan. He walked out, into a waiting car, and went straight to Laguna Beach. For fifteen days he hid there, waiting for his false passport, then flew out of Brazil to Amsterdam. He planned to lie low for a long while, but it was January – midwinter, freezing and snowing.

I arrive in Amsterdam, it's snowing, cold, nobody on the streets, I don't want to stay. I just go inside one travel agent, buy one ticket and fly to Bali.
 – Andre

Now, back on the tropical island, life was again beautiful – full of sunsets, afternoon joints, surfing, dining and dealing. But his lust for whimsical jet-setting would soon flip his life again.

CHAPTER TWENTY

SUA CASA CAI –
YOUR HOUSE FALLS

Rafael wasn't in Bali when Andre flew back. He'd had a long streak of bad luck, busts and rip-offs, which had sent him into a financial tailspin, unable to pay basics like his kids' school fees. So when he'd got a call from his friend Lee, in Amsterdam, asking him to come and 'play a game', Rafael had jumped on a plane, desperately hoping for a win. 'Everybody wanted to do it with me because I know the game.'

Lee was paying all operational costs, but needed someone he could trust to organise the buying, packing and sending. He'd pay Rafael in cocaine, giving him 2 of the 7 kilos being sent. In Amsterdam, he gave Rafael €45,000 to arrange things in Rio. In a few weeks, Rafael had it all set. A Brazilian girl was running with the 7 kilos of coke in Lee's €3000 suitcase – with a false carbon fibre bottom – which he'd had tailor-made by an elderly Dutch specialist.

She flew to Brussels, avoiding Dutch customs, then was supposed to take a train to Amsterdam. But she failed to show up. She simply vanished and things turned sinister.

'I'm gonna kill you, motherfucker,' Lee's Dutch investor screamed down the phone at Rafael, accusing him of a double-cross. 'You don't know who you're dealing with. You can't hide.'

'*Pff*, man, she busted,' Rafael retorted, unsure if it were true.

'You think I'm fucking stupid?' the investor ranted. 'I know you stole the coke, you did bullshit. I'm gonna kill you, I'm gonna burn your eyes with cigarettes.'

> *Everybody becomes Al Pacino, Scarface. All the drug dealers,*
> *they have this. In the end we think they found it in the X-ray*
> *and she bust. It's a lottery.*
> – Rafael

Rafael was more desperate now. His wife was hassling him to hurry up, because she needed cash. Rafael was tired and cold in Europe's freezing winter and wanting to go home to Bali to see his kids, sit on the beach and surf. But when Lee offered him another game, he knew he had to stay and breathe life into his career.

He flew back to Brazil, met another horse, Otto Koester, loaded him with 1 kilo and sent him off. Otto made it, finally breaking Rafael's spell of bad luck. Rafael got $15,000 commission and reinvested it with Lee in another run. Otto was keen to run again too.

Back in Rio, Rafael loaded a backpack with 4 kilos of coke. As soon as it was ready, Rafael drove Otto to Rio's Galeão

International Airport and risked going inside with him to buy a ticket to fly immediately. The flight was full, so they bought a ticket for the following day.

Everything was too crazy, in a hurry. I don't care any more. I pushed to do it quickly, 'Let's do, let's do, fast, fast, let's go today, let's go to the airport now.' I think everything go down because my wife was hurrying me.
– Rafael

The next day, as Otto stood in line waiting to board the plane, there was a sudden commotion. A girl just ahead was pulled aside. They'd found 3.5 kilos of cocaine in her hand luggage. In those first moments of chaos, Otto had a chance to flee. But he decided not to; he felt confident that his bag was well packed and safely checked in. He thought they'd take her and let everyone else board the plane, but police suspected the 17-year-old girl from Cape Verde was a decoy for a larger amount. Suddenly, the window to flee slammed shut – every passenger was a suspect. Cops began checking them one by one, taking their bags off the plane for a rigorous search. They found the coke in Otto's backpack and hit their second jackpot for that flight.

A Brazilian, Otto Koester, 26, who also has Swiss nationality, was carrying 4 kg of cocaine in his baggage. Both [he and the 17-year-old girl] were trying to go to Europe on the same flight, although they had no connection with each other.
– *Federal Police Association Press Agency*, 11 April 2008

Rafael was waiting in his hotel when he got word from Lee that Otto had been busted. Lee had checked the net when Otto didn't show. Rafael felt exhausted. All he had to show for the past six months of hard work were failed projects, guilt over his jailed horses, and bankruptcy.

> *I was still in Rio, hiding myself in some hotel. I was already very depressed because I lose a lot of coke, I put three people in jail, everything gone to hell, then my friend calls me and says, 'You have to get out of the country now, quickly, or they're gonna catch you.' I say, 'Don't say that! Why?' 'Man, you were stupid; you went to buy the ticket with the horse. They have cameras everywhere, big surveillance.' I was depressed, desperate, waiting, thinking any minute now somebody's coming to catch me. It was the worst time in my career.*
> – Rafael

Rafael booked a flight and raced to Rio de Janeiro airport with only hand luggage.

> *I was on the run. I didn't bring anything to make it easy. I throw away many things, clothes, even the laptop I leave in my friend's house because of all the communication, emails and everything.*
> – Rafael

At the airport things went perfectly. He checked in, sailed through immigration and sat down in his tail-end economy seat, breathing a sigh of relief. Now, to hit the safety of the skies ... But his instincts for trouble were sharp and something was wrong; his pulse started racing. Passengers were all seated and the plane wasn't moving. The captain announced, 'I'm sorry we have a problem ...' Rafael tuned out; he didn't need to hear any more words. Two Federal police officers were walking towards him – a black guy and a blonde woman, wearing suits with shiny *Policia Federal* badges slashed across their shoulders. They were checking the seat numbers above the passengers' heads.

Was like slow motion for me ... they come, they come ... three seats to come, then the guy looks in my eyes, I look in his eyes. My heart beat te te te te near to heart attack. I think, 'Fucking done! Okay, take me.' He comes close, looking at me, then doof, he passes, goes to the guy in the seat behind. Was the scariest five seconds of my life.

And then the plane still doesn't take off. I think, now they are going to come back for me. 'More wine, please, I need wine.' I think, 'Why don't we take off? Why doesn't this shit go up?' Was fucking bad time. I was praying, making promises: 'God, I promise if I see my kids again, if I reach Bali safe, I'm gonna stop this shit. Please help me, God, I want to see my kids again. Please, please God.' I didn't realise they were just taking his bag off ... We waited one hour.

I make it to Bali again. Free. But when I come back everything was falling down ... I quit the business. No money, oh ... and then I decide I'm going to sell the house, start to do business, but my brilliant wife doesn't take to losing everything and being normal. She says, 'No, we're not going to sell the house. I'm gonna go to Sweden and do by myself.' I say, 'No, don't do.'

A couple of months before, when I was in Brazil, she tried

to kill herself. She was alcoholic – drink every day. Cut her wrists
in the tower . . . crazy . . . she think I get a girlfriend and left
her, but I was looking to fix our money situation. That's the
price I pay for all the shit.
  – Rafael

Rafael had had enough. He'd seen too many friends ruin their
lives and he wanted to start a normal life. He also desperately
wanted to quit using blow, as he knew that it was his addiction that had kept him in the game for so long, as well as
destroying his lungs. 'One day I say, "Fuck, I'm gonna die. I
can't use this shit any more." He'd tried to abstain while away,
but failed, especially as every time he packed the coke the stuff
leached through his skin or he inhaled the dust in the air. Now,
he was trying hard, and it was exacerbating dark emotions.

In Brazil I try to stop but I get high from touch, packing, you
know. And then when I finish the packing I get depression,
aggressive, shaking hands, heart beat dedededede, and then I
cai do cavalo – fall from the horse. I'm in a party, I get drunk
and then somebody comes, 'You want a line?' . . . The second
I put that shit in my nose I regret it. I feel like shit, paranoid.
The day after my nose is totally blocked, bleeding, with asthma
for two days. I feel to kill myself. And then I say, 'Now, I'm not
going to take this shit any more,' and one week passes, two weeks
and then I cai do cavalo again. I say, 'Today I'm gonna take
one small line to relax,' – and it's like, I take 2 grams; paranoid,
looking out the windows, thinking the police are gonna come
and catch me for the bullshit.

Then I come to Bali, totally broke, I get depression ... oh my god, I'm going to die ... they're going to catch me ... I can't do this any more. Start cry, cry, cry. And fuck, start getting paranoid about everything. They're going to connect me with this guy Otto.

I get this kind of depression from abstinence. Feel like crying. I was shaking, I was aggressive over small things. My kids would do something, 'Ahhh,' I scream ... I never do that, I was mellow, nice, but I find some different behaviour. I was not happy about this. I start crying. You know I never cry. What am I gonna do? The world's going to finish.

– Rafael

Rafael sold the land near his house to pay the kids' school fees and some of their debts. But the house was still mortgaged, as Anna had used it as collateral for a bank loan.

We start getting trouble trouble trouble, no money, can't pay kids' school, no money and she tells me, 'I prefer to go to jail than live like that.' I say, 'What the fuck you talk about? You live in paradise – you have a house, you have kids, you have everything. Let's stop, let's stop,' and my wife was already getting everything ready for a run. She was organising everything with my friend in Brazil, pushing too, call him, call him ... 'No, stop this shit. I cannot do it any more.'

– Rafael

Anna decided to do a run to Stockholm. She flew to Brazil, where the cop Claudio supplied her with almost a kilo of blow, which she packed into the legs of a tripod and sent by DHL to Sweden, where someone was paid to collect it. Then she flew to Stockholm to sell it. It was a win.

Fugitive Andre had also invested and Anna Skyped him, asking him to fly in to collect his cash and party with some Swedish girls.

> *When the shit arrived in Sweden, she calls me, 'Hey, Andre, can you come here to pick up your money?' I say, 'Oh, I don't wanna go to Europe now.' Then she puts three blonde girls on Skype. 'Oh, these are my friends. They're dying to know you, Brazilian boy ... oh yeah, Andre, come here to party.' 'Oh, why not?' I was in Bali almost one year and a little bit bored, needed civilisation ... I think, okay, I go to Europe, get my money, do some parties and come back with euros. Not a big deal.*

But you were still being hunted?
> *Yes, stupid, you know.*
>   – Andre

Rafael asked Andre, 'You sure you can go?'

'No problem, my passport's so good, no worries.'

But Andre didn't make it to Sweden. En route, he was busted in Amsterdam for flying on a false passport and slammed back in a cell. Bali beaches and sunsets were again a beautiful memory, but he expected to be back soon. He'd ostensibly confessed his real name to authorities – Luke Shakira Martins. It was another alias he'd set up with passport and ID papers. His lawyer sent them from Brazil and 'Luke' was sentenced to one month's jail.

The day of his release, the police told him he was being sent back to Bali. They took him to Amsterdam's Schiphol Airport, walked him into a room and took off his handcuffs, saying, 'Right, now you're free.'

'I turn my back to go and two guys come and say, "You are arrested under Interpol, Andre."' Another pair of bracelets was snapped around his wrists. It was a bitter blow.

Andre had checked Interpol's website in Bali, so he knew it had issued a Red Notice for him, but thought he'd outsmarted the Dutch cops with his second false ID. He now guessed they'd taken fingerprints off a prison glass or plate and, through Interpol, discovered he was a Brazilian fugitive. It was in fact his nemesis who'd suspected his real identity. Chief Caieron had sent documents, fingerprints and photographs to the Netherlands' embassy and Interpol to confirm it was Andre. 'They confirmed that he was our guy – and we brought him back. I did all the papers to assure his coming back to Brazil and *chain*.' It took another three months of legal red tape to fly him back home to serve out the rest of his sentence. Of course, Andre had other plans.

Back in Bali, Anna's Stockholm win was a brief respite, but things were getting worse again. Rafael sold his jewellery to help pay the bills, but the bank was threatening to take the house.

Because when I was in Brazil she make so many bills, she borrow money, she borrow money from the bank and give the house paper to guarantee. And then she knows we're going to lose the house, the bank's gonna take, we have two months, and then she was in a hurry to make the money. I say, 'I cannot do this any more. Let's sell the house, stop this shit. Start a normal life; I'm going to get a job.' She says, 'No, we cannot. Let's do one more to cash in.' I say, 'No, don't do it,' but I don't have any power over her. She says, 'I'm going to do this, you pussy, I don't care what you say.' She organises everything. Then she says, 'I'm gonna do this last one, easy, I go myself.' I say, 'When are you going?' She says, 'Tomorrow.' 'What? Tomorrow?'

    – Rafael

Rafael warned her at least not to collect the couriered package – that was a job for a mule.

She was crazy, you know . . . she wanted to do it herself, she wanted to be a mule. I hired the people there to do this job and, after the thing arrives, everything's clear, I fly and get the money. I say, 'Fuck, you are a boss, you cannot do this job. This job is for a mule – you wanna be a mule?' She says, 'Yeah . . . you cannot do anything.'

So she went from Bali to Stockholm, and they send the coke from Peru. And she was calling me because it was delayed one day. I say, 'Abort, abort. Don't take it. Run. Run.' I feel something's wrong. I say, 'Don't ring me, just in case,' and then she start to call me all the time to talk, 'Oh, it's delayed again, they send to Finland.' I say, 'Stop calling. Fuck . . .'

    – Rafael

Five days later, it was Rafael's 45th birthday, and he was having a low-key celebration in his Bali house with half a dozen friends, their kids, some beers and a small cake. His phone rang. It was Anna, so he took it outside. 'Happy birthday, your present's come,' she whooped. It was the news Rafael so desperately wanted to hear. 'I was like, "Thank you, the shit arrived. I can pay my loan, we're not going to lose the house. We're rich again. Goal."'

Rafael went back to his friends, keeping his good news quiet but feeling great relief. It didn't last. His phone rang ten minutes later. It was Anna again. 'What the fuck, it's baking powder,' she yelled down the phone. 'Fuck, you asshole, your friend sent us baking powder.'

In ten minutes, Rafael's world had gone from bright to very dark. He called his friend in Peru, who instantly took the blame, saying his packer had done this once before – stolen the coke and sent baking powder. 'Sorry, Rafael,' he said.

There was nothing Rafael could do. Anna phoned back and he relayed the Peruvian's response. 'Okay, fuck you, fuck you,' she screamed, then hung up. Rafael went back inside to his guests, hiding his emotions until his not-so-happy birthday finished.

Everybody goes home, I try to sleep, and then I start to think, 'Fuck, what's happened?' I try to call Anna. She doesn't answer. And then I fall to sleep. Wake up the next day, try to call, no answer. I don't know what's happened.

For ten days I don't know. I was thinking she fuck up, she start taking coke, get crazy, high like hell inside some apart-

ment, paranoid to call, maybe dead from overdose. I think many things. Maybe somebody killed her to take the stuff. I keep trying to call, nobody answer, nobody answer, nobody answer.

I call all the friends. They go to the apartment where she was – it was locked, nobody there – and then they find the key with friends, go there and the police come: 'What are you doing here?' Then I suspect she's busted.

I contacted my friend – a Swedish buyer, he's supposed to buy the shit – and say, 'Please help me, Anna is there.' After ten days, he calls and says, 'She's inside,' because he has some police connection who tells him. He says, 'Be careful, they're gonna come to you. Be careful with all the evidence.'

When I know she's inside, I panic much more. I say, 'Fuck, they come for me now. She's bust.' Panic, crying, depression, you know ... the kids by myself. What am I going to do with all these kids? I had no money. I have to clean the house, take my computer out of here. I think Interpol is going to come here and take me too. Cry, cry, depression ... was the worst time. I cannot go out to eat – I call for the pizza. I don't shave. I don't shower. I don't even go to the first floor. I stay in the second floor, lay down, sleep, you know ... and cry. Three days. I was in bad shape. Just waiting for somebody to break my door and catch me too.

And then Emily, the mother of my daughter's best friend, comes to pick up her daughter. She asks my son, 'Where's papa?' He says, 'Papa's upstairs.' And then I was there, like ... not crying, but bad shape. And she was, 'Hey, Rafael, hello, how are you? Are you all right?' 'No.' 'What's happened?'

And then I say, 'I'm in deep shit. Anna's in jail.' She goes,

'What?' Then we started have a better conversation and then she says, 'Why do you look like this? I've never seen you like this with a beard. Why don't you shave any more?' I was like, 'I don't give a shit.' I think I'm gonna go to jail, get a problem too.

Did she know you were a drug dealer?

She knew, because her husband was an addict. He bought a lot with me. Certain times she hated me, because I give coke to him.

    – Rafael

Rafael found out the details of the bust. The 1.3 kilos of coke had been discovered in the DHL parcel in Leipzig, Germany, despite being well hidden in a transformer for an electric guitar. The cops switched the cocaine for baking powder, lined the transformer with a fluorescent agent, then sent it on to Anna in Stockholm, where she'd used her real name. Undercover cops watched her accept the parcel, then spied on the apartment for five hours, before bursting in and arresting Anna and her friend, who both had the fluorescent agent all over their hands.

She's stupid … she told me she had somebody to take it. It was bullshit, it was her. Very dangerous … you pay somebody to receive, like a horse.

Interpol was involved in the case. They hack all the phones. They have eyes on her since she stepped in the airport, follow her, record her phone calls. She was hot because we'd been doing there for the last two years before this happened. I was Bali–Stockholm–Amsterdam, Stockholm–Amsterdam, Stockholm–Bali

... she was too. They record everything on the phones. That's why I've never been there after she got caught. Because I'm 100 per cent sure they're going to catch me.

– Rafael

In Bali, Rafael quickly organised a buyer for his house, selling it much more cheaply than its real value, because the bank was calling in its loan. He was sure he'd feel better when he had the cash and could pay his bills, the kids' school fees, their Bali visas. Weeks after Anna's bust, he got the $30,000 deposit and put it in his safe. He thought it would be a good feeling. It wasn't. He collapsed on the floor in front of the safe with the door open, just looking at the stash that once seemed so important.

I think, when I sell the house, I get the money, everything is going to be good. But it was not. I get worse paranoia, worse frustration. I realise, fuck, I sold my property. I'm never going to buy something like this again. I don't have a house. Where am I going to live? Shit. I want it back. I feel like shit. Depression. Once the money looked like it was never going to finish. Now that looks like a dream. How did I lose everything? Before I have a house, land, motorbike, everything. Then I realise, I don't have anything, not even the house. I sold everything. The house was the last thing I had. I thought, ah, at least I have a house. I don't need to pay rent. And then it's gone.

I look at the money in the safety deposit box and start to cry. I think, 'Fuck, what am I going to do with this money? Fuck, poor Anna's in the jail.' I was really crying. Tears. Cry cry cry

cry. Sobbing. Very uncontrolled. I lost my wife. I was scared, I think they're gonna catch me. I was worried what's gonna happen with my kids. Who they gonna live with? Where I'm going to send them? In my mind, I was very sure that soon somebody was going to come and catch me, Interpol or some special police.

Did you take cocaine?

No, no. I don't take. If I take, I feel good.

   – Rafael

Anna was sentenced to five years jail after using the defence that she'd expected a delivery of marijuana, not cocaine, from a South American man, Pedro, whom she'd met in Bali. She claimed Pedro had promised her €5000 to collect and hold the package. She denied Rafael had any involvement.

CHAPTER TWENTY-ONE

SLEEPING LIKE AN ANGEL

At a New Year's Eve party in Bali, almost two months after Anna's arrest, Rafael took his last line of cocaine. He'd just begun a new relationship and a new life as a surf coach.

'I don't have anything. I have to sell lunch to buy dinner.' He was broke but felt happier than he could remember, free from a sense of constant paranoia and foreboding, no longer looking over his shoulder. He'd quit the game and his wild ways, and even if the police still sometimes watched him, he had nothing to fear. A dark cloud had lifted. He was back to surfing every day, living the life he'd come to the island for all those years ago.

When his son won a surf competition, he instinctively felt like ducking out of the shot, then realised that, actually, now he could be photographed.

I was in the podium with him, my son – very happy. And when I look to the public there was like 100 cameras shooting us, and I have this kind of drug dealer feeling . . . But at the same time I was proud, I am not a drug dealer, I can show my face, come, take a picture. Then when I go down, two guys come, 'Hey, Rafael, remember me?' I look. 'Sorry, no.' 'I bought something from you.' I say, 'Shush, I have my son.' My son says, 'Papa, what did the guy buy from you?'

– Rafael

No longer using coke also opened his eyes to the fact that it had been the glue that kept him and Anna together in a fraught relationship. Being free of it also meant he was content to have sex with one woman – his new girlfriend, Emily.

Even when she'd found him that night at his lowest ebb there'd been sexual chemistry – 'I remember I touch her hand. We started to have feeling with each other. But we say "Cannot, no, cannot."' Their feelings were conflicted by the fact that Emily was Anna's friend and her estranged husband, Julio, was Rafael's friend and customer. The two couples had socialised together, but for the past six months Julio had been in a clinic in Brazil for coke addiction. It was complicated, so breaking the news of his new relationship to Anna in jail wasn't easy for Rafael. It went as badly as he'd expected – 'Fuck, she wanted to kill me.'

Late one night about a year later, Rafael got a surprise phone call. It was Andre, who'd just flown back to Bali after his third jailbreak, asking to stay at the beach house. Rafael told him he'd sold it but he'd be waiting outside the Canggu Club. Andre arrived looking like an unlikely escapee, dapper in a buttoned shirt, long pants and leather shoes, with his gap-toothed smile. When they got into the car, Andre ripped from behind his ears the glue which had kept them pinned back to look more like the photo in his false passport.

I run away with the fake passport and the picture is totally different to me. I travelled all the countries, and nobody stopped me. It's crazy.
  – Andre

I remember he has the glue behind the ear. He took out, tuff, tuff. And his ears come back again like this, stick out.
  – Rafael

Andre had escaped from a semi-open prison, a farm. He was able to literally walk out, and the guards discovered him missing only at roll call. In total, he'd now spent four years in jail, and thrown a million dollars at his cause: to make jail life easier, to be moved to less secure prisons in order to escape, and also to appeal his 37-year sentence. Now it had been cut to 12 years, which was why they'd put him on the farm.

On day one, he'd escaped. Again he went to Laguna Beach, surfing for 15 days until his new false passport was ready. The photo was of a younger, fat guy with black hair and a wide jaw. Andre had dyed his hair black and planned to say he'd got sick and lost weight if anyone asked. He took a bus from Laguna to Argentina, where he stayed for a couple of days, then boarded a flight, transiting back into São Paulo, then on to Doha and Singapore on Qatar Airlines.

Always on his toes and ready to tap-dance, he had a plan to reduce his risk. He started chatting to a Chinese girl in the seat next to him. 'How are you? I'm Rodrigo, what's your name?' During the transit in Singapore he grabbed her hand. 'What are you doing?' she asked.

He was ready with a slick reply: 'You're so beautiful, I'd like to walk with you. Let's have fun.' They strolled around the airport like a romantic couple. It was the perfect camouflage.

When I come to take the plane again, the Chinese girl comes with me. I take the passport from her hand and give it together with my passport. And the guy says, 'Oh, okay, going to Bali ... nice.' She would never ever imagine what I'm doing. Every time I do something different, because I know what I need to do for no suspicion. If I go with somebody, especially a girl who has the eyes like that, it's fucking normal, you know an Asian travelling in Asia. When I arrive in Bali, I do the same with her.

– Andre

He breezed into Bali on his false passport, audaciously carrying in his checked-in luggage a tripod loaded with 150 grams of cocaine – 50 grams in each aluminium leg – which he'd sell for $15,000, and a couple of joints.

Were you nervous?

As nervous as if I'm bringing a phone in my pocket. For me it's easy. I don't think about that. I believe in myself, I believe in my job, I know really, really well how that works. I did this so many times here already. I know how to do it. I'm so confident with that.

What did it feel like to arrive back in Bali?

I'm fucking really happy, you know, happy again. But after you do it many times, it feels really normal also. I was prepared,

*maybe I get arrested on the way, maybe São Paulo, maybe some-
where. I was prepared for that also.*

   – Andre

Andre stayed at Rafael's modest rented house but their now
different worlds quickly collided.

*He was so used to being in jail, he talk all the time about kilos
of coke. Was very hard, because I don't belong to this any more,
and sometimes in front of the kids, like, 'Oh, somebody got
busted for this, for that, he take some lines.' The kids say, 'What?'
'Andre, come on.' 'Oh, sorry, sorry.' Not because he want to fuck
me, but he just came from jail.*

   *He says, 'Oh, let's do like this. I'm gonna have new connec-
tions.' I say, 'Uh-uh, I don't want to do any more, man. When you
left here I was another guy. Now I have my business, start in the
surf school, I don't do anything wrong. I even have a Facebook.'*

   *I was very happy I bring him to my house, but Emily was
a little bit afraid. She says, 'Fuck, I want to live with you because
you promised me you were going to stop this shit.' She's totally
against drugs. She says, 'I don't feel safe living together in the
same house with Andre here. Any time the police could break
the door to catch him.' Then she says, 'Oh, Andre, it's better you
find another place to go.' He felt a little bit sad with me.*

   – Rafael

Andre was quickly immersed in Bali's drug world again, getting on his feet by selling Sumatran weed, but soon moving to
quality imported grass, hashish and snow.

Through a Brazilian friend working in Australia, he'd organised an Australian Hells Angels boss to meet cop Claudio in Brazil, to buy 200 kilos of cocaine to send to Sydney. Andre's commission was $2000 per kilo. If it came off, he'd be making $400,000 and eagerly checked his emails for updates.

Meanwhile, he was waiting on a FedEx parcel of hashish from Amsterdam, interviewing an English girl to work as a horse, and meeting with an unlikely horse, a 55-year-old Englishwoman, to buy hashish which she trafficked from India. His phone ceaselessly beeped with messages like, 'The choc is on the island!', or 'Can I buy one surfboard?'

He was also soon trying to get Rafael back working with him, but Rafael started keeping his distance.

I don't approve of this shit any more. And I think, 'If I stay with him, he get problem, going to get for me too.' But I'm clear with him; I say, 'Andre, I don't want to.' 'Oh, let's make money together, it will help you.' I say, 'No, man, I don't want to get involved in this shit.' He knew my view, but he kept trying to push me to make money. I think, 'Are you my friend, or some evil person who wants to fuck me?'

– Rafael

Even seeing Andre's fast return to living in style didn't change his mind. Andre took out a three-year lease on a newly built, two-storey house among rice paddies. The property comprised three bedrooms, two bathrooms, a swimming pool, and was just 200 metres from Canggu beach. He bought a new car, a fake Harley-Davidson, two scooters, a plasma TV and a bunch of new surfboards. He even got braces on his teeth to close a gap in the front that had widened in jail. He invested in a new restaurant on the beach and was living with a rich Indonesian girlfriend. The only thing Andre couldn't do was safely leave Bali.

I'm living now like a movie. I really had to make a choice about my life. Keep this life, or back to normal life. And I chose to keep my life like a movie. Day by day I party, crazy things on the phone, I chose this for my life.

I have already 25 years of really dream life, I can choose where I want to go . . . Now I cannot fly, but before I fly – like I get bored in Bali, so I go to Koh Samui for one week; get bored, I go to Europe for a couple of days. And this life for me is really, really pleasure life. Every day is new things, new feelings, new adventures. I pray to my gods every day, help me another day, another adventure in Bali.

Cos every day for me is a new adventure. Why? Because I don't know what's happening. If some police stop me in the street and ask for my passport, maybe I need to run, maybe I need to pay, maybe . . .

You know what I mean – I don't know what to expect in the next second. This is my day-by-day now. But this really really doesn't make me sad, this excites me. I don't know what new thing's going to happen tomorrow. Maybe I am here, maybe I need to run away – every day is different feeling. I believe so much the life just flows away.

– Andre

Although Rafael was out of the game, it hadn't stopped snowing in Bali. The Island of the Gods was still full of rich expats and tourists wanting the buzz of intoxication – the parties on the beaches or in the five-star hotels kept going, but discretion had replaced blatant, arrogant indulgence.

As long as there was a thriving market, there would be those ready to gamble their lives for a fast buck. A European guy sold snow to expats; Barbara, the Botox-faced woman, kept coke hidden in a hollowed-out Bible, and people still called Rafael sometimes, asking for his help to sell their kilos. For a while, there'd been a scarcity, but now it was snowing in Bali, with the price a sky-high $350 a gram. But Rafael refused to slip back.

He was reminded often of the life he'd left behind, as it still frenetically whirled around him. When 56-year-old English-woman Lindsay Sandiford was busted at Denpasar Airport with 4.7 kilos of coke in the lining of her suitcase, at least two of his friends had to flee overseas.

She give up so many people, she talk.

When I see the news last week, I was thinking, 'Fuck, Andre must be panicking, because he buys hashish from this woman.' I don't give a shit. I go to sleep. Andre comes, 'Oh, be careful, the island's hot,' and I say, 'I have nothing to be afraid of.' I remember how I felt when it was my stuff that was bust; heart beat, no sleep. Now I sleep like an angel.

– Rafael

AFTERWORD

SNOWSTORM

Three weeks after the Englishwoman was busted, another dealer's life in Bali exploded. The Brazilian surfer who went down had been close to Rafael and others in Bali for years – and his bust caused panic.

The dealer had been careful. Always. One sultry afternoon he was riding his motorbike, beside his partner in this run, to pick up a DHL parcel containing a backpack loaded with nearly 1 kilo of coke. He'd paid a Balinese taxi driver to collect it and bring it to him at the front of some surf bungalows near Canggu beach – familiar turf.

The two bikes approached the waiting taxi. As soon as the Brazilian took the parcel, his life blew up. It was sudden frantic commotion. Police dressed like surfers burst from behind the gate. The Brazilian wheeled the bike around, but a cop grabbed his shirt, shouted, 'Stop' and put a gun to his back. The dealer kept accelerating. The cop fired a warning shot into the air. The dealer revved, trying to break the cop's grip. Then, it was over. The cop whacked him in the back of the head with his gun and he fell off his bike.

He wound up on the ground, with no hope of escape, four of the cops kicking and punching him. Young Balinese surfers came running out of the bungalows to see what was going on. They wanted to defend their surfer friend, but backed off fast when the men yelled, 'Police'.

The other dealer involved in the run had luckily escaped, not only the police clutches, but two bullets that were aimed directly at him as he tore off.

Police took the Brazilian to his beach house, where they found his girlfriend, a gardener and a maid. They handcuffed the dealer to a shower pipe, then ransacked his house, searching for more drugs and going through his phone, his computer and his photos.

Police wanted information; they wanted other dealers – especially the one who'd eluded them back at the scene. They interrogated the captives, pushing the gardener:

'Who was the guy who escaped?'

'I don't know anything.'

They hit the gardener in the face, giving him a black eye.

'Where are his friends? You know his friends?'

'No, I don't know anybody, I don't know anything.'

He was actually Rafael's gardener, on loan to the Brazilian to beautify a new garden with his 'magic hands', but his friend held his tongue, saving Rafael from certain interrogation.

The dealer remained handcuffed to the shower pipe, released only occasionally for a beating and questions: 'Who you going to sell to?', 'Who is your friend?' and 'Who sent this?'

I think they beat him very bad, but he didn't get any stitches or bruises. They know how to give you pain but no evidence.

   – Rafael

The house was now swarming with cops. They'd discovered a stash of cash in a safe, and used some of it to buy a box of beer and food. They were walking around in the guy's floral board shorts, floating in his swimming pool on his surfboards and watching his plasma TV, while the maid, the girlfriend, the gardener and the dealer were held prisoner in the bathroom.

Bad news spread fast. Another Brazilian friend of Rafael's had watched the whole drama through his window and called him 10 minutes after the bust. Rafael's instant reaction was panic.

I near to get heart attack. I think, 'Shit, they are going to come to me.' My heart beat dededede. But when I think calm and clear, I say to myself, 'Relax, man, you did the right thing, you didn't get involved. That's it.'

I go surfing in Uluwatu the day after in the morning cos I was, like, 'Aah, I need to surf.' I cancel my class. When I come out from the water, was 22 missed calls. I say, 'Fuck.' I have to put my phone off, because all the Brazilian community, everybody call me, 'Where is the guy?' 'What's happened?' 'What did he have, coke?' I say, 'Fuck, man, I don't know.' Then my surf partner was pissed off with me because I answer. He say, 'Don't answer the phone, man. Fuck, you're going to get in trouble.'

   – Rafael

In Bali, there was panic. The beach in Canggu was swarming with undercover cops, and the dealer's friends, customers, partners and sellers were all getting strange phone calls. Some fled to other islands; others flew overseas. The dealer's main seller, a European man, nearly fainted when someone broke the news to him.

He lose the colour in his face. You know, like he say, 'What? Ahhhh,' nearly crying. 'I have to go, I have to go.' I think he already left Bali now – he's very afraid.
    – Rafael

Rafael drove past the dealer's house on his way to the beach, and saw at least eight cops lounging back on their bikes out the front with their long hair, moustaches and board shorts.

The next day he noticed his friend's new car, his fake Harley and two scooters were gone, but there was a silver van in the driveway, which police would use to drive their captive to the airport en route to Jakarta. But before snatching him from his Bali life, they all huddled together with the drug dealer for a photo.

He was the hunting trophy.
    – Rafael

Later, the police returned to the house and swiped everything, from his furniture, clothes and leather shoes to his quiver of custom surfboards. When a friend called in later on, the place was stripped bare (though he later got some of it back with the help of an influential Balinese friend). The dealer's girlfriend was too scared to stay there and had slept at the gardener's house.

The cops were still searching, phoning and interrogating his contacts.

After his instinctive panic, Rafael relaxed, but with so much heat familiar feelings flared when he noticed someone riding closely behind him, with a helmet shield obscuring his face. Rafael tore off, zigzagging through the traffic until he lost him – realising it was probably just old instincts dying hard. But his number was in the busted dealer's phone, and many people knew they were old friends, so he braced for a bang on his door.

For two days, I just wait for the police to come to my house. I have some smoking papers, you know, so I clean everything and then I was ready for them, but this time I feel so comfortable. I say, 'They cannot fuck me, I don't have anything to do with this shit.' My girlfriend was freaking out; she regrets to be with me, because I have this kind of friend. She near to leave me. 'I have a kid, soon the police gonna come here, better I move.' I say, 'Do what you want. It's me – you think I'm doing something with this guy?' 'No, I'm sure you don't.' 'Then shut up, be quiet, nothing is going to happen, wait and see.'

So, are you a little bit worried?

Actually no, I don't have anything to do with this shit. Since the day he get this problem, everybody called me saying, 'Oh, be careful, be careful.' I say, 'Careful of what, man? I don't have anything to do with this shit.' It's a funny feeling, because I've been so much closer, this one is so far away. I'm not scared at all. I sleep like a baby, I eat like a horse. I don't give a shit, because I know this time I did the right thing. I don't give a chance for them to involve me.

– Rafael

The day before the bust, the Brazilian dealer had gone to Rafael's house and asked him to make a few calls to help him sell a kilo of snow due on the island the next day.

He comes to my house with his girlfriend and says, 'Oh, tomorrow I'm going to get this shit, 1 kilo, it's already in Hong Kong.'

He says, 'Come on, Rafael, you make a couple of calls and you can make some money.' I straight away say, 'No, man, I don't want to get involved – are you crazy? No way, José. All my buyers, they're in jail or dead, everybody fuck up. Forget it. Keep your money, man, buy land, get out of this shit.' He says, 'I will give you some cash, because you need it to pay the school.' I say, 'No, no, I don't want to know. Don't tell me, please, man. Be careful, man.'

But he tells me it's coming with DHL. I say, 'Are you crazy? Anna got busted with this shit. Be careful, man.' 'No, it's okay. No chance they catch me. I have this taxi driver. But if something happens, you know what to do.' I say, 'Come on, nothing's going to happen, don't talk like this.' And then, the day after, bang, bust.

– Rafael

You are living the dream until you bust and all the reality comes so fast and so bad; no more beach, just cops around, asking a million questions at the same time.

This game is fucking dangerous.

– Busted drug dealer

EPILOGUE

Rafael

The busts that kept happening were a constant confirmation to Rafael that he had done the right thing. Despite struggling for cash these days, he felt happier than ever.

Friends say, 'Now you are a different person, you are the real Rafael. Before you have something evil. Even your eyes are different now. I hear a lot, 'Oh Rafael ... man, you look so different, I don't know why but you look very nice.' Now, actually I'm fit again, I go to the beach every day, I surf, you know ... I can socialise in normal places, I can have straight friends, I can talk about normal business.

In the end, after all the glamour, I don't feel proud. I try to forget this shit. Because I don't think it's cool. I poison people here with this shit just for money, nothing else. Poison people, fuck families, even make people die from overdose. I like to show off in that time. For what?

Now, I have different value for life. I don't wanna have a nice car, I don't wanna have a gold necklace, I don't wanna go to five-star hotels. My goal now is to have a job, get money to raise my kids, working as a surf instructor, have a quiet, normal life. And try to show the new generation that's not a good choice. That's the thing now in my heart.

When I see young guys coming to Bali, to meet me to try to do some drug business, they look at me with shining eyes. They think I have an island, I have an aeroplane, because in the surfing world in Brazil they make so much bullshit about me. 'Hey, Rafael, I wanna bring some coke – can you help me?'

I need to say, 'Don't do that, because maybe you focus on me, you wanna be like me; have a nice house, fuck all the girls, ba ba ba ba. You don't have so much of a good life in the end. You have only three options: jail, hospital or cemetery – one of these three.'

They get shocked, because I say, 'Man, forget this shit. I know what I'm talking about because I've been there and then in the end I get fucked.' Then I start, 'Remember the house I have before?' – because they have seen it in magazines – 'Where is the beautiful house? Where are the motorbikes? Where is my family, my kids? My nice remote control car? Everything gone to hell. My wife is in jail. I suffer with all that, you know. I suffer when I see friends of mine getting caught, because all of them get killed, murdered, or busted.

'I'm gonna tell you something ... If you do this, you might make money, the devil gonna give you a lot of money with the coffee spoon for a long time, but when he take, he gonna take with a big spoon all at once. Whooo ... You gonna be broke ... You gonna get shot ... You're crazy, man, forget this shit.' That's my goal now, to change their minds.

And now you enjoy teaching surfing?

I love it. You know, that's my life. I love to go to work, yes! I'm going to give a surf class. I go very happy; I'm gonna go to the

ocean, I'm gonna swim, I'm gonna teach people to surf. I'm
lucky. Most of my gang is not here any more. They are all dead,
jail, the very bad end.

Around 15 years I play. Now, I just want a simple and happy
life. Now I know who are my real friends. Before, I have many
people there just to suck. Just to eat, to drink for free. I don't
realise.

I scramble to live day by day but I'm still free, healthy and
alive. I have my girl I love, my beautiful kids, surfing. I'm healthy
and I'm happy – much happier than before. I don't need to hide
myself – I'm Mr Rafael now, the teacher, surf guru.

Marco

Marco spends his days now on death row in a maximum-security prison on Nusakambangan Island, dubbed Indonesia's Alcatraz. The sun-kissed tropical island is lush with an ugly scar of seven prisons slashed across it. It's also where executions take place; where in 2008 the Bali bombers, terrorists Amrozi, Samudra and Mukhlas, were taken from their cells to a clearing and shot dead by a 12-sniper firing squad.

Now Marco awaits the same fate.

Incredibly, most of the time he's upbeat and optimistic. In jail, he plays tennis, listens to music, and cooks when he gets ingredients brought in by a rare visitor. 'I make good food, believe me.'

As in his trafficking days of taking insanely audacious risks, he's still a reckless rule-breaker in jail. 'I'm a troublemaker. I've been moved 56 times in here. I've been in every cell. They even put me in the kitchen.'

But the reality of his desperate situation swarms around him. Most of his fellow inmates are on life or death sentences. His compatriot Rodrigo Gularte is failing to cope with the drawn out, torturous wait for execution and spends most of his time in the Christian church praying, crying and confused.

The other Brazilian here, Rodrigo, get crazy. He's always talking to himself, he doesn't change his clothes any more. But there is nothing I can do. He reads the Bible, goes to the church.

He tried to burn himself to death, didn't he?
Yeah, in the other jail he try, but not professional.

Despite Marco's bravado, his own fear and loneliness are inescapable. American big-wave surfer Gabriel recalls one emotional conversation when Marco called to say goodbye when Gabriel was being released from Bali's Kerobokan jail.

He started off saying, 'Hey, whoa . . . you're getting released.' I'm like, 'Yeah.' He was happy for me, but then he broke down, he lost it. I was on the phone going, 'What do I do? What do I say?' I couldn't speak to him; I didn't have a thing I could say . . . what could I tell him? I was going home. So I didn't say anything, he went silent and then he hung up. He didn't say goodbye.
– Gabriel

It's perhaps Marco's way of staying sane that he's convinced himself that, with so many nationalities now on death row in

Indonesia, international pressure will ensure they don't get shot dead.

I'm sure. The Brazil embassy works hard. French guy, Dutch guy, Swiss guy, many people here, from Nepal, from Pakistan, from India, from America, from Australia, on death sentence.
   – Marco

But in June 2012 it looked like political pressure would fail to save him; that Marco would be the first westerner executed in Indonesia, when the *Jakarta Post* ran a story that he was to be executed in coming weeks. The story was based on quotes from an Indonesian prosecutor, Andi DJ Konggoasa, who also claimed that Marco's final request was for a bottle of Chivas Regal whisky.

That bit sounded believable enough, prompting a Brazilian friend in Bali to consider making the long and emotional trip to the island to take him a bottle.

But no officials had told Marco anything, he knew only what was in the media. A month earlier he'd signed some unofficial looking paper brought in by an attorney who'd jokingly asked what his last request was. 'Three bottles of Chivas whisky and two women', he'd answered with typical Marco sass.

But the story turned out to be false. Until the Indonesian government announced a decision on Marco's second clemency application, made in 2008, by law, he would not be shot. BBC Brazil reported that the Brazilian Ambassador had had this confirmed by the Indonesian Attorney-General. The ambassador then travelled to the penal island to reassure Marco.

Were you scared?

No problem, no problem. My embassy is here all the time. You see they already put [Schapelle] Corby's sentence down five years.

Marco still believes one day he'll walk free. After all, he's beaten seemingly unbeatable odds before.

All my family already die – my father, my mother, my brother, my grandmother, my two uncles; eight people already die. But you know, Marco is still alive. No worry, no worry. Because for sure I'm going to go out from here.

Marco has also outlived his best friend from childhood, Beto, who all those years ago used to drop his pliable young friend off at the bottom of the *favelas* to run up and fill his lunch box with the 'white' stuff. Beto died of a cocaine over-dose.

Although the harsh third-world prison has not yet broken Marco's indefatigable spirit, it's taken a toll physically. His injured leg always hurts and lack of health care has resulted in gum disease and all his teeth falling out.

I want to go home ... I'm very tired. People don't care about me here. Look, I have no teeth. I have to ask them all the time to bring me to a dentist, but they say you give me $1000 and I don't have the money.

Incredibly, visiting Marco isn't depressing. Ask him, 'Hey, sing that song again, Marco,' and he bursts into, 'I never can say goodbye, every time I think … ' then he stops and asks earnestly, 'I don't know, what kind of song do you want? Aretha Franklin or something else?'

Juri

The Italian jeweller, who was busted in Bali with 5.26 kilos of cocaine in his surfboard bag – on Carlino's failed run to help Marco – lives in the same prison as Marco, but with better prospects. His life sentence was cut to 15 years. His expensive wink paid off and, with annual sentence cuts, he could be home in Italy next year.

Fox

After stealing Rafael's cash and selling behind his back, Rafael reckons Fox made between €300,000 and €400,000 profit. He then fled to Tahiti, built an oceanfront mansion in surf mecca Teahupoo, bought a boat and started growing marijuana from seeds he bought in Amsterdam – with a business plan to control the island's dope supply.

But he was busted with 35 kilos of marijuana and is now in a Tahitian prison.

I was thinking to go there and fix him, but I forgive him. He's paying for his mistake already – he's in jail, I'm surfing.
– Rafael

Borrador – Jose Henrici

Missing Englishwoman Kate Osborne's ex-boyfriend Jose

Henrici, aka Borrador, didn't return to Bali. No one is absolutely certain of his fate, but it's believed he died from a cocaine overdose in a cheap hotel with a prostitute, after serving a couple of years in jail in the jungles of Peru.

The Diaz brothers

After fleeing Bali following Kate Osborne's suspected murder, Poca and Mario never returned to the island, but continued dealing. There's no trace of them now, but it's believed Mario died of leukaemia in Peru and Poca was strangled to death in Brazil over a $50,000 drug deal dispute.

> *For a period of time everybody was happy and living life on top of the world and the karma started. If you look back, most had some tragic . . . real bad tragedy.*
> – Alberto

Psychopath

Psychopath, aka Fabio, served two years in jail in Amsterdam for collecting the FedExed parcel of cocaine. After getting out, he met a millionaire girlfriend who bought him a new Mercedes and today supports him.

Fabio

The gregarious Fabio who ran the bar on Legian beach left Bali after it got too hot for him, not long after police snatched him off the beach and took him at gunpoint to Rafael's house. He became a *favela* guide in Rio.

Tota

Hells Angel Tota was shot dead in front of a trendy bar in Rio in a dispute over slot machines.

As Tota had stood drinking beer out the front of the bar Carolice, at 3 am, two men drove up in a silver Peugeot. One man got out of the car, disguised in a red balaclava, and started shooting.

Tota was hit in his head and stomach, and was killed instantly. Two of his friends were shot in the feet and legs. Pandemonium broke out on the streets, with patrons from the many busy bars running for cover, or throwing themselves on the ground.

Rio police had no doubts that the two men had gone to the spot to execute Tota in part of the 'slot machine war'. It was well known Tota lived next door to the bar.

Chino

Chino was busted for ecstasy production in the country to which he'd fled after escaping Bali. He is now in jail while his interminably long drug trial is heard. If convicted, he faces a mandatory death sentence.

Operation Playboy

Chief Caieron has worked for the Brazilian Federal Police since 1996, and personally instigated Operation Playboy in 2004.

The very beginning of Playboy Operation took place when I started to see – in the daily newspaper – that young folks from our city [Florianópolis] and state [Santa Catarina] were being arrested in Europe with 3, 4, 5 kilos of cocaine. So, someone, somehow with somebody else, was recruiting and hiring those young guys to do this, and those guys couldn't be far from me. The challenge? Start to search, to find and put all the pieces together.

Once we started to investigate, we decided to call 'Playboy Operation' because we saw what kind of guys – high middle-class – were involved in those activities.

In six years Operation Playboy resulted in the arrest of more than 20 people who were exporting cocaine to Europe and Bali and returning to Brazil with ecstasy and dope.

Carlino

Carlino didn't slow down after his horses got life and death sentences; he got busier. Until the day he was busted.

Rafael had finished the drug game, but was watching his friend still perilously playing.

It was only me and him still standing – from all the group but Carlino was dealing a lot. Doesn't give a shit, like in Ku De Ta. He was too arrogant, like a big boss. He was asking for it the way he play, and then he say, 'Rafael, can you help me?' I say, 'What?' 'You have any coke in Brazil, cheap, good stuff?' I say, 'Forget it man, everybody's in jail, I cannot help you. Stop this shit. Come on, Carlino, it's no good man. Make your villa.' He was on the way to making a villa.

And then he goes to Brazil but he makes a big mistake. He goes on the same flight with the horse. And then they catch the horse in France, the horse points to him, and they catch him.

So is he in jail in France now?

Yeah, I hear he tried to kill himself because I hear in Paris it's very hard in the jails, fighting all the time, the black people crazy, the Cameroon gang there, very strong, many rapes, not a nice jail to stay. I think Carlino gets ten years.

— Rafael

Marco Froes

Marco Froes, Andre's horse, who was busted with 3 kilos of cocaine at Florianópolis Airport about 90 minutes before Andre's second arrest, and who Andre suspects worked a sting with the police to trap him, is now in a witness protection programme.

Diego Amaral

Diego served no more than two years in jail for trafficking 8 kilos of cocaine. He was given leniency for turning police informant against his boss, Andre — giving Chief Caieron the information and evidence he needed to prosecute one of the big Playboys.

Diego's got the law benefits ... guess he stayed no more than two years in prison, maybe less.

— Chief Caieron

Alberto

Alberto served 18 months in Bali's Kerobokan Prison, leaving there a confused and disturbed man, keener than ever to do one last big drug deal, then quit cashed up. Instead, he met people who opened his eyes to another way. Before long, he was looking back at his drug career with shame and remorse.

I still regret all the shit that directly or indirectly people suffered because I was a tool, a mechanism, a piece of the machine. If I could go back in time, I would never get involved.

Thank god I met the right people and started getting more spiritual and started to realise you don't need much to be happy.

Now, I just try to live my life without doing any harm to anyone, and just try to help people when I can. And thank god I have a business that is helping people, helping people to surf good waves, helping people to have a good time.

There are a lot of people – especially young people – if you say, 'There is death penalty in Indonesia,' they still say, 'Yeah, but there's a lot of people still doing it and I can do it too.' But they have no idea the cost of that Russian roulette that they are going to start playing.

Most people get involved because of the money, but it comes together with the glamour, the power kick and all the shit and it's not until you finish – when you look back – that you see it was all fantasy, all a big cloud of bullshit you were living.

And sometimes, unfortunately, it takes people going through the worst to learn that. If my story helps any of those kids to think twice before doing something stupid, this alone for me is worth everything.

Andre
Andre's most recent whereabouts cannot be revealed. Stay tuned!

ACKNOWLEDGEMENTS

First, thank you to all the people who spoke to me; sharing details of their lives and giving me unique material to paint a picture of Bali's drug underworld.

Special thanks to the charismatic Rafael, who revealed deeply personal and graphic details, much of which he's now ashamed – although he still gets excited with a sparkle in his eye as he relives the moments. Like most of the dealers I interviewed, Rafael had never spoken to anybody about much of what he was telling me.

Thanks to Andre and Alberto for the long days of compelling interviews, and to Marco who I talked to in jail several times and spoke to on the phone regularly for months. I hope he is freed one day – as is his belief. He divides opinion among those who know him, but the one thing everyone agrees on is that he is a very funny guy. He often made me laugh. Amazing, considering his situation.

Thanks to Chino, who I tracked down on trial in another country where he's facing mandatory death if convicted of the drugs charges against him. When Chino first saw me walk into the courtroom, he later told me, he thought I was with Interpol. But I explained I was a journalist, writing a book, and had flown in especially to see him and his reply was, 'I'm honoured'. I had lunch with him a couple of times at court, and visited him in jail. He was very polite and friendly, almost always smiling, and clearly liked by those around him. We continued talking on the phone afterwards.

Hopping over to the other side of the law: thanks to Operation Playboy boss Chief Fernando Caieron, who is passionate about his job and the arrests that were made during his Playboy Operation. Chief Caeiron sent me endless emails answering hundreds of questions, as I tried to connect the dots – in one of them he even joked about the many emails. *'Hope you're doing pretty good!!!! By the way, do you know how many emails we've changed? (lol) Fernando Caieron.'* His emails were often colourful, and showed his sense of humour.

Thanks also to Detective Chief Inspector Bill Whitehead, of Cumbria police in the UK, who also spent a lot of effort emailing answers to my queries about the Kate Osborne case.

Thank you to Indonesian translator Desi Mandarini, Portuguese translator Daniela Ortega, and Swedish researcher Axel Johansson.

And a huge thank you to those friends and family who read random chapters during the writing of *Snowing in Bali*, especially Caroline Frith, Sue Rose and James Foster, who among others gave me their blunt critiques – I'm always guided by your opinions. And thanks also to James for using his hawk-eye to help me in the editing process.

Thank you to staff at Pan Macmillan; to freelance editor Mark Evans for doing the first edit, Editorial Assistant Alex Lloyd for his help with the picture section, and huge thanks to Managing Editor Emma Rafferty, who also edited *Hotel K*, and who is undoubtedly one of the best in the business – and lovely to work with.

And finally, thank you very much to non-fiction publisher Tom Gilliatt. I wrote this at the end of *Hotel K*, and it's true again – *Snowing in Bali* is unlikely to have been written without Tom's belief and enthusiasm, and the total free rein he gives me to go out and produce a book.

ALSO AVAILABLE

HOTEL K

The Shocking Inside Story of Bali's Most
Notorious Jail

Kathryn Bonella

Welcome to Hotel Kerobokan, or Hotel K, Bali's most notorious jail. Its walls touch paradise; sparkling oceans, surf beaches and palm trees on one side, while on the other it's a dark, bizarre and truly frightening underworld of sex, drugs, violence and squalor.

Hotel K is the shocking inside story of the jail and its inmates, revealing the wild 'sex nights' organised by corrupt guards for the prisoners who have cash to pay, the jail's ecstasy factory, the killings made to look like suicides, the days out at the beach, the escapes and the corruption that means anything is for sale. The truth about the dark heart of Bali explodes off the page.

Quercus
www.quercusbooks.co.uk

COMING SOON

HASH

The Chilling Inside Story of the Secret
Underworld Behind the World's Most Lucrative Drug

Wensley Clarkson

For millions of people across the world, lighting up a joint is
no more controversial than having a cup of tea. But in *Hash*
Wensley Clarkson explores the dark and sinister side of this
multi-billion pound business: one fuelled by a brutal underworld network of dealers, hitmen, drug barons, drug mules,
bent cops and even terrorists.

Sex, intimidation, bribery and murder are all employed in a
quest for staggering profits. Travelling from the lawless Rif
mountains in Morocco, to darkened warehouses in Spain protected by heavily armed gangsters, and exploring the real story
on both sides of the law, this is a revelatory roller-coaster ride
through the secret world of Hash.

PUBLISHED JUNE 2013

Quercus

www.quercusbooks.co.uk